THE NEW WEALTH ORDER

THE MONEY GAME THEY NEVER TAUGHT YOU

SPEAKER SINGH

ISBN
Paperback 979-8-90362-256-6
Hardcase 979-8-90560-515-4

CONTENTS

PART 1

THE OLD WEALTH LIE

Chapter 1

THE SALARY MYTH

*From **The New Wealth Order***

— by Speaker Singh

I'm going to begin this book by saying something that sounds rude… until you sit with it long enough to realize it's actually kindness:

"A salary is not security. It's a system."

For more than a decade, I've had the privilege of working closely with people most of the world calls "successful"- millionaires, business owners, founders, senior executives and families with wealth that quietly moves across countries, currencies and asset classes.

And across every city, every boardroom, every family office, one pattern kept repeating -

The truly wealthy never confuse income with wealth.

And the financially stressed almost always do.

I've seen people earning seven figures a month living one bad quarter away from panic.

And I've seen people with modest salaries sleep peacefully because they built ownership.

This chapter is not meant to insult salary earners. Most honest wealth journeys start with a salary. Even mine did.

This chapter is meant to **wake you up**.

Because the biggest financial trap in the modern world is not poverty. The biggest trap is the illusion of safety.

And nothing creates that illusion faster than a monthly credit message:

"Salary credited."

It feels like control.

It feels like stability.

It feels like proof that life is working.

But for most people, the salary is not freedom.It's a leash.

A simple question that exposes the salary myth.

Let me ask you something—no judgment, just clarity:

If your salary stopped today, how long could you maintain your lifestyle?

- One month?
- Three months?
- Six months?
- One year?

Most people avoid this question because the answer is uncomfortable. But the New Wealth Order is built on uncomfortable honesty.

If your life collapses the moment your salary pauses, then you don't have stability.

You have **dependency**.

And dependency is always expensive, be it emotionally, financially or psychologically.

Now, what a salary really is?

Let's strip the emotion away and define salary in plain language:

A salary is a contract. You exchange your time, skills and obedience to a hierarchy for predictable cashflow. That's it!.

A salary is not evil. A salary is not shameful. A salary is simply **linear income,** meaning- you work, you get paid.

The myth begins when society teaches you this dangerous sentence:

"If you have a stable salary, you are safe."

No. A salary does not make you safe. It makes you **reliable** to your employer, to the bank, to the EMI system, to the lifestyle machine.

Safety comes from something else: **Safety comes from ownership, reserves and multiple income streams.**

The carrot-and-stick system nobody talks about. Now I'm going to say this bluntly, because soft language keeps people asleep: **The salary system is the world's most successful carrot-and-stick model.**

You've seen this method in leadership, politics and even parenting:

- **The carrot:** reward
- **The stick:** fear
- **The result:** compliance

In salary life, the carrot is obvious:

- Monthly pay
- Bonuses
- Promotions
- Incentives
- Titles
- "Employee of the Month"
- That sweet sentence: *"We're proud of your performance."*

But the stick is always there too:

- Ratings
- Appraisals
- Targets
- Office politics
- Layoffs
- "Restructuring"
- "Cost optimization"
- "Role redundancy"
- "Not a cultural fit"
- "We're exploring other options"

The stick doesn't have to hit you every day. It just needs to be visible in the room. That's how fear works.And here is the real psychological trick:

The carrot arrives monthly while the stick is unpredictable.

So you become addicted to the carrot and terrified of the stick.

That's why people stay trapped in jobs they hate. That's why people accept disrespect.

That's why people quietly surrender their dreams. Because the salary isn't just money.

It becomes your oxygen.

In my journey, I've watched brilliant people, mostly capable people,delay investing, delay building assets, delay starting something of their own because the salary had trained them into one mindset:

"Don't move. Don't take risks. Don't disturb the system."

The New Wealth Order requires the opposite mindset:

"Build assets quietly until salary becomes optional."

THE FIRST MISUNDERSTANDING: INCOME IS NOT WEALTH

Let me make this beginner-friendly.

Income is what you earn like your salary, business income, commissions, freelance income, etc.

Wealth is what you keep and own. Wealth is your **net worth**.

And net worth is simple:

Net Worth = Assets - Liabilities

- **Assets** put money into your life (or grow your value): investments, rental properties, business ownership, land, equity, productive assets.
- **Liabilities** pull money out of your life: loans, credit card debt, consumer EMIs, obligations you must pay to "maintain your status."

A salary is not an asset.A salary is **fuel**.

But always remember, fuel is useful. But fuel is not the destination.

THE SECOND MISUNDERSTANDING: "IF INFLATION IS LOW, I'M FINE"

Here's a truth most people never fully absorb -

Modern economies are designed for prices to rise over time.

In India, the monetary policy framework targets headline inflation around **4%** with a tolerance band of **±2%** (meaning the target range is 2% to 6%).

Even without becoming an economist, you need to understand what this implies:

Your money is designed to lose purchasing power.

That means if your salary is the only engine in your financial life, you are running on a treadmill that slowly speeds up.

And inflation isn't just a theory, it appears in official CPI (Consumer Print Index) prints. For example, India's CPI inflation for **December 2024** was reported at **5.22% year-on-year** (provisional) in MoSPI's press release.

Under the new CPI series (base year 2024=100), the first print reported **2.75% year-on-year** for **January 2026** (provisional).

Inflation moves up and down in the short term. But zoom out and you'll see the long-term direction: upward.The World Bank's data shows India's consumer inflation (annual %) at **5.0% for 2024** (most recent value shown).

The simple impact of inflation (no jargon)

If your family lifestyle costs ₹50,000 per month today, inflation doesn't ask for permission.

It will quietly make that same lifestyle cost:

- ₹55,000
- ₹60,000
- ₹70,000
- and eventually much more

Not because you became luxurious.Because the currency got weaker.

This is why "saving" without investing is not safe.It is a slow surrender.

THE THIRD MISUNDERSTANDING: "MY SALARY WILL KEEP INCREASING"

Yes, salaries increase. But here's what most people miss.**A raise is not wealth. In simple words, a raise is often just a cost-of-living adjustment while wearing makeup.**

For context, salary hike surveys in India often sit in high single digits. For example,

- WTW forecast a **median salary increase of 9.5% in 2025** (similar to 2024 actual).
- Aon projected **around 9% salary increase for 2026**, citing **8.9% actual salary growth observed in 2025**.

Now let's humanize what happens next, what I've observed again and again in my experience.

When people get a raise, they don't use it to buy freedom.They use it to buy *a larger lifestyle.*

New phone. Better car. Bigger rent. Better society. More dining. More "deserved" expenses.

And the biggest trap: **new EMIs**.

So the raise doesn't reduce stress. It increases it.Because the brain starts thinking:

"If I earn more, I can afford more fixed obligations."

That is the moment your salary stops being income.It becomes a **debt-support system**.

You don't feel richer.You feel more trapped.

THE SALARY-TO-EMI PIPELINE

Let's talk about the real system.

In the old wealth order, the hero was the employee.

In the modern world, the hero of the banking system is a very specific person,

A salaried borrower with predictable EMIs.

Because that person is easy to model. Easy to lend to. Easy to profit from.

Here's the pipeline I've watched destroy financial peace in thousands of lives,

1. Get a salary
2. Get a credit card
3. Get "pre-approved" loans
4. Get a car on EMI
5. Get lifestyle subscriptions
6. Get a home on maximum eligibility

7. Upgrade again because "promotion"
8. Keep investing "later"
9. Panic when something breaks

The most dangerous part is not the home loan.

The most dangerous part is what happens **before** the home loan:

Your emergency fund stays weak.

Your investments stay inconsistent.

Your spending becomes permanent.

And your salary becomes the only pillar holding the entire building.

The national reflection (this isn't just personal failure)

ICRA reported that deterioration in household savings in FY2023 was driven by a sharp decline in **net financial savings to a 43-year low of 5.3% of GDP**, alongside a surge in financial liabilities as households borrowed to fund consumption and housing purchases.

And the RBI's Financial Stability Report (as summarized by Reuters) highlighted that India's household debt stood at **41.9% of GDP** (in that snapshot) with **non-housing retail loans** forming **over half** of household debt as of March 2025 and rising delinquencies in some retail segments.

Let's translate that into everyday language.A large number of people are borrowing not to build freedom but to maintain lifestyle. That's the salary myth at scale.

"But my job is stable" — the most expensive belief

In my experience managing wealth across different markets, I've learned one rule:

If your financial plan requires your job to behave perfectly for 30 years, it's not a plan. It's a prayer.

The world of work is changing fast.

The World Economic Forum's *Future of Jobs Report 2025* summarizes what employers expect between 2025 and 2030:

- Job creation and destruction due to structural transformation could amount to **22% of today's total jobs** over 2025–2030.
- Workers can expect **39% of existing skill sets** to be transformed or become outdated over the same period.
- **59 out of 100** workers would need training by 2030 (in the report's simplified illustration).
- **40% of employers** anticipate reducing staff where AI can automate tasks.

Now, I'm not here to scare you with AI headlines.I'm here to restore your dignity.

Because the only way to be truly calm in a changing world is to build a financial life that can survive change.

Layoffs aren't a theory either. Crunchbase's tech layoffs tracker reports:

- **More than 191,000** layoffs in 2023
- Layoffs continued in 2024 and 2025, with **over 127,000** reported in 2025 (in their tally), and continuing into 2026.

Whether you work in tech or not, the message is universal:**No paycheck is immortal.**

So why do people build lifestyles as if it is?

Because the salary myth is emotional,not logical.

THE EMOTIONAL SIDE OF THE SALARY MYTH

The salary myth survives because it feeds three powerful human needs:

1. **Status**

Salary is socially measurable. It becomes your ranking in family functions.

2. **Identity**

"I am my job title" becomes "I am my worth."

3. **Approval**

Parents relax when you get a job. Society claps when you get promoted.

But here's the brutal truth:

Approval does not pay your EMIs.

Approval does not build your retirement.

Approval does not protect your family in a crisis.

Ownership does!

WHAT I NOTICED AMONG MILLIONAIRES AND BILLIONAIRES

Let me share something from my journey.When I sit with ultra-successful people, people who've built real wealth, they almost never start a conversation with:

"How do I get a higher salary?"

They start with questions like:

- "How do I allocate capital?"
- "How do I protect downside risk?"
- "What's the opportunity cost?"
- "How do I build cashflow?"
- "How do I buy time?"

- "How do I structure real estate efficiently?"
- "How do I diversify across geographies and currencies?"

Their language is different because their mental model is different.

They don't think like employees.They think like owners.

And this is the core of The New Wealth Order:

Your salary is not your identity. It is your raw material.

TWO STORIES FROM MY EXPERIENCE

I'm going to share two stories. Details are blended and anonymized to protect privacy. But the patterns are real.

Story 1: The high-income illusion

I once worked with a senior professional, let's call him **Arman**.

Arman earned extremely well. The kind of salary that makes relatives behave politely.He looked wealthy.

But when we mapped his financial life, the truth was simpler:

- Big fixed costs
- Maximum EMIs
- Lifestyle matched income perfectly
- Low liquidity
- Scattered investments
- Overconfidence in job stability

He wasn't rich.He was **expensively dependent**.

Then life happened, a business slowdown, a restructuring, and suddenly his role wasn't "needed" the same way.

His salary stopped, but his obligations didn't.That moment is why I am aggressive about this topic.Because I've watched what it does to good families:

A salary myth doesn't just damage money.It damages relationships, self-esteem, mental health, and peace.

Story 2: The quiet asset builder

Now let's talk about **Neha**.Neha didn't have a dramatic salary. But she had a dramatic strategy.

From early in her career, she made one decision:

"I will not allow my salary to become my only pillar."

So she built:

- An emergency buffer
- Automated investing
- Controlled lifestyle growth
- Skills that increased her earning power
- And eventually, real estate exposure based on numbers, not emotion

Years later, Neha had something rare:

Choice....

She could leave a job without fear.

She could negotiate without desperation.

She could handle shocks without panic.

Neha didn't become free because she earned the most.

She became free because she built ownership early.

THE REAL ESTATE TRAP INSIDE THE SALARY MYTH

Now we need to talk about the most common "wealth move" in the Indian mind:

"Buying property means I'm set."

Sometimes that's true. Real estate can be a powerful tool.

But here is the New Wealth Order distinction:

A home can be emotional wealth

But not always financial wealth

A house becomes financial wealth when it:

- increases your net worth sustainably
- fits your cashflow safely
- doesn't destroy liquidity
- doesn't block investing in other assets
- doesn't make you hostage to your salary

In my experience, people don't just buy property. They buy **validation**.

And validation is expensive.

You buy the biggest home you're eligible for, not the smartest home you can afford.

Then you spend the next 20 years working to keep it.

That is not ownership.

My perspective from managing assets on three continents, that is **reverse ownership** - the home owns you.

In The New Wealth Order, real estate is not about showing people you made it.

It's about building:

- cashflow (rent)
- long-term value
- stability
- and optionality

If your property purchase makes you panic every month, it wasn't a wealth move.

It was a status move.

THE NEW WEALTH ORDER LENS: WHAT SALARY IS ACTUALLY FOR....

This is the turning point.In this book, I'm not asking you to hate salary.I'm asking you to **use salary correctly**.

In The New Wealth Order, salary has five jobs:

Job 1: Run life with dignity

Basic living, family responsibilities, health.

Job 2: Build protection

Emergency fund, insurance, buffers. If life punches you, you don't collapse.

Job 3: Kill bad debt

Bad debt is the stick in the carrot-and-stick model. Remove the stick.

Job 4: Buy assets consistently

This is where wealth begins: disciplined ownership.

Job 5: Buy freedom

You invest until your life is not controlled by one employer, one paycheck, one month.

The old wealth order says: **increase salary**.

The new wealth order says: **convert salary into assets**.

THE "SALARY MYTH TEST" YOU CAN DO TODAY......

If you do nothing else after reading this chapter, do this test.

1. Your Financial Oxygen

How many months can you live if income stops?

2. Your Fixed-Cost Ratio

How much of your monthly income is already promised to someone else?

(EMIs, rent, subscriptions, lifestyle obligations)

3. Your Ownership Ratio

How much of your monthly income is buying assets?

If your ownership ratio is near zero, your future is being built on hope.

And hope is not a strategy.

WHY THIS CHAPTER MAY FEEL UNCOMFORTABLE

Because it attacks a belief you were raised to respect:

"A good job is safety."

I respect good jobs. I respect hard work. I respect professionalism.

But I also respect truth.

And the truth is:**A job is a single point of failure.**

The New Wealth Order is about removing single points of failure in your financial life.

CLOSING: THE SENTENCE THAT CHANGES EVERYTHING

Let me leave you with a sentence I wish someone had drilled into my mind earlier in life:

Your salary should fund your freedom, not your lifestyle inflation.

If you build your life on salary alone, you are always one event away from fear.

But if you convert salary into assets quietly, consistently, intelligently and then one day you wake up and realize something beautiful:

Your job is no longer your master.It becomes your choice.And choice is the highest form of wealth.That is the New Wealth Order.

READER NOTE

This chapter is educational and meant to build financial awareness and decision-making clarity. It is not personalized investment advice. Before acting on any strategy, consider your risk tolerance, obligations, time horizon, and local regulations—and consult a qualified professional if needed.

Chapter 2

THE SAVINGS ILLUSION

From The New Wealth Order — by Speaker Singh

There's a sentence I've heard in almost every country, in almost every income bracket, in almost every language - especially from good, hardworking, responsible people:

"At least I have savings. I'm safe."

I understand why people say it. I respect the intention behind it.

Savings feels like discipline. It feels like adulthood. It feels like protection.

But after more than a decade of advising millionaires and billionaires across different markets, I'm going to tell you the truth - clean and direct:

Savings can protect you from a shock.But savings alone will not protect you from time.

And time is the most expensive force in finance.This chapter exists because the world has changed, but our "middle-class money rules" haven't.In the old world, saving money in a bank account and in fixed deposits felt like the responsible path. In the new world, that same habit when overused quietly turns into a financial trap.

Not because saving is bad.Because saving is not the same as building wealth.

And if you mix these two concepts, you'll work hard for decades and still feel like life is running faster than you.That feeling is not your imagination.That feeling is math.

A STORY FROM MY JOURNEY: THE DAY I STOPPED ROMANTICIZING "SAFETY"

Years ago, early in my career, I met a wealthy family who had already "won" the money game - business ownership, real estate, diversified investments, global exposure, the kind of financial structure most people never see from the outside.

During a conversation, I casually said something like:"Let's keep a big portion safe in cash and deposits."

The head of the family smiled,not arrogantly, just knowingly and said:

"Speaker Singh, cash is not an investment. Cash is waiting."

That line stayed with me.

Because that's what the wealthy understand very early:

- Cash is for stability.
- Assets are for growth.
- Ownership is for freedom.

The poor are forced to think about survival.

The middle class is taught to worship "savings."

The wealthy are trained to master allocation.

This chapter is where I train you to see money the way owners see it—without confusing comfort for strategy.

WHAT IS THE SAVINGS ILLUSION?

The Savings illusion is the belief that:

1. Money in the bank is "safe," therefore it is "smart."
2. If you save enough, you will become wealthy.
3. Low risk = no risk.
4. A fixed return means a guaranteed future.

Here's the reality:Savings is not wealth. Savings is delayed spending.

Savings is a parking lot. Not a factory.

A factory produces value. On the other hand, a parking lot stores value and charges you for it, silently.

Yes, savings gives you peace for emergencies.But if you try to build a lifetime of prosperity using only savings, you are trying to win a marathon with a water bottle.

You won't lose in one day.You'll lose slowly. Quietly. Politely. Over the years.

That's why it's dangerous because you don't feel the damage immediately.

The "safety" you feel is emotional — the loss you face is mathematical.Saving feels safe because it has low volatility.

Your bank balance doesn't jump up and down like the stock market.

Your fixed deposit statement doesn't scare you.

But the real enemy of long-term wealth is not daily volatility.The real enemy is loss of purchasing power.And purchasing power is what actually matters.

Because you don't eat your bank balance.

You eat what your bank balance can buy.

THE THREE SILENT TAXES THAT DESTROY SAVERS....

If you remember only one section from this chapter, remember this:

Savers pay three invisible taxes.

1. Inflation Tax

Inflation is the gradual rise in prices over time.

India officially follows flexible inflation targeting—4% CPI inflation with a tolerance band of ±2% (2% to 6%).That means inflation is not an accident; it's a policy reality you must plan around.

And inflation isn't steady. Look at the range even in recent official data:

- India's CPI inflation for December 2024 over December 2023 was 5.22% (provisional).
- Under the revised CPI series (base year 2024=100), inflation for January 2026 over January 2025 was reported at 2.75% (provisional).

One month, inflation is mild. Another month, it bites.

That's why I don't want you to "plan" using one inflation number. I want you to understand the rule:

Over time, prices rise.And cash that doesn't grow faster than prices becomes weaker.

Even global datasets reflect persistent inflation: India's consumer inflation for 2024 is shown at 5.0% in World Bank data.

So if your savings earn less than inflation, your money is not growing—your money is shrinking.

2. Tax Tax Tax

Most people forget this: even if you earn interest, you may not keep all of it.

In India, interest on bank deposits is generally taxable under "Income from Other Sources". The Income Tax Department's own tutorial lists interest on bank deposits under this head.

Meaning: your interest is not "free money."It's income and it gets treated like income.

So when someone says, "My FD gives 7%," the real question is:

How much is left after tax?

3. Opportunity Cost Tax

This is the tax nobody sees because it doesn't appear on a statement. Opportunity cost is what you could have earned if your capital was allocated better.

This is where the Savings Illusion turns deadly.

Because saving doesn't just fail to make you rich.Saving often prevents you from building assets early—when time matters most.

Time is compounding's oxygen.And if you suffocate compounding for 10 years because you wanted "safety," you may end up paying for that decision for the next 30.

The bank is not your financial guardian, in fact, it's a business.

Let's make something clear without hatred, without drama:Banks are not charities. Banks are spreading businesses.They take your money at a lower rate, and they lend it at a higher rate.

That difference is their oxygen.

Look at the reality of deposit returns versus lending returns (RBI data as reported by Business Standard):

- Weighted average lending rate (fresh rupee loans) of scheduled commercial banks: 8.71% in November 2025
- Weighted average lending rate (outstanding loans): 9.21% in November 2025
- Weighted average domestic term deposit rate (fresh deposits): 5.59% in November 2025
- Weighted average domestic term deposit rate (outstanding deposits): 6.73% in November 2025

You see what's happening?

Your deposit is not "resting."

Your deposit is working.

Just not for you at the same speed.

And savings accounts are an even clearer example of the illusion. For instance, SBI's savings account interest rate (as shown on its own website) was 2.50% p.a. across balances, effective 15 June 2025.

Now compare that to inflation periods like December 2024's 5.22% CPI print.

That gap is not a small gap.

That gap is a wealth leak.

"But money in the bank is safe." Is it?

It's safer than keeping cash under your mattress.

It's useful for liquidity.

It's essential for emergency reserves.

But "safe" has a precise meaning.In India, deposit insurance exists, and that's good. But it is limited.

RBI's own FAQ states that each depositor in a bank is insured up to ₹5,00,000 (principal + interest), in the same right and capacity, in certain failure/merger scenarios.

Now here is the part that most people never think about:

If you have ₹20 lakh sitting in one bank, the "insured" part is ₹5 lakh.The rest is trust.

And as a recent Livemint report notes, DICGC insurance covers 97.6% of total bank accounts, but only 41.5% of the value of deposits, meaning the big money is not fully covered.

So yes! Banks are critical institutions.But blind faith is not a strategy.In The New Wealth Order, we don't run on faith.We run on structure.

THE MOST DANGEROUS LIE: "AT LEAST MY MONEY WON'T GO DOWN."

Let me be aggressive here, because this sentence destroys futures:

If your money "doesn't go down" in number but goes down in purchasing power, it still went down.You just didn't see it.It's like a slow health issue.The report looks "fine" until the day it's not.

Savings protects you from visible pain.

But it exposes you to invisible decay.

THE GLOBAL PROOF: WHY "CASH FOR DECADES" IS A LOSING ASSET CLASS

Let me give you one of the clearest global snapshots of the savings illusion.NYU professor Aswath Damodaran publishes long-term historical returns for the U.S. market.

According to his table, $100 invested at the start of 1928 would have grown (by end of 2025) approximately to:

- S&P 500 (incl. dividends): $1,157,598.95
- 3-month T-Bills (cash-like): $2,578.30

Read that again.

$100 became over $1.15 million in productive ownership (equities).

The same $100 became about $2,578 in "safe" cash-like bills.

That is not a small difference.

That is the difference between:

- ownership compounding, and
- cash slowly surviving.

Cash is not evil.But cash is not how wealth scales.

Now let's look at India's version of the same reality: compounding exists, but volatility scares people away.In India, the opportunity is massive because growth is massive.

For example, the Nifty Indices whitepaper reports that from June 30, 1999 to June 30, 2025, the Nifty 50 delivered an annualized return of 14.04% with annualized volatility of 21.94%.

Let me translate this in human language:

- Equity ownership has historically had strong long-term growth potential.
- But it is emotionally difficult because it moves up and down.

The Savings Illusion survives because people confuse:

- volatility (movement) with
- risk (permanent loss/failure to meet goals).

Sometimes the biggest risk is not volatility.Sometimes the biggest risk is staying "safe" in low-return instruments while your goals get more expensive every year.

THE CARROT-AND-STICK SYSTEM BEHIND THE SAVINGS ILLUSION

Just like the Salary Myth, the Savings Illusion also has a carrot-and-stick model.

The stick: fear

- "Markets are gambling."
- "Real estate is risky."
- "Business can fail."
- "Gold can fall."
- "You'll lose everything."

Fear keeps people parked.

The carrot: comfort

- "FD is guaranteed."
- "At least you'll get interest."
- "At least your money is safe."
- "At least nothing will happen."

Comfort keeps people complacent.So the system trains you to do this:

Work hard → save money → feel safe → repeat → retire hoping it's enough.

And then one day reality arrives:

- education costs
- medical costs
- home upgrades
- inflation
- family responsibilities
- longer life expectancy
- unexpected shocks

Suddenly, your "safe" savings starts feeling small.Not because you were irresponsible.Because you were operating under an outdated rulebook.

REAL PEOPLE. REAL OUTCOMES. TWO STORIES (LOSS + SUCCESS)

Story 1: The "FD Champion" who lost to time

(Details changed to protect privacy, but the pattern is real.)

Rakesh was a disciplined saver. The kind of person families admire.

For years he did this:

- salary came
- expenses controlled
- fixed deposits created
- savings account always "healthy"

He felt proud—and he should have, because discipline is rare.

But here's what went wrong:

He treated saving as the end goal, not the starting point.When his children reached college age, he discovered something painful:

His money had grown in rupees.But the cost of education has grown faster.

Then came a medical event in the family.

Suddenly he had to break deposits, pay tax on interest, and use capital at the worst time.

His biggest shock wasn't the event.His biggest shock was realization:

"I saved for decades… and I'm still financially vulnerable."

This is the savings illusion in one sentence: You can do everything right and still lose if your "right" is based on an old map.

Story 2: The quiet investor who built breathing space

A woman I'll call Neelam (again, anonymized).

She wasn't earning extraordinary money at the start. But she had extraordinary clarity.

From my experience, wealthy families don't "save more."They allocate better.

Neelam did three things early:

1. She built a real emergency fund (not an emotional one).
2. She invested consistently (small amounts, regularly).
3. She didn't chase shortcuts—she focused on compounding.

She still kept savings.But she stopped treating savings as "wealth."

Years later, she had what most people truly want:

- lower anxiety
- higher resilience
- more choices
- and the ability to handle shocks without breaking her future

She didn't become free through luck.She became free because she stopped worshipping savings and started building ownership.

THE REAL ESTATE ANGLE: SAVINGS CAN DELAY YOUR PROPERTY DREAM IF YOU PARK TOO LONG

Now let's bring this home—literally.

Many people try to buy real estate like this:

1. Save for down payment
2. Keep it in savings/FD "until it's enough"
3. Then buy property

There's nothing wrong with saving for a down payment. That's responsible.

But here's the trap I've watched repeat:

While you're saving slowly...

the property market moves.

And if property prices (or even rents) rise faster than your deposit returns, your "safe" savings becomes a treadmill.

You keep running, but the goalpost moves.Now, I'm not saying "buy property at any price."That's foolish.

I'm saying: in the New Wealth Order, you must understand the difference between:

- saving for a near-term goal (smart)
- parking long-term wealth in low-growth instruments (self-sabotage)

Real estate itself has risks—liquidity risk, tenant risk, legal risk, leverage risk, project risk.

But real estate also has one advantage that saving doesn't:It is an asset with utility and scarcity characteristics.

In the New Wealth Order, you don't blindly worship property either.

You evaluate it like an owner:

- cashflow
- Location quality
- Legal clarity
- Leverage safety
- time horizon
- exit options

The most misunderstood concept: "I'm not an investor. I'm a saver."I hear this constantly, and I want you to understand what you are really saying:"I prefer emotional comfort over long-term purchasing power."That is not an insult. That is human.

But it's also a warning.Because the world punishes comfort if comfort blocks growth.

Let me give you a simple framework I teach:

Savings is for:

- emergencies
- short-term goals
- stability
- liquidity

Investing is for:

- long-term goals
- beating inflation
- building net worth
- financial independence

If you use savings for what investing is meant to do, you will feel "safe"... right until the day you don't.

THE NEW WEALTH ORDER RULE: DON'T CONFUSE SAFETY WITH PROGRESS

Here's how I explain it to clients—especially those transitioning from middle-class thinking to owner-class thinking:Savings is protection. Investing is progress.

Protection without progress becomes stagnation.

Progress without protection becomes chaos.

We need both. But in the right proportions.

The "Real Return" test (simple, powerful, life-changing)

Every time someone offers you a "safe" return, ask this:

1. What is my nominal return? (the stated interest rate)
2. What is inflation likely to be over my horizon?

3. What tax might apply to that interest?
4. After all that, what is my real return?

You don't need to be perfect. You need to be awake.

Even with conservative thinking, you'll realize why many savers feel stuck despite "doing everything right."

The Savings Illusion isn't just financial — it's psychological

Here's the emotional damage it causes:

- You keep waiting for "enough."
- You delay investing because you're "still building savings."
- You delay opportunities because "FD maturity is next year."
- You fear market volatility more than purchasing power loss.
- You begin believing wealth is only for "risk takers."

In reality, wealth is for:

- consistent allocators
- disciplined owners
- patient builders

Not gamblers.

WHAT THE WEALTHY DO DIFFERENTLY WITH "SAVINGS"

Let me humanize this with what I've observed working with high-net-worth families.

They still keep cash.But they keep it with purpose, usually in buckets:

***Bucket 1:** Operating Cash (0–3 months)*

This is money for daily life and business operations.

Bucket 2: *Safety Reserve (3–12 months)*

This is insurance against disruption: job loss, business downturn, health issue.

Bucket 3: *Opportunity Cash ("dry powder")*

This is cash held specifically to buy assets when opportunities appear.

Everything beyond these buckets is expected to do a job:

Grow. Compound. Protect purchasing power. Build freedom.

They don't keep large sums in savings accounts because it feels good.

They keep cash strategically, and they deploy it.That's the mindset shift this chapter is designed to install in you.

PRACTICAL BLUEPRINT: HOW TO KEEP SAVINGS WITHOUT FALLING FOR THE ILLUSION

This is the actionable part.

Step 1: *Decide your "sleep-well number"*

This is the minimum amount you need in liquid, low-risk instruments to sleep peacefully.

For some, it's 3 months of expenses.

For others, it's 6–12 months.

The number depends on:

- job stability
- business stability
- dependents

- health situation
- EMI burden

Step 2: *Separate your money by purpose (not by emotion)*

Create separation so you don't mix:

- emergency money
- lifestyle money
- investment money
- down payment money

When money has a clear purpose, you stop making emotional decisions.

Step 3: *Stop keeping long-term money in short-term instruments*

If your goal is 10–20 years away, then parking all of it in savings and fixed deposits is not "safe."

It is financially naive.

Step 4: *Learn basic asset allocation*

In this book, we will go deeper into:

- equities (index funds, diversified ownership)
- real estate (cashflow + appreciation frameworks)
- debt instruments (smart stability)
- gold (strategic hedge, not obsession)
- global diversification (where appropriate)

But the foundation is this:Allocate based on time horizon, not fear.The brutal truth,but said with care.

If you are reading this and thinking:

"Speaker Singh, I've saved my whole life. Are you saying I was wrong?"

No.

I'm saying you were disciplined—now upgrade your strategy.

Savings is not wrong.

Over-reliance on savings is wrong.

Because the world has changed:

- inflation realities
- taxation realities
- deposit rates realities
- life expectancy realities
- opportunity realities

The New Wealth Order is not about disrespecting safety.It's about respecting time.

CLOSING: THE SENTENCE THAT ENDS THE SAVINGS ILLUSION

Here is the lines I want in your bones:

Savings protects your present.

Investing protects your future.

Ownership protects your freedom.

Keep savings. Build reserves. Be responsible.But do not confuse a parked car with a moving journey.Because money that just sits… eventually sits out your dreams.

And in The New Wealth Order, we don't let time defeat us.

We build assets.

We build ownership.

We build a financial life that can outlast inflation, outlast shocks, and outlast the old rules.

That's the point. That's the revolution.

READER NOTE (IMPORTANT)

This chapter is educational and meant to build financial literacy and long-term thinking. It is not personalized financial advice. Taxes and rules can change; always verify current regulations and consider your personal situation before acting.

Chapter 3

INFLATION VS THE MIDDLE CLASS

The Silent Tax That Turns Hard Work Into Slow Poverty

*(From **The New Wealth Order** by Speaker Singh)*

Let me start with a line that will make some people uncomfortable:

If you are middle class and you're not actively fighting inflation, you are not "playing safe." You are donating your future quietly, monthly, automatically.

In my journey working with wealthy families, business owners, and high-performing professionals across countries I've learned one brutal truth that separates the rich from the struggling:

The rich plan for inflation.

The middle class prays inflation won't notice them.

And inflation always notices.Most people think inflation is a headline—some number on the news. In real life, inflation is your grocery bill attacking your salary. Inflation is your child's school fees growing faster than your increment. Inflation is rent increasing while your "fixed" budget stays polite.

In this chapter, I'm going to show you simply, clearly, and aggressively, how inflation is structured to punish the middle class *more than anyone else*, and how the **New Wealth Order** mindset builds systems that don't just survive inflation... they use it.

1. INFLATION ISN'T PRICES RISING. IT'S MONEY DYING.

Let's make it easy.

If last year, ₹100 bought you:

- 2 kg of something

and this year ₹100 buys you

- 1.8 kg of the same thing,

Then the thing or commodity didn't "become expensive."**Your money became weak.**

Inflation is not just "costlier things." Inflation is **the declining purchasing power of currency**, the rupee buying less over time.In India, policymakers explicitly operate with an inflation framework where the target is **4%**, with a tolerance band of **2% to 6%** (for the April 2021–March 2026 period).That means inflation isn't an accident. It's a managed reality.

Now listen carefully:A controlled amount of inflation is considered "normal" for economies. Fine.

But here's the part most middle-class households don't understand:

Inflation is not "equal."

The inflation number you see is an **average**.

Your life is not an average.

A household that spends a big portion on food, fuel, rent, education, and health **feels inflation more sharply** than someone whose biggest spend is "vacations and luxury."

Inflation doesn't hit everyone equally. It never did. It never will.

2. THE MIDDLE CLASS GETS HIT FROM BOTH SIDES

In my experience, the middle class is trapped in a very specific structure:

Side 1: Income is slow.

Most middle-class income comes from:

- salaries
- fixed professional income
- small business cash flows that are fragile

These don't adjust instantly.

Side 2: Expenses are fast.

Middle-class expenses are dominated by:

- food
- rent/housing
- education
- healthcare
- EMIs
- transport
- utilities

These adjust instantly.So inflation creates a cruel daily reality:

Your income negotiates once a year.

Your expenses renegotiate every week.

And inflation is an expert negotiator.

3. THE DIRTY SECRET: INFLATION IS A REGRESSIVE TAX

In plain language:

Inflation acts like a tax that hurts the lower and middle-income groups more.

Why?Because people with lower incomes:

- hold more of their wealth in **cash or bank deposits**
- spend more on **essentials**
- have fewer inflation-hedging assets (equity, businesses, real estate, global diversification)

This idea isn't motivational talk; it's widely recognized in serious economic research.

A major working paper on **inflation inequality in India** shows something most people intuitively feel but rarely see in research form:

- **Inflation volatility is higher for poorer households than for richer households**
- inflation has **persistently remained higher for poor households**

It also highlights that inflation burden is uneven, and that the poorest households can experience **higher effective inflation rates**.

This is not a small technical detail.It means two families living in the same city can face *different inflation realities*—because their consumption baskets are different.

And when you look at consumption weights, the difference becomes obvious: poorer households typically have a **much higher share** of spending tied to food, while richer households have more flexibility and more "miscellaneous" spending.

So when food inflation spikes, the poor and middle class don't just feel "some impact."

They feel a **budget earthquake**.

4. INDIA'S INFLATION REALITY: THE HEADLINE VS THE KITCHEN

Let's put real numbers on the table.

- India's CPI inflation for **December 2024** (year-on-year) was **5.22%** (provisional).
- Food inflation (CFPI) in that same month was **8.39%**.

Now stop. Read that again.

Headline inflation: 5.22%

Food inflation: 8.39%

This is why middle-class households feel like the official number is "lying."

It's not exactly lying.

It's averaging.

But your thali doesn't care about averages. Your kitchen inflation is personal.

5. THE CPI ITSELF IS CHANGING—BECAUSE INDIA IS CHANGING

One of the smartest things India has done statistically is update inflation measurement to reflect changing consumption patterns.

In **February 2026**, India released the **first CPI press release on base 2024=100**, based on the **Household Consumption Expenditure Survey 2023–24**.

That first reading reported:

- **2.75%** year-on-year CPI inflation (Jan 2026 over Jan 2025)

And the new series includes:

- more divisions (moving toward COICOP classification)
- more granular data
- additions like **rural housing** and digital-era expenses like streaming services

Media reporting around the revision also notes a major shift:

Food's weight in the CPI basket drops sharply (from ~46% to ~37%), reflecting that household spending patterns are changing.

And this is important for you as a reader because it proves something:

Even governments admit one truth:

Inflation is not one number. It depends on what people buy.

So if you still treat inflation like a simple "5% problem," you are underestimating the enemy.

6. THE MIDDLE-CLASS SQUEEZE: THE 4 BIG INFLATIONS THAT HURT YOU MOST

In my experience, middle-class financial stress doesn't come from "one big expense."

It comes from **four relentless inflations** that keep returning like monthly EMIs:

1. Kitchen Inflation (Food)

Food is frequent, emotional, unavoidable.

And it spikes hard during supply shocks.

2. Roof Inflation (Rent + Housing Costs)

Even if "CPI housing" looks low in a report, real rent pressure in many cities feels high to working families.

3. Health Inflation (Medical Costs)

One medical emergency can erase years of disciplined savings.

4. Education Inflation (Fees + Coaching + Competition Costs)

For Indian parents, education is not optional. It's identity, pride, and future security.

Middle-class families don't just buy education.

They buy *hope.*

And inflation makes hope more expensive every year.

7. THE GLOBAL INFLATION SHOCK WAS A WARNING SHOT

If anyone thinks inflation is "only an Indian problem," they haven't studied recent history.

In 2022, inflation erupted across developed economies too:

- United States: CPI rose **9.1%** (June 2022, year-on-year), the largest 12-month increase since 1981.
- United Kingdom: CPI rose **11.1%** (October 2022, year-on-year).
- Euro area: annual inflation reached **10.6%** (October 2022).

Now here's why I'm bringing this into a book aimed at Indian readers:

Because inflation is not loyal to any country.

It is loyal to conditions such as energy shocks, food shocks, currency pressure, policy mistakes, global wars or supply disruptions.

If it can hit the US, UK, and Europe that hard... it can hit any nation.

And when inflation rises, **wages rarely keep up**.

The ILO's Global Wage Report (2022–23) captured the reality clearly:

- global monthly wages fell in real terms to **-0.9%** in the first half of 2022 (and **-1.4%** excluding China)

That is inflation beating earnings on a global scale.And once inflation outruns wages, the middle class enters what I call:

The "Invisible Pay Cut" era

You didn't get fired.

You didn't get a salary reduction.

But your lifestyle got downgraded anyway.

8. INFLATION VS SALARY: THE MIDDLE-CLASS ILLUSION OF PROGRESS

This is where the middle class gets emotionally trapped.

You get a raise. You feel proud.

But inflation quietly steals the meaning of that raise.

Here's a simple example:

- Salary increases by **8%**
- Inflation is **6%**

Your real purchasing power increase is not 8%.It's approximately:

$(1.08/1.06) - 1 \approx 1.9\%$

So you celebrated an 8% hike… and inflation said,

"Cute. I'll take most of that."

In my journey, I've seen people work harder every year yet feel poorer every year. They think something is wrong with them.Nothing is wrong with them.

What's wrong is the strategy:

- earning only in **linear income**
- saving in **low-growth instruments**
- ignoring **asset ownership**
- delaying investing because of fear

The bottom line is inflation punishes fear.

9. INFLATION VS SAVINGS: WHY "KEEPING MONEY SAFE" CAN BE DANGEROUS

The middle class loves the word "safe."

Safe FD.

Safe savings.

Safe bank balance.

But inflation changes the meaning of safety.If inflation is 6% and your money earns 0% (cash), then every year:**you lose 6% purchasing power.** Even if your money earns 6%, you may still lose—because taxes exist.

So the question isn't:

"Is my money safe?"

The real question is:

"Is my purchasing power safe?"

Because inflation doesn't steal your money directly.It steals your **future options.**

10. INFLATION AND DEBT: SOMETIMES IT HELPS YOU. USUALLY IT HURTS YOU.

There's a popular finance myth:"Inflation is good if you have loans."

This is only true **in a specific scenario**:

- you have **fixed-rate** long-term debt
- your income rises with inflation
- your EMI stays the same

Then inflation reduces the *real burden* over time.

But here's the middle-class reality I see more often:

- loans are often **floating rate**
- when inflation rises, interest rates can rise
- EMIs increase
- stress increases

Inflation doesn't just raise your grocery bill.

It can raise your EMI too.

That's why inflation and debt is a dangerous combination for families that are already living close to the edge.

And there's another uncomfortable truth:

Inflation doesn't only increase prices.

It increases **borrowing behavior**.

A credible Indian research summary from ICRA highlights that:

- household net financial savings fell to a **43-year low of 5.3% of GDP in FY2023** (from 7.3% in FY2022)
- linked to a surge in financial liabilities as households borrowed for consumption and housing purchases

This is what inflation does socially:

It converts the middle class from "savers" to "borrowers" without them realizing when it happened.

11. THE REAL WAR: CONSUMER INFLATION VS ASSET INFLATION

Now we enter the heart of **The New Wealth Order**.

Most middle-class people fight inflation only on the expense side:

- coupon codes
- cheaper brands
- cutting outings
- delaying purchases

That's survival.

But the wealthy fight inflation on the ownership side.

They own:

- businesses that can raise prices
- assets that rise with inflation (or ahead of it)
- equity stakes
- real estate
- productive systems

This is a different game.

Middle class: "How do I reduce my expenses?"

Wealthy: "How do I increase my ownership?"

And yes, ownership comes with risk.

But ignoring ownership comes with a guaranteed risk: **slow poverty.**

12. REAL ESTATE: INFLATION'S FAVORITE ASSET (WHEN DONE RIGHT)

The Global Reality + Why Dubai Deserves a Special Lens

Let me speak plainly, from my experience managing wealth for high-net-worth families across multiple markets:**Inflation doesn't destroy everyone equally. It punishes the people who only "save" and rewards the people who "own."**And when it comes to ownership, real estate is one of inflation's most misunderstood weapons.

But first, let's kill the fantasy.

Real estate is not magic.

Real estate is not always profitable.

Real estate is not "buy anything, anywhere, anytime."

Real estate is **a system**. And like any system, it pays people who understand structure and punishes people who buy with emotion, ego, or social pressure.

12.1 The two engines of real estate returns (simple, powerful)

When readers hear "real estate return," most think only one thing:

"Property price badhega… appreciation."

That is only half the game.

Real estate returns usually come from two engines:

Engine 1: Cashflow (Rental Yield)

Rental Yield = annual rent ÷ property price

It's the *income* component.

Engine 2: Capital Growth (Appreciation)

This is the *price* component.

And a third force quietly shapes your real result:

Engine 3: Costs + Taxes + Currency

- transaction fees
- maintenance/service charges
- vacancy periods
- financing costs (interest)
- taxes (if any)
- currency movement (if investing internationally)

In the New Wealth Order, we never say:

"Dubai gave 20%" or "London gave 5%."

We ask a more intelligent question:

What is the total return after costs, after vacancy, after fees, after reality?

Because that's the number that changes your life.

12.2 Why real estate often protects against inflation

Real estate has an "inflation relationship" that salaries and savings do not.

Here's why:

- **Land is limited** (you can print currency, you can't print location)
- **Replacement cost rises over time** (cement, steel, labor, approvals, infrastructure)

- **Rents often rise with incomes, population growth, and city expansion**
- **Leverage can amplify outcomes** (good leverage builds wealth; reckless leverage destroys it)

And this isn't just theory. Even global research shows housing behaves very differently across cycles and countries.

For example, BIS data shows that **global real (inflation-adjusted) house prices were down year-on-year in 2025**, highlighting how interest rates and policy can cool markets even when inflation exists.

Translation:

Real estate is not a straight line. It's a cycle.

Inflation is persistent. Real estate is cyclical.

That's exactly why strategy matters.

12.3 A quick world tour: what global real estate looked like recently

Now let's ground this in numbers—because the middle class doesn't lose due to lack of motivation.

They lose due to lack of **measurement**.

Snapshot: recent residential price growth (examples from major markets)

These are not "forecasts." These are documented index-based figures:

- **United States:** Case-Shiller U.S. National Home Price Index showed **~1.4% year-on-year** in **Nov 2025** (percent change from year ago).

- **United Kingdom:** Nationwide reported annual UK house price growth slowing to **0.6% in Dec 2025**.
- **Singapore:** URA reported **private residential property prices rose 3.3% for the whole of 2025**.
- **India:** RBI's All-India House Price Index (HPI) rose **3.1% year-on-year in Q4 FY25** (Jan–Mar 2024–25).
- **Dubai:** ValuStrat reported **Dubai residential capital values up ~19.8% in 2025**, with villas outperforming apartments.

Now pause and absorb the pattern.While many mature markets showed *low single-digit* growth, **Dubai printed double-digit growth** in that period.

This does **not** mean Dubai "always" grows faster.

It means Dubai, in that cycle, became a magnet for global capital and demand.

And that's where the New Wealth Order must pay attention.

12.4 The yield reality: Dubai is playing a different cashflow game

Here's the part most people outside Dubai don't understand:

In many global "trophy cities," rental yields are often low—especially in prime locations—because prices are extremely high. Savills, in a prime residential world cities report, noted prime yields around **3.15% in 2024** (as a global prime benchmark).

Now compare that with Dubai.

A UAE Residential Property Price Report by Reidin (Jan 2025 edition) showed **Dubai gross rental yields around ~7.0%** for the overall residential market in that snapshot.

And on the apartment level, the same report's charts show Dubai apartment gross rental yields around **~7.4%–7.5%** around Dec 2024–Jan 2025.

This is not a minor difference.

That is a **different wealth model**:

- In many global cities, real estate is often a "store of wealth" (low yield, slow cashflow).
- In Dubai, real estate can be both **a store of wealth and a cashflow engine**, depending on what you buy and where.

And Savills explicitly calls Dubai **"a standout destination"** for prime residential property, citing **capital value growth (6.8%)** and **record rent growth (23.5%)** in that year.

So when I tell a reader, "Dubai deserves serious attention," I'm not selling dreams.I'm reading the signals of **cashflow + demand**.

12.5 Why Dubai stands out in the New Wealth Order (the 5 advantages)

From my journey and from the data, Dubai has five structural advantages that make it extremely relevant for the next chapters of this book.

Advantage 1: High global visibility + global buyer demand

Dubai has positioned itself as a global business and lifestyle hub. When global capital moves, it looks for:

- safety
- infrastructure
- liquidity

- regulation
- ease of ownership
- and future growth narratives

Dubai's real estate sector also hit a major milestone in 2025: **over 270,000 transactions worth AED 917 billion**, according to Dubai's government communications.

That is not a small local market anymore. That is a global-scale property economy.

Advantage 2: Yield strength (cashflow matters in inflation)

As shown earlier, Dubai has shown **higher gross yield profiles** than many prime world markets in recent snapshots.

In inflationary periods, cashflow matters because it:

- cushions volatility
- supports EMIs if leveraged
- gives you resilience even if prices go sideways for a while

Advantage 3: Tax structure (a very real advantage for net returns)

This is where many investors wake up.

The UAE government platform states the UAE **does not levy income tax on individuals**.

PwC's UAE tax summary also notes that since there is no personal income tax, **capital gains tax is not imposed on individuals** in the UAE.

Now, pause and understand what this means in investor language:

It's not only about "how much you earn."

It's about **how much you keep**.

Yes! Dubai still has costs:

- Dubai Land Department fees (commonly structured as a **4% fee** in sale registrations, with other admin fees; DLD services list the 4% fee in their sale registration guidance).
- ongoing service charges exist, and Dubai Land Department provides a **Service Charge Index** service via RERA framework to check approved fees for jointly owned properties.

So Dubai isn't "free." But the tax structure can be a meaningful tailwind for **net ROI**.

Advantage 4: Residency pathway via real estate

Dubai ties long-term residency options to investment in a way many markets don't.

Dubai Land Department's investor Golden Visa service states that a real estate investor owning property with a purchase value ≥ AED 2 million can apply for a **10-year renewable residence permit** (with family sponsorship options; mortgaged property has conditions).

This matters because residency reforms change demand. Demand changes price and rent dynamics.

Advantage 5: Transparency signals

Dubai Land Department maintains public-facing portals for **real estate transaction data** and related datasets.In global investing, transparency is not just convenience, it reduces blind risk.

12.6 The honesty clause: Dubai is strong, but it is not invincible

Now let me protect the reader from the most dangerous thing in investing: **overconfidence.**

Dubai has had an extraordinary run. But cycles exist.Reuters reported that **Fitch** warned Dubai real estate prices could face a **double-digit decline** (up to ~15%) due to supply coming online, after strong post-pandemic gains.

Does that mean you shouldn't invest?

No.

It means you must invest like an adult:

- with a margin of safety
- with conservative leverage
- with cashflow focus
- with location logic
- with an exit plan
- with a long enough time horizon

Because the New Wealth Order is not built on hype.

It is built on **systems that survive both booms and corrections.**

12.7 Speaker Singh's rule: "Emotion buys headlines. Systems buy freedom."

Here is my practical rule—simple enough for a beginner, sharp enough for a serious investor:

If you buy real estate as an emotion, inflation will punish you.

If you buy real estate as a system, inflation can become your ally.

Buying as emotion looks like:

- "Everyone is buying there"
- "My cousin doubled money"
- "This developer is famous"

- "I love the view" (view is not cashflow)
- "I'll manage later" (later becomes expensive)

Buying as a system looks like:

- clear goal: cashflow vs appreciation vs mixed
- legal clarity
- realistic rent assumptions
- vacancy buffer
- service-charge awareness
- conservative financing
- liquidity and exit plan
- and a purchase price that makes sense *today*, not only in fantasy

12.8 A Dubai-focused "Return Framework" I want readers to use

When Dubai is done right, the strength usually comes from **stacking advantages**, not betting on one.

Dubai Total Return Stack (conceptual)

1. **Rental yield** (income)
2. **Capital growth** (cycle-dependent)
3. **Tax efficiency** (how much you keep)
4. **Currency factor** (AED is pegged to USD; FX can help or hurt depending on your home currency)
5. **Residency + lifestyle demand** (not a "return," but a demand stabilizer)

And here's the discipline:**Do not assume all five will work perfectly at the same time.**

But if 3 out of 5 work, you still get a strong structure.

12.9 A simple example (to make this beginner-friendly)

Let's do a clean example—no drama, just math.

- Property price: AED 1,000,000
- Annual rent: AED 70,000
- Gross yield: 70,000/1,000,000 = **7%**

Now reality enters:

- service charges
- maintenance
- occasional vacancy
- agent fees
- registration/transfer costs (like DLD fees)

So your **net** yield might become, say, 5%–6% depending on the building and area.This is why smart investors don't ask:

"How much return will I make?"

They ask:

"What is my net yield after real costs, in a conservative scenario?"That's how you build wealth without needing luck.

12.10 How this changes the rest of the book (important for the reader)

From this point onward, **Dubai will not be a side mention** in *The New Wealth Order*.

Dubai will be one of our core case studies for global wealth building, because it sits at a rare intersection of:

- strong global demand
- investor-friendly structure

- yield potential
- and a real, functioning transaction market

In the next chapters, I will guide the reader through:

- **Dubai vs India** as a wealth engine: cashflow vs long-term domestic growth
- **How to analyze Dubai locations** (demand nodes, infrastructure corridors, rental depth)
- **Off-plan vs ready property** (where people win, where they get trapped)
- **Leverage strategy in Dubai** (how to use loans without becoming a slave)
- **How global investors structure property ownership** (risk control + clarity)
- **A "Dubai Due Diligence Checklist"** that protects beginners from expensive mistakes

Because the goal is not to "convince you."The goal is to upgrade you into an investor who can **verify**.That is the New Wealth Order.

13. THE NEW WEALTH ORDER PLAYBOOK: HOW THE MIDDLE CLASS WINS AGAINST INFLATION

Now we bring this chapter home with action- simple, understandable, and practical.

Step 1: Calculate Your Personal Inflation

Your inflation is not CPI.

Your inflation is **your household basket**.

Track:

- rent/maintenance
- groceries
- school fees
- medical spends
- transport
- insurance
- EMIs
- family support

You'll discover something shocking:

You may be living at 8–12% "personal inflation" even when CPI says 5%.

Step 2: Protect the Base (So Inflation Can't Destroy You With One Shock)

You cannot invest confidently if one emergency can wipe you out.

The base includes:

- emergency fund
- insurance (health + life)
- elimination of toxic debt (credit cards, high-interest personal loans)

Step 3: Stop Parking Long-Term Goals in Short-Term Instruments

Your child's education fund is not a savings account goal.

Your retirement is not an FD goal.

Inflation eats low-growth money first.

Step 4: Own Inflation-Responsive Assets (Not Just Earn Income)

The New Wealth Order is based on one sentence:

Don't only earn money. Own what money chases.

Money chases:

- businesses
- productive assets
- ownership stakes
- real assets
- innovation
- land in growing corridors
- well-run companies
- infrastructure themes

Step 5: Build "Multiple Income Engines"

In my journey, the single biggest hedge against inflation I've seen is not a stock.

It's a human.

A person who can:

- increase skill value
- change industries
- build side income
- negotiate powerfully
- sell, consult, freelance, build a brand
- create assets (content, IP, distribution, real estate deals, partnerships)

Inflation cannot easily defeat a person who upgrades their income faster than inflation upgrades their expenses.

14. TWO STORIES FROM MY EXPERIENCE (NAMES CHANGED)

Story 1: The Saver Who Did Everything "Right"

A middle-class couple—disciplined, honest, hardworking—saved monthly for years.

They avoided "risk." They loved FDs. They loved safety.

Ten years later, they had a respectable corpus.

But their real dream—buying a better home and funding their child's future—was still far away.

Why?

Because:

- their money grew slowly
- prices grew steadily
- and the gap kept widening

They didn't fail.

Their strategy failed.

Story 2: The Builder Who Used Inflation Instead of Fearing It

Another client—similar income range—did something different.

They:

- built an emergency base
- bought one well-located asset with conservative leverage

- kept investing consistently
- upgraded skills, increased income, created a second income stream

Over time, inflation raised:

- rents
- asset values (cyclically, not linearly)
- business opportunities

They weren't lucky.

They were positioned.

Inflation rewards positioning.

15. WHAT I WANT YOU TO REMEMBER

Let me end this chapter with a truth that may sting, but will save you years:

Inflation is not an event. It is a system.

And the middle class suffers because they treat it like weather.

The New Wealth Order treats inflation like a war.

Not because we want fear.

Because we want clarity.

If you understand inflation:

- you stop blaming yourself
- you stop chasing only salary increments
- you stop worshipping "safety" that is actually slow loss

- you start building ownership
- you start investing with structure
- you start becoming inflation-resistant

And that is the beginning of wealth.

CHAPTER TAKEAWAYS (READ THIS TWICE)

- Inflation is the silent tax that erodes purchasing power—even when your salary rises.
- Inflation is unequal: poorer households can face higher effective inflation and higher volatility.
- India has experienced meaningful inflation (e.g., CPI 5.22% Dec 2024; food inflation 8.39%).
- India's CPI measurement is evolving (base 2024=100; first Jan 2026 reading 2.75%), reflecting changing consumption patterns.
- Global inflation shocks (US 9.1%, UK 11.1%, euro area 10.6% in 2022) prove inflation can erupt anywhere.
- Wage growth often lags inflation; real wages can fall during inflation spikes.
- Middle-class finances are vulnerable when savings fall and borrowing rises.
- The New Wealth Order response is ownership + systems + compounding—not just "cut expenses."

Chapter 4

WHY MOST PEOPLE STAY FINANCIALLY STUCK

The Invisible Loop That Keeps You Working Hard but Moving Nowhere

*(From **The New Wealth Order** — by Speaker Singh)*

Let me start with a truth that sounds harsh, but it's the kind of harsh that saves people:

Most people don't stay financially stuck because they are lazy.

They stay stuck because they are running on a financial operating system that was designed for a world that no longer exists.

In my journey—working with millionaires, billionaires, founders, senior executives, and families whose money moves across countries and asset classes—I've noticed something very uncomfortable:

Two people can earn the same income… and live completely different financial destinies.

One becomes free.

The other becomes stressed.

One builds assets.

The other builds EMIs.

One sleeps peacefully.

The other keeps checking the bank app like it's a heartbeat monitor.

And the difference is not intelligence.

The difference is **structure**.

This chapter is about the structure that keeps people stuck—and the structure that sets people free.

Because financial stuckness is not a "money problem."

It is a **system problem**.

1. WHAT "FINANCIALLY STUCK" ACTUALLY LOOKS LIKE

Before we solve it, we must define it in normal human language.

You are financially stuck when:

- your salary increases, but your net worth doesn't
- your lifestyle improves, but your peace decreases
- your expenses become permanent, but your income remains fragile
- your savings exist, but one emergency can erase years of progress
- your retirement is a vague hope, not a written plan
- your financial decisions are mostly emotional, reactive, or fear-based
- you are one disruption away from panic

Here is the brutal part:

You can be financially stuck at ₹30,000/month.

And you can be financially stuck at ₹3,00,000/month.

Stuckness is not about income level.

Stuckness is about **how your money behaves.**

2. THE FINANCIAL STUCKNESS LOOP

Most people's lives follow the same loop, month after month, year after year:

1. **Earn salary**
2. **Pay EMIs/rent**
3. **Spend on life + lifestyle**
4. **Save "whatever is left"**
5. **Feel safe because balance looks okay**
6. **Delay investing because fear/confusion**
7. **Inflation quietly makes future goals costlier**
8. **Repeat**

This is why the middle class feels like they're working harder every year, yet the finish line keeps moving.

Because they are not failing.

They are repeating a loop.

And loops don't create freedom.**Systems create freedom.**

3. THE #1 REASON PEOPLE STAY STUCK: THEY CONFUSE INCOME WITH WEALTH

Let me say this in the simplest way possible:

Income is what you earn. Wealth is what you own.

Most people measure success by salary, because salary is public, socially respected, and easy to compare.

But the wealthy measure success by:

- assets
- cashflow
- ownership
- allocation
- risk control
- time

This is why I aggressively teach this in *The New Wealth Order*:

Your job is not to earn more. Your job is to convert what you earn into what you own.

Because income stops when you stop.

Ownership can continue.

4. THE #2 REASON: INFLATION QUIETLY BEATS "MIDDLE-CLASS DISCIPLINE"

The middle class is taught discipline like this:

"Save money. Don't take risks. Be responsible."

That advice sounds noble. But inflation doesn't care about nobility.

India's policy framework itself targets positive inflation (4% with a tolerance band of 2%–6%). That means inflation is not a rare accident; it's a long-term reality you must plan around.

Now combine inflation with the middle-class habit of parking long-term money in low-return instruments and you get this:

You did the "right thing"... and still feel like you're losing.

That is not your imagination.

It's math.

5. THE #3 REASON: THE MIDDLE CLASS IS BEING SQUEEZED BY DEBT

This is where it becomes serious.

When savings don't rise fast enough, many households bridge the gap with borrowing. And borrowing is not always evil—but **consumption borrowing** is a silent trap.

India's household net financial savings fell to very low levels in FY2023, with analysis noting a sharp decline to a 43-year low ~5.3% of GDP, alongside a surge in household financial liabilities (borrowing).

At the same time, India's household debt has been rising. RBI's Financial Stability Report (as summarized by Reuters) put household debt around **41.9% of GDP**, and highlighted that **non-housing retail loans** form **over half** of household debt—meaning a large part of household debt is not home loans, but consumption-like borrowing (personal loans, credit cards, auto loans, etc.).

This matters because **non-housing debt doesn't usually create lasting assets**—it creates obligations.

And obligations have one job:

To keep you working even when you are tired.

You don't need a villain to stay stuck.

A few EMIs are enough.

6. THE #4 REASON: "EMERGENCY SHOCKS" RESET YEARS OF PROGRESS

This is one of the most important truths I learned in my experience:

The middle class doesn't collapse because of one big mistake.

They collapse because they have no buffers.

A single medical event.

A job disruption.

A family responsibility.

A business slowdown.

A legal issue.

A house repair.

A sudden relocation.

And suddenly the savings disappear.

This isn't only India. This is global.

In the U.S. Federal Reserve's Survey of Household Economics and Decisionmaking, **63% of adults** said they would cover a hypothetical **$400 emergency expense** using cash or the equivalent (unchanged from 2023), meaning **a large minority still could not** cover it that way.

In the UK, the Financial Conduct Authority's Financial Lives Survey has highlighted low financial resilience as a major issue (reported and discussed widely, including summaries pointing to roughly a quarter of adults with low financial resilience).

So if you've ever felt, "I saved for years but one event broke me," understand this:

You didn't fail.

You were under-protected.

And under-protection creates stuckness.

7. THE #5 REASON: FINANCIAL LITERACY IS DANGEROUSLY LOW (AND THE WORLD IS NOT FORGIVING)

Most people don't stay stuck because they love being stuck.

They stay stuck because they don't understand money well enough to make confident decisions.

Globally, the OECD/INFE 2023 international survey found that **only 34% of adults** across participating countries/economies reached the minimum target score on financial literacy (70 out of 100). Digital financial literacy was also weak, with only **29%** reaching the minimum target score on digital financial literacy.

And when you zoom into older global benchmarks like the S&P Global FinLit Survey (largest global measure of basic financial concepts), India has historically scored low—around **24%** of adults being financially literate in that survey's India result.

Now I want you to understand why this matters:

When literacy is low, people tend to do one of two things:

1. **They avoid investing** ("It's risky, I don't understand")
2. **They gamble emotionally** ("Tip, WhatsApp, YouTube, get-rich-quick")

Both paths keep you stuck.

The New Wealth Order demands a third path:

Learn enough to allocate capital calmly.

Not as a genius. As an adult.

8. THE #6 REASON: PEOPLE BUILD LIFESTYLES FIRST AND ASSETS LATER

This is where ego becomes expensive.

As income rises, many people don't increase investments first.

They increase:

- rent
- car
- gadgets
- travel
- subscriptions
- "status maintenance"

Then they say:

"I'll start investing when I earn more."

But the same lifestyle expansion will consume the next raise too.

So the person doesn't become wealthier.

They become **more expensive to maintain**.

In my experience, this is the tragedy of the modern middle class:

They don't lack earning potential.

They lack **allocation discipline**.

The wealthy don't "save what's left after spending."

They **spend what's left after investing**.

That is not motivation.

That is mathematics.

9. THE #7 REASON: WORK IS CHANGING FASTER THAN MOST CAREERS ARE ADAPTING

Here's a hard truth:

Many people are stuck because their income engine is fragile.

The global labor market is shifting and skill requirements are changing.

The World Economic Forum's *Future of Jobs Report 2025* highlights that:

- on average, **39%** of workers' existing skill sets are expected to be transformed or become outdated over **2025–2030**
- the same period is expected to see major job churn (creation + displacement), reflecting structural transformation in the labor market

So if your plan is:

"I'll keep doing what I do for 25 years and salary will handle everything,"

then you're not planning.

You're hoping your industry stays loyal to you.

Industries are not loyal.

They are competitive.

This is why the New Wealth Order includes a strong career principle:

Your skills must compound the way your investments should.

10. THE #8 REASON: PEOPLE TREAT INVESTING LIKE ENTERTAINMENT, NOT LIKE ENGINEERING

This is where money gets destroyed.

When people don't have a system, they start doing random things:

- buying assets only when everyone is excited
- selling assets only when everyone is scared
- chasing last year's winners
- falling for "guaranteed return" traps
- trusting influencers more than data
- mistaking speculation for investing

And scams flourish in this environment—globally.

For example, UK-focused reporting has pointed to large numbers of people losing money to investment/pension fraud, and regulators have introduced tools to help consumers verify firms.

This is why The New Wealth Order is aggressive about one rule:

If you cannot explain why you bought it, you didn't invest. You gambled.

Investing is not a mood.

Investing is a process.

11. THE #9 REASON: THE WEALTHY OWN ASSETS — THE STUCK OWN ONLY CURRENCY

This is the uncomfortable structural truth behind modern inequality:

Wealth concentrates because assets compound.

Globally, wealth is extremely concentrated. The World Inequality Report 2022 estimates the top 10% owns about **76%** of global wealth, while the bottom 50% owns about **2%.**

In India, research by the World Inequality Lab has found high concentration at the top (e.g., top 1% wealth share around **~40%** in recent estimates).

Now let's translate this into everyday language:

- The wealthy don't just earn income. They own **what produces income**.
- The stuck don't just lack money. They lack **ownership**.

So the stuck fight inflation with coupons.

The wealthy fight inflation with assets.

That's the game.

12. THE MISSING LEVER MOST PEOPLE IGNORE: GEOGRAPHY AND CURRENCY DIVERSIFICATION

Most middle-class investors think like this:

"India is my life. India is my job. India is my money plan."

There is nothing wrong with loving your home country.

But wealth doesn't ask where you were born.

Wealth asks:

- where capital is treated best
- where rules support investors
- where demand is rising
- where cashflow is strong
- where risk is manageable
- where currency exposure makes sense

In my experience, one of the fastest ways people break out of stuckness is by upgrading from "local thinking" to **global allocation thinking**—even if they start small.

And this is exactly why Dubai will be a recurring case study in the coming chapters of this book.

Not because it's perfect.

Because it is a **real-world laboratory** of modern wealth strategy.

13. DUBAI AS A NEW WEALTH ORDER CASE STUDY: WHY IT MATTERS FOR ESCAPING STUCKNESS

Let's keep this practical and grounded.

Dubai's real estate market recorded **over 270,000 transactions worth AED 917 billion in 2025**, described officially as the strongest performance to date.

Now add the cashflow lens:

A UAE residential property report by Reidin showed Dubai gross rental yields around **~7.0%** in early 2025 snapshots, with apartment yields around **~7.4%–7.5%** in that period.

And the capital growth lens:

ValuStrat reported Dubai residential values up around **19.8% year-on-year** in its Jan 2026 update (with villas outperforming apartments).

Savills has also described Dubai as a standout destination in prime residential markets, citing **capital value growth (6.8%)** and **record rent growth (23.5%)** in that year's context.

Now here is the adult truth:

Dubai is not a guaranteed straight line.

No market is.

Fitch, for example, warned of potential **double-digit declines** (up to ~15%) tied to a large pipeline of supply.

So why am I still positive about Dubai as a *case study*?

Because the New Wealth Order is not built on "always up."

It's built on **structure**:

- yield + demand depth
- transparency and transaction volume
- global investor interest
- strategic, conservative leverage

- cashflow discipline
- risk awareness

Dubai is one of the clearest modern markets where readers can learn how global capital behaves—and how smart investors position themselves without emotional blindness.

And yes, we will take this forward in the next chapters too.

14. TWO STORIES FROM MY EXPERIENCE (ONE LOSS, ONE ESCAPE)

Story 1: The "good life" trap (financial loss story)

I worked with a professional—let's call him **R**. Strong salary. Strong designation. Big social respect.

But his structure was weak:

- EMIs everywhere
- lifestyle grew faster than assets
- savings existed, but investment system didn't
- everything depended on monthly income continuity

Then life happened:

A job disruption. Not permanent—but long enough.

His biggest pain wasn't the lost salary.

His biggest pain was this realization:

"I have built a lifestyle, not a balance sheet."

And that is what stuckness looks like:

You appear successful, but you are financially fragile.

Story 2: The "quiet builder" (success story)

Another client—call her **N**—had a modest start.

But her system was world-class:

- emergency base first
- toxic debt avoided
- automated investing
- annual increase in ownership ratio
- skills upgraded like an asset
- real estate approached as numbers, not emotion
- and later: global exposure added thoughtfully, including Dubai as a cashflow-oriented diversification lens

She didn't become free overnight.

She became free in a way that lasts:

quietly, structurally, permanently.

That is the New Wealth Order.

15. THE NEW WEALTH ORDER ESCAPE PLAN: HOW READERS STOP BEING STUCK

This is the part you can use immediately.

Step 1: Know your real numbers (not your feelings)

- Net worth (assets – liabilities)
- Monthly fixed costs
- "Financial oxygen": how many months you can survive without income
- Ownership ratio: how much of your income buys assets monthly

Step 2: Build the base

- emergency fund
- insurance (health + life as appropriate)
- eliminate toxic debt (credit card revolving, high-interest personal loans)

Step 3: Make investing a system, not a decision

Most people fail because they "decide" every month.

Owners don't decide repeatedly.

They automate and follow process.

Step 4: Learn the minimum literacy needed to not be manipulated

Because global research shows most adults don't meet basic financial literacy benchmarks.

You don't need a PhD.

You need immunity.

Step 5: Build at least one cashflow asset strategy

- equity ownership (diversified)
- real estate cashflow strategy (local and/or global)
- business/side income systems
- intellectual property systems

STEP 6: UPGRADE YOUR INCOME ENGINE

Because skills are shifting and job structures are changing.

Step 7: Think globally as you grow

Not because India isn't enough—India is powerful.

But because diversification protects you from:

- currency risk
- policy shifts
- local cycles

And because global hubs like Dubai provide a live example of how cashflow + capital growth + investor-friendly infrastructure can work—when approached with discipline.

CLOSING: THE SENTENCE THAT ENDS FINANCIAL STUCKNESS

Let me end this chapter with the line I want readers to underline:

Most people stay financially stuck because they build income first and hope wealth will appear later.

The New Wealth Order builds ownership first—using income as fuel.

You don't escape stuckness by motivation.

You escape stuckness by replacing the loop with a system.

And from here onward, we will build that system—step by step—using:

- equities
- real estate (including Dubai as a strategic global lens)
- cashflow frameworks
- and risk intelligence

That is what this book is.

Not inspiration.

Instruction for freedom.

READER NOTE

This chapter is educational and intended to build financial understanding. It is not personalized financial advice. Real estate and market investments involve risk, including potential loss and illiquidity. Always verify current laws/tax rules, use due diligence, and consider professional guidance for your specific situation.

PART 2

THE NEW RULES OF MONEY

Chapter 5

INCOME VS ASSETS

Why Earners Stay Busy... and Owners Get Rich

(From ***The New Wealth Order*** *— by Speaker Singh)*

Let me begin this chapter with a sentence that may irritate people who worship salary slips:

Income is not wealth. Income is fuel.

And if you keep collecting fuel but never build an engine, you'll spend your life "moving" without ever *arriving*.

From my journey—working with millionaires and billionaires, founders, real-estate investors, senior executives, and families who think in decades, not months—I've seen this pattern everywhere:

- The middle class chases income.
- The wealthy chase ownership.
- And the difference between those two pursuits is the difference between a life of stress... and a life of choice.

This is Part 2 of *The New Wealth Order*, because Part 1 was about the traps: salary myths, savings illusions, inflation's attack on the middle class, and why people stay stuck.

Now we move into the antidote.

Now we move into the **new rules**.

And the first rule is the one that changes everything:

If your plan is only "earn more," you are playing the wrong game.

Your plan must be: earn → convert Symbol own.

1. THE TWO TEXT MESSAGES THAT SEPARATE THE TWO WORLDS

In my experience, most people build their self-worth around one message:

"Salary Credited."

It feels like security.

It feels like validation.

It feels like life is stable.

But the wealthy get emotionally calmer from different messages:

"Rent Received."

"Dividend Credited."

"Profit Distribution."

"Interest Payment Received."

"Capital Gain Booked."

Why?

Because salary is a **single pipeline**.

Assets are **multiple pipelines**.

The New Wealth Order isn't about disrespecting jobs.

It's about refusing to remain dependent.

Because a job can be a beautiful starting point.

But if a job is your entire strategy... then your entire life is one fragile line.

And fragile lines break.

2. SIMPLE DEFINITIONS (SO EVEN A BEGINNER BECOMES DANGEROUS)

Let's make this chapter easy to understand even for a reader who has never studied finance.

Income

Money you receive for work, time, skill, service, or effort.

Salary. Consulting fees. Business revenue (if you are personally required every day).

Income is active.

You must show up.

Asset

Something that can (1) put money in your pocket, and/or (2) increase in value over time.

Examples:

- equity (stocks, index funds)
- real estate (rental income + appreciation potential)
- business ownership
- bonds/interest-bearing instruments
- intellectual property (royalties, licensing)

Assets can be active or passive—but the key is: they are *owned.*

Liability

Something that pulls money out of your pocket continuously.

Examples:

- consumer loans taken for lifestyle
- credit card debt
- expensive cars bought for status
- "assets" you can't maintain that become cashflow negative

Now here is the New Wealth Order lens:

The middle class measures life by income.

The wealthy measure life by net worth.

And net worth is simple:

Net Worth = Assets – Liabilities

If your income rises but your net worth doesn't… you are getting busier, not richer.

3. WHY INCOME FEELS POWERFUL BUT KEEPS YOU TRAPPED

Income has a special power: it's immediate.

You work.

You get paid.

You feel progress.

But income has four hidden weaknesses that keep people stuck.

Weakness 1: Income is linear

Most income grows in straight lines:

increment → promotion → increment → promotion.

But most meaningful wealth grows exponentially through compounding.

Weakness 2: Income is fragile

A job loss, a health event, an industry shift, a business slowdown—income can pause overnight.

Weakness 3: Income is taxed first (in most systems)

Across the world, earned income is usually the easiest thing for governments to tax.

Weakness 4: Income loses to inflation if it's not converted into assets

Even when your salary increases, your purchasing power can still fall if inflation and lifestyle rise faster.

This is not theory. The global wage story itself proves how fragile income is.

The ILO's Global Wage Report 2024–25 notes:

- **global real wages grew 1.8% in 2023** and projected **2.7% in 2024**, after –0.9% in 2022 when inflation outpaced wage growth.

So even globally, wages can *literally go backward* in real terms when inflation spikes.

And here's another brutal line from the same ILO release that reveals why ownership matters:

- the **lowest-paid 10%** earn **0.5%** of the global wage bill, while the **highest-paid 10%** earn nearly **38%** of it.

Translation: even within the "income world," the game is unequal.

So if income is unequal and fragile… why do most people still chase it like it's the final destination?

Because they were trained to.

4. THE WEALTHY UNDERSTAND SOMETHING MOST PEOPLE NEVER LEARN:

Income is what you use to buy assets. That's it.

Let me say this like I would say it to a client sitting across my table:

Your salary is not your identity.

Your salary is your *seed capital.*

The rich do not "love money" more than you.

They love **systems** more than you.

Their system is simple:

1. generate income
2. convert income into assets
3. let assets generate more income
4. repeat until income becomes optional

The middle class often does the reverse:

1. generate income
2. convert income into lifestyle
3. hope savings will be enough
4. repeat until retirement becomes fear

This is not a motivation issue.

This is an architecture issue.

5. THE OWNERSHIP GAP IS WHY THE RICH GET RICHER (DATA, NOT DRAMA)

People love to turn wealth into morality stories.

But the New Wealth Order is not a morality book.

It's a reality book.

Global inequality data shows how ownership concentrates.

The World Inequality Report 2022 states:

- the **poorest half** of the global population owns about **2% of total wealth**
- the **richest 10%** own about **76% of global wealth**

That's not because the top 10% "work 38 times harder."

It's because the top 10% owns assets that compound.

This is why I push this message aggressively:

If you don't build ownership, you will always be financially polite.

And the world does not reward polite. It rewards positioned.

6. PROOF THAT ASSETS CRUSH CASH OVER TIME (THE COMPOUNDING EVIDENCE)

Now I want you to see a number that should permanently destroy the savings-worship mindset.

NYU professor Aswath Damodaran publishes historical return tables showing the compounded value of $100 invested in different instruments.

According to his updated table (January 2026), **$100 invested at the start of 1928** would have become by **end of 2025** approximately:

- **$1,157,598.95** in the S&P 500 (including dividends)
- **$2,578.30** in 3-month T-bills (cash-like)

Read that slowly.

That is not "small difference."

That is not "some advantage."

That is the difference between:

- **ownership compounding**, and
- **money surviving**.

Now, I'm not saying everyone should only buy U.S. equities.

I'm saying the concept is universal:

Over long periods, productive assets tend to outperform cash-like parking.

And India has its own proof.

The Nifty 50 whitepaper reports that from **June 30, 1999 to June 30, 2025**, the Nifty 50 delivered:

- **14.04% annualized return**
- **21.94% annualized volatility**

Translation: yes, ownership moves up and down.

But over time, ownership has historically been a powerful wealth engine.

This is a New Wealth Order rule:

Volatility is the price of entry.

Compounding is the reward for staying disciplined.

7. THE "INCOME TRAP" I SEE EVERY WEEK (FROM MY EXPERIENCE)

Let me share a pattern from my journey.

I have met people who earn extremely high incomes—doctors, senior executives, global consultants, celebrities, even high-paid traders—who are still financially fragile.

They look successful.

But their wealth architecture is weak.

How?

Because their money is trapped in three places:

1. **Lifestyle expansion** (bigger home, bigger car, bigger obligations)
2. **Illiquid emotional purchases** (status real estate, vanity investments)
3. **Wrong "safety"** (too much cash, too many low-return instruments)

Then one disruption hits:

- job change
- health issue
- recession
- business slowdown
- family emergency

And suddenly their "high income" becomes irrelevant.

Because income without assets is like:

- a powerful engine
- installed on a vehicle with no fuel tank
- and no spare tires

It will run… until it doesn't.

8. THE NEW RULES OF MONEY: YOU MUST BUILD "ASSET PAYROLL"

This is the concept that separates earners from owners.

In The New Wealth Order, I teach people to build **Asset Payroll**.

That means:

You build enough cashflow from assets so your life doesn't collapse if your job pauses.

Asset payroll can include:

- rent from real estate
- dividends
- interest income
- business profit distributions
- royalties
- REIT distributions
- global property income (yes, including Dubai when done correctly)

And here is the aggressive truth:

If your entire life is funded by one salary, you are not secure.

You are dependent.

Security is not "stable job."

Security is "multiple income engines."

9. REAL ESTATE VS THE WORLD: WHY LOCATION AND CYCLE MATTER

Now we bring in real estate, because real estate is where most Indians emotionally believe "wealth lives."

But as I said earlier in this book:

Real estate is not magic.

Real estate is not always profitable.

Real estate is not "buy anything, anywhere, anytime."

Real estate is cyclical.

BIS data shows that in **Q2 2025, global house prices declined in real terms by 0.8% year-on-year**, with different outcomes in advanced vs emerging markets.

Meaning: inflation exists, but property does not always rise in inflation-adjusted terms. Policy, rates, supply, demand—everything matters.

Now let's look at how different markets behaved recently, just to teach the reader what cycles look like:

- **United States:** Case-Shiller National index showed **1.4% year-on-year** change in **Nov 2025**.
- **United Kingdom:** Nationwide reported annual growth slowed to **0.6% in Dec 2025**.
- **Singapore:** URA reported private residential prices increased **3.3% for the whole of 2025**.
- **India:** RBI all-India HPI rose **3.1% year-on-year in Q4 FY25**.
- **Dubai:** ValuStrat reported **19.8% annual appreciation** in its Jan 2026 update.

Now listen carefully:

I'm not presenting these numbers to say "Dubai always wins."

I'm presenting them to show the reader what intelligent investors do:

They compare markets. They compare cycles. They compare yield. They compare demand.

They don't buy property like religion. They buy it like strategy.

And this is where Dubai becomes extremely relevant in the New Wealth Order conversation.

10. WHY DUBAI MATTERS IN THE INCOME VS ASSETS CHAPTER

Because Dubai is a real-world example of what happens when:

- global capital flows into a hub
- demand rises
- transactions deepen
- yields stay attractive (in many segments)
- and policy supports long-term residency and investor participation

Dubai's government communications reported that in **2025**, Dubai's real estate sector achieved:

- **over 270,000 transactions**
- **AED 917 billion** in value

That scale matters.

Because liquidity matters.

If you cannot sell, you don't truly own an asset—you own a locked box.

Now let's talk yield, because yield is what turns real estate from "hope" to "engine."

A Reidin UAE residential property report (Jan 2025) showed:

- **Dubai residential market gross rental yield ~7.00% (Jan 2025)**
- **Dubai apartment gross rental yield ~7.50% (Jan 2025)**

That is gross yield, not net.

Net will reduce after service charges, maintenance, vacancy, fees.

But the point stands:

In many mature "trophy cities," yields can be low.

Dubai, in this cycle, has shown yield strength in many segments.

And yield strength is what helps real estate become **asset payroll**.

This matters for the reader because:

Income is fragile. Cashflow assets reduce fragility.

Now add tax structure to the discussion (because net return is what matters, not marketing return):

- The official UAE government platform states the UAE **does not levy income tax on individuals**.
- PwC's UAE individual tax summary notes that since there is no personal income tax, **capital gains tax is not imposed on individuals** (for UAE national or resident individuals).

And Dubai Land Department states that a property investor with purchase value ≥ AED 2 million can apply for a **10-year renewable Golden Visa** (with conditions).

Again: this is not a "guarantee of profit."

But it is a structural advantage in global allocation discussions.

This is why Dubai will remain a central case study in upcoming chapters.

Because the New Wealth Order is global.

Money has no passport loyalty.

Capital goes where it is treated well.

11. THE CREDIBILITY CLAUSE: DUBAI IS STRONG, BUT CYCLES STILL EXIST

Now, because I'm writing this book to build intelligent investors—not blind followers—I must say this clearly:

Dubai can correct. Dubai can cool. Dubai can punish emotional buyers.

Reuters reported that **Fitch** forecast a potential **double-digit decline** (up to **15%**) in Dubai real estate prices in **2H 2025 into 2026**, driven by a surge in supply (about **210,000 units** projected).

This is exactly why the New Wealth Order rule is:

Don't buy Dubai. Buy a deal.

Don't buy hype. Buy cashflow + location + legal clarity.

Dubai is not a shortcut to wealth.

Dubai is a market—one that can be powerful when approached with discipline.

12. THE INCOME VS ASSETS REALITY:

why income makes you feel "safe," but assets make you actually "free"

Here's the cleanest explanation for beginners:

If you stop working today...

- **Income stops.**
- **Assets may continue.**

That's it.

That's the entire difference between:

- a financially stressed life, and
- a financially flexible life.

Income is like oxygen.

You need it.

But oxygen is not the destination.

Oxygen is what helps you build the ship.

Assets are the ship.

13. THE NEW RULES OF MONEY: 9 LAWS I WANT THE READER TO ADOPT

Law 1: Your first goal is not "more income." It's "more ownership."

Chase income if you must—but convert it.

Law 2: Every raise must increase your asset-buying power

If your lifestyle consumes every raise, you are not progressing—you are just upgrading your cage.

Law 3: Build protection first, then growth

Emergency fund. Insurance. Toxic debt elimination.

Then build assets aggressively.

Law 4: Stop saving "whatever is left."

Owners invest first and live on the remainder.

Law 5: Learn the difference between "good debt" and "stupid debt"

Debt that buys productive assets can be strategic.

Debt that buys lifestyle is slavery.

Law 6: Make investing a system, not a decision

Most people lose because they "decide" emotionally every month.

Owners automate. Owners allocate. Owners rebalance.

Law 7: Understand total return

For any asset, look at:

- cashflow (yield)
- appreciation
- costs
- taxes
- liquidity
- risk

Law 8: Diversify across asset classes and geographies

This is why Dubai becomes relevant:

- it can add cashflow potential
- and global exposure
- if done with discipline

Law 9: Your life must not depend on one income line

Build multiple engines.

Because one engine failure should not destroy your family's future.

14. TWO STORIES FROM MY EXPERIENCE (ONE WARNING, ONE BLUEPRINT)

Story 1: The "High Income, Low Net Worth" tragedy

(Details changed to protect privacy, but the pattern is real.)

A client—let's call him **A**—earned what most people dream of. He was respected, successful, admired.

But he had:

- huge lifestyle costs
- multiple EMIs
- minimal real investing discipline
- "savings" that looked big but weren't big enough for his obligations
- and no asset payroll

Then his industry faced turbulence. His income reduced.

And the truth hit him like a slap:

"My income looked like power... but my net worth was weak."

He wasn't a bad person.

He wasn't irresponsible.

He was simply trained to chase income like a trophy.

And trophies don't pay bills.

Assets do.

Story 2: The "Medium Income, High Ownership" escape

A woman—call her **N**—didn't start rich. She started structured.

She did this:

1. emergency base first
2. automated investments monthly
3. annual increase in asset allocation
4. avoided lifestyle inflation traps
5. later added real estate with a cashflow lens
6. later explored global diversification as net worth grew

She didn't become free overnight.

But she became free in the only way that lasts:

quiet, disciplined, boring compounding.

That is the New Wealth Order.

15. THE BEGINNER'S BLUEPRINT: HOW TO SHIFT FROM "INCOME LIFE" TO "ASSET LIFE"

Here's the step-by-step plan I would give to a reader who is new, confused, and afraid of investing.

Step 1: Calculate your "Survival Cost"

How much money you need per month to run your life.

Step 2: Build a 3-layer foundation

1. Emergency fund
2. Health insurance + life cover (as appropriate)
3. Remove toxic debt

Step 3: Create your "Ownership Ratio"

Every month ask:

What percentage of my income bought assets this month?

Not saved. Bought assets.

Even 10% is a start.

But the goal is to increase.

Step 4: Start with simple, diversified ownership

In India, for many beginners, broad equity exposure can be a logical learning path (with risk awareness).

The goal is not to "win fast."

The goal is to build an ownership habit.

Step 5: Add real assets when your foundation is stable

Real estate—done correctly—can become a cashflow engine.

And global markets like Dubai can become a case study for how yield + demand + international capital flows behave—when approached with discipline and due diligence.

Step 6: Reinvest cashflow

This is where compounding becomes violent (in a good way).

Cashflow that you spend becomes lifestyle.

Cashflow that you reinvest becomes freedom.

16. THE AGGRESSIVE TRUTH I WANT TO LEAVE IN THE READER'S MIND

Let me end this chapter with the line that defines Part 2:

If your entire plan is salary increments, you will remain a worker in the economy.

If your plan is asset ownership, you become an owner in the economy.

The New Wealth Order is not about being reckless.

It's about being realistic.

Because the world doesn't reward effort alone.

It rewards **ownership + allocation + compounding + patience**.

So here is your identity choice:

- **Earner**: respected, busy, taxed, fragile
- **Owner**: calm, positioned, resilient, compounding

Your job is not to pick one forever.

Your job is to **graduate**.

Use income as fuel.

Convert it into assets.

Build asset payroll.

And make your future so strong that you never again fear a single paycheck.

That is the New Wealth Order.

READER NOTE

This chapter is educational and not personalized financial advice. All investing involves risk, including loss of capital and illiquidity (especially in real estate). Cross-border investing can add legal, tax, and currency complexity—always verify current rules and consult qualified professionals for your situation.

Chapter 6

CAPITAL ALLOCATION STRATEGY

**Why the same income creates poverty for some…
and freedom for others**

(From ***The New Wealth Order*** *— by Speaker Singh)*

Let me begin this chapter with the most offensive truth in personal finance—offensive because it's accurate:

Most people don't have an "income problem."

They have a capital allocation problem.

They earn. They save. They invest "sometimes."

But they don't allocate capital like a decision-maker.

And in my journey—more than a decade managing wealth conversations with millionaires and billionaires across different markets—I can tell you this with absolute clarity:

The wealthy don't win because they know a secret stock.

They win because they know where money should live, why it should live there, and when it should move.

That is capital allocation.

And if you want to enter **The New Wealth Order**, you must stop behaving like a consumer of money and start behaving like the **CFO of your family**.

Because money doesn't respect emotions.

Money respects structure.

1. WHAT "CAPITAL ALLOCATION" REALLY MEANS (SIMPLE DEFINITION, POWERFUL IMPACT)

Capital allocation strategy is one thing:

Where each rupee goes—by design, not by accident.

Every rupee you earn must go into one of these destinations:

1. **Consumption** (today's lifestyle)
2. **Protection** (emergency fund, insurance, stability)
3. **Debt reduction** (removing obligations that eat your future)
4. **Investment** (assets that fight inflation and build ownership)
5. **Opportunity capital** (dry powder for rare moments)

Most people allocate like this:

"First I live my life… then whatever remains, I save or invest."

The wealthy allocate like this:

"First I build the future… then I live from what remains."

Same money. Different destiny.

That's the New Wealth Order mindset.

2. THE BIGGEST MYTH: "INVESTING = PICKING STOCKS"

Let me be aggressive because this misunderstanding keeps people poor for decades:

Investing is not stock-picking. Investing is allocation.

Stock-picking is a *small* layer inside the larger system.

Your real wealth outcome is driven by three decisions:

1. **Asset allocation** (how much in equities, debt, real estate, gold, cash, global assets, etc.)
2. **Implementation** (which products/vehicles, costs, taxes, liquidity)
3. **Behaviour** (staying disciplined, not panic-selling, not chasing hype)

People obsess over #2 and #3 while ignoring #1.

That is like arguing about which brand of fuel to buy while you never built the engine.

3. RESEARCH THAT SHOULD END THE DEBATE: ALLOCATION DOMINATES YOUR EXPERIENCE

There's a famous set of studies in institutional investing that many professionals refer to (and many people misunderstand).

Brinson, Hood, and Beebower's work ("Determinants of Portfolio Performance") examined how much a portfolio's policy (asset mix) explained the **variability** of returns over time.

Vanguard has also published a detailed discussion explaining what these studies actually mean—and what people incorrectly claim they mean.

Here's the beginner-friendly translation:

- **Your target mix** (for example, 60% equity/40% bonds) tends to explain a large share of the up-and-down movement of your portfolio over time.
- This does **not** mean "asset allocation explains 90% of your final wealth." That's a common misunderstanding, and even Vanguard explicitly calls out this misconception.

But here is the key point that remains true:

If your asset allocation is wrong for your goals, nothing else can save you.

Not stock tips. Not YouTube. Not a "hot sector." Not a "guaranteed plan."

Capital allocation is the foundation.

4. THE NEW WEALTH ORDER RULE: WEALTH IS BUILT BY POLICY, NOT BY MOOD

Most people invest based on mood:

- "Market is high, I'll wait."
- "Market is falling, I'm scared."
- "Gold is moving, buy gold."
- "Dubai is booming, buy Dubai."
- "Crypto is trending, I don't want to miss out."

This is emotional allocation. It creates random results.

Owners allocate by **policy**:

- clear goals
- time horizon
- risk capacity
- liquidity needs
- diversified buckets
- rebalancing rules

This is engineered allocation. It creates repeatable results.

5. THE TRUTH ABOUT RETURNS: ASSETS BEAT CASH OVER TIME (HISTORY IS LOUD)

Let's destroy the "I'll keep it safe in cash forever" mindset with one brutal dataset.

NYU professor Aswath Damodaran's historical returns table shows what happened to **$100 invested at the start of 1928**, by end of 2025:

- S&P 500 (incl. dividends): **$1,157,598.95**
- 3-month T-Bills (cash-like): **$2,578.30**

This is not a small gap.

This is the difference between:

- owning productive assets
- and parking money in "safety" for life

Now, I'm not saying "buy only U.S. stocks."

I'm saying the principle is universal:

Over long time periods, productive assets have historically outperformed cash-like parking.

India has its own evidence. The Nifty 50 Whitepaper reports that from **June 30, 1999 to June 30, 2025**, the Nifty 50 delivered:

- **14.04% annualized return**
- **21.94% annualized volatility**

Volatility is the entry fee.

Compounding is the reward.

6. GLOBAL PROOF (125 YEARS): THE "LAW" OF RISK AND RETURN IS UNDEFEATED

If you want world-class capital allocation, you must stop thinking in 2–3 year timelines.

UBS's Global Investment Returns Yearbook (built on the Dimson–Marsh–Staunton dataset) is considered a major authority on long-run asset performance.

A Cambridge summary of the Yearbook's findings reports that over the long run (1900–2024), annualised **real** returns were roughly:

- **5.2%** for worldwide equities
- **1.7%** for bonds
- **0.5%** for bills (cash)

And UBS's media note highlights that global stocks delivered an annualized **real** return of **3.5%** in the 21st century and an **equity premium vs cash** of **4.3%**.

Translation for the reader:

- Ownership has historically been rewarded, but not smoothly.
- Cash has historically felt safe, but it quietly loses purchasing power.
- Your job is to allocate across assets so you can survive bad cycles and still capture long-run compounding.

7. CAPITAL ALLOCATION IS NOT ABOUT "MAXIMUM RETURN." IT'S ABOUT SURVIVAL + GROWTH

If you only chase return, you will eventually blow up.

From my experience advising wealthy families, the first priority is not return.

The first priority is: don't die financially.

That means:

- never be forced to sell assets in a panic
- never be forced to borrow at terrible rates
- never allow one emergency to erase 10 years of progress
- never concentrate your entire future into one asset class

So in the New Wealth Order, capital allocation has two objectives:

1. **Resilience** (you can take shocks)
2. **Compounding** (you can grow over time)

8. SPEAKER SINGH'S CAPITAL ALLOCATION FRAMEWORK: THE 5 BUCKETS

This is the framework I use to simplify complex wealth conversations.

You don't need finance jargon.

You need clear buckets with clear jobs.

Bucket 1: The Oxygen Bucket (Liquidity)

Job: Keep you alive.

This is:

- emergency fund
- short-term needs
- predictable expenses
- "sleep-well money"

Rule: This bucket is not to get rich. It's to prevent poor decisions.

Bucket 2: The Stability Bucket (Defense)

Job: Reduce volatility and provide stability.

This includes:

- high-quality debt instruments
- conservative fixed-income exposure
- instruments aligned to near-term goals

This bucket reduces the probability of panic.

Bucket 3: The Growth Bucket (Offense)

Job: Beat inflation and build ownership.

This includes:

- diversified equity exposure (domestic + possibly global as appropriate)
- long-horizon assets that can compound

This bucket is where wealth is born.

Bucket 4: The Real Assets Bucket (Inflation Relationship)

Job: Anchor value in scarcity/utility assets.

This includes:

- real estate (cashflow + appreciation potential)
- selective gold exposure (not obsession—strategy)

Real assets protect against certain inflation regimes, but they are cyclical and require intelligence.

Bucket 5: The Opportunity Bucket (Tactical/Optional)

Job: Capture rare opportunities without destroying the core plan.

This bucket is small, controlled, and rule-based.

If you don't have rules, this bucket becomes gambling.

9. THE STEP-BY-STEP CAPITAL ALLOCATION STRATEGY (THE ACTUAL SYSTEM)

Now let's engineer it, like a professional.

Step 1: Define your time horizons (this changes everything)

Allocate by *when you need the money*.

- 0–2 years: liquidity + high stability

- 3–7 years: balanced stability + growth
- 8–15+ years: growth heavy (with risk management)

When people ignore horizon, they commit the biggest mistake:

They invest long-term money in short-term vehicles (low growth) OR short-term money in high-volatility assets (panic selling).

Step 2: Calculate your "financial oxygen"

Ask one question:

If your income stops today, how many months can you survive without selling long-term assets?

That number decides whether you are resilient or fragile.

Step 3: Decide your risk capacity (not your ego)

Risk tolerance is psychological. Risk capacity is mathematical.

- If you have no emergency fund, your risk capacity is low.
- If you have heavy EMIs and dependents, your risk capacity is lower.
- If your job is unstable, risk capacity is lower.
- If you have long time horizon and strong buffer, risk capacity rises.

Capital allocation is not about bravery.

It's about math.

Step 4: Build a strategic asset allocation (your "policy portfolio")

This is your long-term target mix.

Vanguard repeatedly emphasizes that the mix of assets largely defines the range of returns you can expect, and disciplined adherence matters.

You are not creating a "perfect portfolio."

You're creating a portfolio you can stay with for years.

Step 5: Implement with low friction (costs, taxes, liquidity)

The best allocation fails if implementation is sloppy.

You must account for:

- fees and commissions
- tax leakage
- liquidity constraints
- lock-ins
- transaction costs

A "high return" that you can't access when needed is not wealth.

It's a trapped number.

Step 6: Rebalance (because markets will move your portfolio without permission)

Rebalancing is not about being smart.

It's about staying aligned to your risk profile.

Vanguard explicitly states rebalancing is primarily about **risk management**, not about scoring maximum returns.

And Vanguard research notes that without rebalancing, allocations drift—often creating much higher risk than intended (for example, a 60/40 portfolio drifting heavily toward equities over long periods).

Step 7: Protect retirement from "sequence risk"

This is where average investors get destroyed.

Sequence-of-returns risk matters most when retirement begins in a bad market sequence; withdrawals during early losses can permanently damage the portfolio.

So allocation must evolve as your timeline changes.

10. WHAT CAPITAL ALLOCATION LOOKS LIKE IN REAL LIFE (3 ARCHETYPES)

These are not "recommendations." They are educational archetypes to help readers think clearly.

Archetype A: The Protector (stability-first)

- high liquidity needs
- low risk capacity
- near-term obligations

Allocation leans toward Buckets 1 and 2, with smaller growth exposure.

Archetype B: The Builder (growth-first)

- strong emergency base
- long horizon
- stable income engine

Allocation leans toward Bucket 3 (growth), with rules for Bucket 1 and 2 so panic never forces selling.

Archetype C: The Owner (multi-engine)

- diversified across equities + real estate + fixed income
- rebalancing discipline
- opportunity capital reserved

This is where wealthy families usually live: not extreme, but structured.

11. THE REAL ESTATE LESSON: WHY PROPERTY MUST BE ALLOCATED LIKE A BUSINESS

Real estate is where emotion becomes expensive—especially for Indian families.

But global data shows something important:

Property markets do not move uniformly.

Policy, interest rates, supply, and cycle matter.

BIS reported that in **Q2 2025**, aggregated global house prices adjusted for consumer prices fell **0.8% year-on-year**, marking continued global decline in real terms.

In the U.S., Case-Shiller data shows home price growth around **1.4% year-on-year** in **November 2025**.

In the UK, Nationwide reported annual house price growth slowed to **0.6%** in **December 2025**.

That's the reality of mature markets in that period: often low single-digit growth.

Now compare that with Dubai in the same cycle…

12. DUBAI AS A CASE STUDY INSIDE CAPITAL ALLOCATION (WHY IT KEEPS SHOWING UP IN THIS BOOK)

I will be clear: **Dubai is not magic.**

But Dubai is strategically important in modern capital allocation—especially for investors who are ready to think globally.

Dubai's government communications reported that the real estate sector in **2025** recorded:

- **over 270,000 transactions**
- **AED 917 billion** in value
- and described it as the strongest performance to date.

Now look at the two return engines:

Engine 1: Cashflow (yield)

Reidin's UAE Residential Property Price Report shows Dubai apartment **gross rental yields** around **~7.41% (Dec 2024) to ~7.50% (Jan 2025)** in its snapshot charting.

Engine 2: Capital growth (cycle-dependent)

ValuStrat reported annual appreciation of **19.8%** (Jan 2026 update, year-on-year) on its ValuStrat Price Index.

Savills also called Dubai a standout prime destination, noting prime yields and highlighting Dubai's prime capital value growth and record rent growth in that report context.

That is why Dubai gets attention in The New Wealth Order:

Because in that cycle, Dubai showed a rare combination of transaction depth, strong rent dynamics, and strong price dynamics.

But I will not let you become blind.

The adult warning: Dubai can correct

Reuters reported Fitch's view that Dubai real estate prices could face a **double-digit decline (up to ~15%)** in late 2025 into 2026 due to a surge in supply (with **210,000 units** projected), after a strong post-pandemic rise.

So what is the New Wealth Order approach?

Allocate to Dubai like an investor, not like a fan.

- focus on yield quality
- conservative leverage
- realistic vacancy assumptions
- service charges and net yields
- location logic
- legal clarity
- exit plan

Dubai is not a "bet."

Dubai is a **sleeve** inside a global real-assets allocation—when your financial base is strong.

13. A GLOBAL "CORE PORTFOLIO" IDEA (WHY 60/40 STILL MATTERS CONCEPTUALLY)

Even if you never use a classic 60/40, the principle matters:

Balance growth with stability so you can stay invested.

J.P. Morgan's Guide to the Markets (daily edition dated Jan 26, 2026) illustrates how $100,000 compounded over 20 years under different mixes, with "stocks," "bonds," and "60/40 portfolio" shown as separate outcomes.

You don't need to memorize the numbers.

You need the lesson:

- Too aggressive → panic and emotional selling
- Too conservative → inflation slowly eats your future
- Balanced allocation → higher chance of staying consistent

14. THE CAPITAL ALLOCATION MISTAKES THAT KEEP PEOPLE AVERAGE FOREVER

From my experience, these are the mistakes that destroy families:

Mistake 1: "All-in one asset"

- all real estate
- all gold
- all fixed deposits
- all equities
- all one market (only India, only Dubai, only US)

Concentration can create wealth for a few—but it destroys many because timing becomes everything.

Mistake 2: "I'll invest later when I have more money"

No.

You invest now so you have more money later.

Mistake 3: "I only buy when I feel confident"

Confidence usually arrives after prices rise—meaning you buy expensive.

Mistake 4: Ignoring net returns

Gross yield is not net yield.

Headline return is not real return.

Marketing return is not your return.

Mistake 5: No rebalancing rule

Without a rule, you become a slave to emotions.

Mistake 6: Using leverage without a buffer

Leverage without cash reserves is not strategy.

It's fragility.

15. TWO STORIES FROM MY JOURNEY (ONE LOSS, ONE BREAKTHROUGH)

Story 1: The high-income trap (loss story)

A client (details changed) earned extremely well.

But he allocated money like a lifestyle consumer:

- big EMI commitments
- minimal emergency base
- heavy concentration in one "safe" bucket
- and emotional investing when friends talked about markets

Then came a disruption: income slowed for a period.

He wasn't ruined because his salary reduced.

He was ruined because his **allocation had no shock absorber**.

That's the point:

Income protects you month-to-month.

Allocation protects you decade-to-decade.

Story 2: The calm allocator (success story)

Another client started with normal income—nothing extraordinary.

But she built a ruthless allocation habit:

- emergency base first
- automated investments
- annual step-up
- diversified across buckets
- never chased hype
- rebalanced with rules
- later added real assets with a cashflow lens and global diversification thinking

She didn't become rich fast.

She became financially unbreakable.

That is the New Wealth Order.

16. SPEAKER SINGH'S CAPITAL ALLOCATION COMMANDMENTS (WRITE THESE DOWN)

1. **Your salary is seed capital. Treat it with respect.**
2. **Protect first, then grow.**
3. **Diversify across buckets, not across rumors.**

4. **Cash is not wealth. Cash is oxygen.**
5. **Equities are not gambling. Random behavior is gambling.**
6. **Real estate is not a religion. It's a spreadsheet.**
7. **Dubai can be powerful—but only inside a disciplined global allocation.**
8. **Rebalance to control risk, not to show intelligence.**
9. **Your goal is not maximum returns. Your goal is maximum consistency.**
10. **If you can't explain why you own it, you don't own it—you're trapped in it.**

CLOSING: THE LINE THAT DEFINES THIS CHAPTER

Let me end with the sentence that separates the old world from the new:

Old Money Rule: "Earn more."

New Wealth Order Rule: "Allocate better."

Because most people don't lose money by being unlucky.

They lose money by letting money live in the wrong places for too long.

So from this chapter onward, you are not just an earner.

You are an allocator.

A builder.

A strategist.

And when you master capital allocation, the market stops being a casino...

...and becomes a tool.

READER NOTE

This chapter is educational and intended to build financial thinking, not personalized investment advice. Investing involves risk, including loss of capital and illiquidity (especially real estate). Cross-border investing adds legal, tax, fee, and currency complexity. Always verify current rules and seek qualified professional guidance for your specific circumstances.

Chapter 7

CAPITAL ALLOCATION, COMPOUNDING, AND RISK MANAGEMENT

The Wealth Trinity: Where Money Goes. How Money Grows. How Money Survives.

*(From **The New Wealth Order** — by Speaker Singh)*

Let me open this chapter with something I learned the hard way in my journey—over a decade in rooms where people don't *talk* about wealth, they **command** it.

The wealthy don't obsess over returns first.

They obsess over *structure* first.

Because a high return without a structure is just a good year that ends in a bad decade.

This is why the New Wealth Order has a simple, aggressive thesis:

Wealth is built by three powers working together:

1. **Capital Allocation Strategy** — where your money lives
2. **Compounding Power** — how your money multiplies
3. **Risk Management** — how your money survives shocks

Miss one… and the other two eventually collapse.

Most people never get wealthy not because they don't earn enough—but because they don't understand this triangle.

And I'm going to say it bluntly:

If you treat money emotionally, money will punish you logically.

1. THE NEW WEALTH ORDER TRIANGLE (THE RULES NOBODY TAUGHT YOU)

Imagine a triangle.

Corner 1: Allocation

If money goes to the wrong place, compounding can't happen.

Corner 2: Compounding

If compounding is weak (or interrupted), wealth stays small.

Corner 3: Risk

If risk destroys you once, compounding resets to zero.

This is the tragedy of the middle class worldwide:

- they allocate by habit, not by plan
- they interrupt compounding with panic
- they ignore risk until risk humiliates them

In my experience, wealthy families do the opposite:

- they allocate with written policy
- they protect compounding like it's sacred
- they treat risk management like oxygen

That's the difference between "earning money" and "keeping money."

2. CAPITAL ALLOCATION STRATEGY

Why the same salary creates freedom for one person… and struggle for another

Let me speak in beginner-friendly language:

Capital allocation means you decide—*before the month begins*—where each rupee will go.

Most people do it backwards:

"Let me pay expenses… then I'll invest whatever is left."

The wealthy do it forward:

"Let me invest according to policy… then I'll live from what remains."

Same income. Different destiny.

Here is the New Wealth Order truth:

Your financial life is not defined by your income.

Your financial life is defined by your allocation.

2.1 The 5-Bucket Allocation System (Speaker Singh Method)

From my experience, the cleanest way to build real wealth is to give every rupee a job.

Bucket 1: Oxygen (Liquidity)

Job: Keep you alive without selling assets.

This is your emergency fund + near-term needs.

If you don't have Oxygen, you will sell good assets in bad times.

That single mistake destroys decades.

Bucket 2: Shield (Protection)

Job: Stop disasters from becoming bankruptcy.

This includes insurance planning (health, life as appropriate), and safety buffers.

Bucket 3: Stability (Low-volatility money)

Job: Reduce panic. Provide predictable support for medium-term goals.

You do not keep Stability to become rich.

You keep Stability so you don't behave stupidly.

Bucket 4: Growth (Ownership)

Job: Beat inflation and build net worth.

This is typically diversified equity exposure for long-horizon goals.

India's own long-run index evidence shows why ownership matters: the Nifty 50 Total Return Index delivered **~14.04% annualized return** from **June 30, 1999 to June 30, 2025**, with **~21.94% annualized volatility**.

Translation: the growth engine moves up and down. But over time, it has historically compounded.

Bucket 5: Real Assets + Opportunity (Inflation-linked + Tactical)

Job: Add real-world asset exposure (like real estate) and keep controlled "dry powder" for rare opportunities.

But here is the New Wealth Order warning:

If your Opportunity bucket has no rules, it becomes a gambling bucket.

2.2 Rebalancing: The Discipline That Stops Your Portfolio From Becoming a Monster

Over time, markets shift your allocation without asking permission.

A portfolio that started balanced can silently drift into high risk.

That's why sophisticated investors rebalance—not to show intelligence—but to **control risk**.

Vanguard's guidance is unusually clear:

the purpose of rebalancing is **to manage risk, not maximize returns**.

This is a New Wealth Order principle:

You don't rebalance to predict markets.

You rebalance to avoid becoming overexposed right before a downturn.

3. COMPOUNDING POWER

The most powerful wealth force... and the most fragile

If allocation is the "where," then compounding is the "how fast."

Compounding is simple:

- money earns returns
- returns earn returns
- time does the heavy lifting

But compounding has an enemy: **interruption**.

The market doesn't destroy most investors.

Bad behavior destroys most investors.

The global proof: assets vs cash over long periods

NYU professor Aswath Damodaran's historical return table shows what happened to **$100 invested at the start of 1928** by end of **2025**:

- S&P 500 (with dividends): **~$1,157,598.95**
- 3-month T-Bills (cash-like): **~$2,578.30**

Read that again.

That is not a "small advantage."

That is **a different universe**.

And if you zoom out globally, UBS's Global Investment Returns Yearbook summary (via Cambridge) reports annualised **real** returns over **1900–2024** roughly around:

- **5.2%** for worldwide equities
- **1.7%** for bonds
- **0.5%** for bills

This is why the New Wealth Order says:

Cash is oxygen. Not wealth.

It helps you survive—but it doesn't usually help you win long-term.

3.1 The "Time Advantage" Example (Simple, Indian, Real)

Let me give you an example in plain math (illustrative only, not a promise).

Assume someone invests **₹10,000 per month**.

If the portfolio returns an average of **~12% per year** (illustrative), the future value after **20 years** is roughly **₹99 lakh**.

If it returns **~10% per year** (illustrative), the future value after **20 years** is roughly **₹76 lakh**.

Now here's the violent truth of compounding:

Starting earlier can beat investing longer.

If Person A invests ₹10,000/month for **10 years** and then stops, but leaves the money to compound for the next **20 years**, they can end up with **more** than Person B who starts 10 years late and invests for 20 years (again, illustrative math).

This is why wealthy families push the young generation to start early.

Because time is the only asset you can't buy later.

3.2 The "Hidden Compounding Killer": Costs

People obsess over returns and ignore fees like they're dust.

Fees are not dust. Fees are termites.

Vanguard illustrates that even seemingly small cost differences can create huge differences over long periods (example: expense differences like **0.3% vs 1.2%** over decades).

New Wealth Order rule:

If you can't control markets, control friction.

Costs. Taxes. Bad loans. Bad products. Bad behavior.

4. RISK MANAGEMENT

The part everyone ignores… until life forces them to learn

Let me say something that will make you uncomfortable:

Most people don't actually want wealth.

They want the *feeling* of wealth.

Because real wealth requires tolerating discomfort:

- volatility
- patience
- boring discipline
- delayed gratification
- saying no to hype
- building buffers instead of showing off

The New Wealth Order defines risk properly:

Risk is not volatility.

Risk is **permanent loss.**

Risk is:

- selling at the bottom because you ran out of cash
- being forced to exit because EMIs are choking you
- leverage exploding during a slowdown
- legal mistakes in real estate
- concentration in one asset
- trusting the wrong people
- ignoring cycles

Volatility is normal.

Permanent loss is usually self-created.

4.1 The Market Will Humble Everyone (Historical Reality)

If you want compounding, you must accept drawdowns.

The S&P 500 fell about **56.8%** from peak (Oct 2007) to trough (Mar 2009) in the Global Financial Crisis according to compiled historical bear market data.

This is why risk management is not optional.

Because when markets fall hard, the question is not:

"Is my portfolio down?"

The question becomes:

"Will my life force me to sell?"

That's the difference between a temporary decline and a permanent loss.

4.2 Diversification: The Brutal Academic Proof Most People Don't Know

Here's a truth that shocks beginners:

Most individual stocks underperform cash-like returns over long horizons.

Hendrik Bessembinder's research found that "most individual US common stocks" have buy-and-hold returns below one-month Treasury bills over their lifetimes, and that broad equity gains are driven by a **minority of stocks**.

And the global evidence summary from ASU's W. P. Carey notes that across **1991–2020**, the majority of stocks underperform one-month U.S. T-bills, and a tiny fraction of firms account for essentially all net wealth creation.

What does that mean for you?

If you are not professionally skilled at stock selection, broad diversification is not "safe."

It is *mathematically intelligent.*

You diversify because you want exposure to the few winners that create most of the wealth.

4.3 Behavioral Risk: Your Mind Is the Most Expensive Asset Manager

Why do people sell at the bottom?

Because pain is louder than logic.

Kahneman and Tversky's Prospect Theory explains that people tend to feel losses more intensely than equivalent gains—this drives irrational decisions under stress.

In my experience, this is the greatest hidden cost in investing:

Not fees. Not taxes.

Fear.

The New Wealth Order is designed to reduce fear by design:

- emergency buffers
- proper allocation
- diversified ownership
- rebalancing rules
- conservative leverage
- clear time horizon

So you don't rely on willpower.

You rely on structure.

4.4 Sequence Risk: When Timing Hurts More Than Return

Sequence-of-returns risk matters especially when you are withdrawing (retirement, education, major expenses).

Vanguard's research explains how retiring near bear markets can create a wide range of outcomes depending on the return sequence—even with the same long-run averages.

New Wealth Order translation:

When you start withdrawing, risk management becomes more important than return chasing.

5. THE SPEAKER SINGH RISK PROTOCOL

The 12 rules I teach to protect compounding

1. **Never invest emergency money in volatile assets.**
2. **Never use leverage without liquidity buffers.**
3. **Never concentrate your entire future into one asset class.**

4. **Never buy what you cannot explain in one paragraph.**
5. **Never confuse a bull market with intelligence.**
6. **Always know your "forced-sale risk."** (How long you can survive without selling.)
7. **Rebalance to manage risk, not to look smart.**
8. **Treat costs like cancer—small today, lethal later.**
9. **Build protection first, then growth.**
10. **Stay diversified unless you have proven skill.**
11. **Stress-test your plan for bad years, not good years.**
12. **If your plan requires everything to go right, it is not a plan. It is fantasy.**

6. DUBAI AS A NEW WEALTH ORDER CASE STUDY

Allocation + Compounding + Risk — in one real market

Now let's talk about Dubai the right way.

Not like fans. Like strategists.

Dubai matters in The New Wealth Order because it's one of the clearest modern examples of:

- global capital flows
- high transaction depth
- strong rental dynamics (in certain periods/segments)
- the role of policy + infrastructure + population growth
- and how real assets can become "asset payroll"

Dubai's official communications reported that **2025** recorded:

- **270,000+ transactions**
- **AED 917 billion** in transaction value

That scale matters because liquidity matters.

The cashflow lens (yields)

Reidin's UAE Residential Property Price Report (Jan 2025) showed Dubai **residential gross rental yield around ~7.00%**, and **apartment gross rental yields around ~7.50%** in that snapshot.

The appreciation lens (cycle-dependent)

ValuStrat reported **19.8% annual appreciation** in its Jan 2026 update of Dubai residential values.

So yes—Dubai can look extremely attractive in a strong cycle.

But the New Wealth Order does not worship cycles.

It respects cycles.

The adult risk warning (supply + correction risk)

Reuters reported Fitch's view that Dubai prices could face a **double-digit decline (up to ~15%)** in the second half of 2025 into 2026, tied to a large projected supply pipeline.

So how do intelligent allocators approach Dubai?

They do not "buy Dubai."

They buy a deal inside Dubai, with a risk framework.

6.1 The Dubai Allocation Rule (Speaker Singh)

Dubai is not your whole plan.

Dubai is a **sleeve** inside your Real Assets bucket—allocated after your foundations are strong.

And Dubai must be evaluated with **net yield**, not gross yield.

Gross yield is marketing.

Net yield is reality.

When calculating net yield, you must factor:

- service charges
- maintenance
- vacancy assumptions
- agent/management fees
- transaction costs
- mortgage costs (if any)
- your home-country tax obligations (if applicable)

Dubai Land Department provides a **Service Charge Index** inquiry tool (RERA-approved fees for jointly owned properties).

That matters because service charges can quietly destroy "great yield" stories.

6.2 The Dubai Risk Checklist (Non-negotiable)

If you want Dubai to strengthen your compounding—not threaten it—these are the checks:

1. **Legal clarity**: title deed/developer record/escrow compliance
2. **Location logic**: not "hot area," but supply-demand logic
3. **Net yield math**: real rent minus real costs
4. **Liquidity**: exit plan before entry
5. **Leverage discipline**: conservative borrowing, strong buffers

6. **Service charges verified** via official tools
7. **Cycle awareness**: understand boom vs normalisation vs correction risks
8. **Currency awareness**: AED exposure implications for your full portfolio
9. **Tenant profile + vacancy risk**: don't assume constant occupancy
10. **Developer vs secondary risk differences**: avoid blind off-plan emotion

Dubai can be powerful—when you buy like a CFO, not like a tourist.

6.3 UAE tax lens (but don't get drunk on it)

One reason global investors consider Dubai/UAE is the personal tax structure.

The UAE official platform notes the UAE does **not levy income tax on individuals**.

PwC's UAE summary also states there is currently **no personal income tax** in the UAE.

But listen carefully:

Tax advantage is a spice, not the meal.

A bad deal in a tax-free place is still a bad deal.

And readers must remember: your own country's tax rules may still apply depending on residency and reporting obligations.

6.4 Residency incentive lens (Golden Visa)

Dubai also links certain real estate investment thresholds with long-term residency pathways.

Dubai Land Department states that a real estate investor owning property with purchase value ≥ AED 2 million can apply for a **10-year renewable residence permit** (Golden Visa investor route), subject to requirements.

Again: this is not a "return."

It's a structural consideration for global allocators.

7. TWO STORIES FROM MY EXPERIENCE

(Details changed for privacy, but the patterns are real.)

Story 1: The "Return Addict" who got destroyed (loss story)

A client—let's call him **K**—was obsessed with returns. He wanted the fastest path.

He allocated like this:

- emergency fund: thin
- investments: concentrated
- debt: heavy
- risk management: none
- belief system: "markets always come back fast"

Then a downturn hit. Nothing unusual—just a normal cycle.

But because his structure was weak, he faced the worst sentence in wealth-building:

"I have to sell."

Not because the asset was bad.

Because he had no oxygen.

He sold at the wrong time. He locked in loss.

And the most painful part?

He didn't lose money only.

He lost **time**.

That is the real cost of poor risk management: it steals your years.

Story 2: The "Allocator" who became unbreakable (success story)

Another client—call her **R**—did something boring and powerful.

She built the New Wealth Order triangle:

- Allocation: bucket system, written plan
- Compounding: automated, long-horizon ownership
- Risk: buffers, diversification, conservative leverage, rebalancing

Over time she built asset payroll.

Later—only later—she explored real assets and global diversification as a *sleeve*, with net-yield math, not hype. Dubai was evaluated as:

- cashflow potential
- market depth
- and policy structure

—but still with cycle awareness and risk controls

Her wealth didn't explode overnight.

It did something better:

It became stable.

And stability is the platform from which freedom is built.

8. THE NEW WEALTH ORDER SUMMARY

The three rules to tattoo in your brain

Rule 1: Allocation decides your destiny

A portfolio is not "what you bought."

A portfolio is "how your money is distributed."

Rule 2: Compounding rewards consistency, not intelligence

If you keep interrupting, you reset the machine.

Rule 3: Risk management protects compounding

You don't get wealthy by never falling.

You get wealthy by never getting forced out.

And I'll end with the sentence I want every reader to remember:

The poor chase returns.

The middle class chases safety.

The wealthy chase structure.

That structure is the New Wealth Order.

READER NOTE (IMPORTANT)

This chapter is educational and not personalized financial advice. All investing involves risk, including loss of principal. Real estate can be illiquid and involves legal, operational, vacancy, and market-cycle risks. Cross-border investing adds additional legal, tax, and currency considerations. Always do due diligence and consult qualified professionals for your specific situation. **PART 3 – THE ASSET FRAMEWORK**

PART 3

THE ASSET FRAMEWORK

Chapter 8

STOCKS & EQUITY INVESTING

The Ownership Engine of The New Wealth Order

(Narrated in the voice of Speaker Singh)

Let me start this chapter with a sentence that will offend the old mindset—because it destroys the comfort story we were raised on:

If you don't own productive assets, you will spend your life funding someone else's freedom.

That is not poetry. That is the math of capitalism.

In my journey—more than a decade in wealth rooms with millionaires and billionaires across different countries—one truth repeats itself in every language:

They don't work for money the way the middle class does.

They make money **work for them** by owning **assets**—and the most powerful, scalable ownership asset ever created for the common person is **equity**.

Because equity is simple:

- You buy shares.
- You own a slice of a business.
- And if the business grows over time, your ownership grows in value.

Yet most people treat stocks like:

- gambling
- tips
- fast money
- "one multibagger" fantasy
- a place to prove intelligence

And then they wonder why the market "doesn't work."

No.

The market works beautifully.

It just doesn't reward **confusion**.

This chapter will make you dangerous—in a good way.

- You'll understand what equity really is.
- Why it has historically created wealth (and why it can also destroy careless people).
- How serious investors approach it.
- And how you—an everyday Indian investor—can build an equity framework that actually fits the New Wealth Order.

1. WHAT A STOCK REALLY IS (BEGINNER-SIMPLE, BUT LIFE-CHANGING)

A stock is not a "ticker."

A stock is not a "price on an app."

A stock is not a "hot tip."

A stock is **ownership**.

When you buy equity, you are buying a claim—through shares—on:

- a company's future profits
- a company's assets
- a company's growth
- and in many cases, dividends (cash paid out of profits)

The price moves daily, sometimes violently, because humans panic and celebrate daily.

But the real driver of long-term wealth is this:

Over time, stock prices follow business reality.

If the company's profits rise sustainably, the value rises.

If the company rots internally, eventually the price collapses.

That's why equity is not a "market game."

Equity is a **business ownership game**.

2. HOW EQUITY MAKES MONEY (THE 2 ENGINES)

Equity returns come from two sources:

Engine 1: Capital appreciation

If the company becomes more valuable, your shares become more valuable.

Engine 2: Dividends

Some companies distribute part of profits to shareholders.

Now here's an important concept beginners miss:

Total Return = Price Return + Dividends (reinvested)

That's why long-term index performance is often measured with a **Total Return Index (TR)**—it assumes dividends are reinvested, showing the real compounding experience.

India's own Nifty 50 whitepaper explains this clearly and reports that since June 30, 1999 to June 30, 2025, the **Nifty 50 Total Return (TR) INR** delivered an **annualized return of 14.04%** with **21.94% annualized volatility**.

That single statistic contains the full truth:

- Strong long-term growth potential
- But not a smooth ride

If you want the reward, you must respect the volatility.

3. "WHY EQUITIES CREATE WEALTH" — THE GLOBAL EVIDENCE (NOT HYPE. HISTORY.)

I don't want you to believe in stocks because influencers say so.

I want you to respect stocks because 125 years of global history screams the same message:

Ownership has been rewarded. Patience has been paid.

The UBS Global Investment Returns Yearbook public summary (based on the Dimson–Marsh–Staunton database) shows that over 1900–2024:

- Equities produced higher long-run returns than bonds, bills, and inflation in both the US and UK, and it reports annualized **nominal returns of 9.7% for equities** vs **4.6% for bonds, 3.4% for bills,** with inflation at **2.9% per year** for that period.

And if you want a brutal, unforgettable demonstration of compounding:

NYU's Aswath Damodaran data shows the value of **$100 invested at the start of 1928** grew to:

- **$1,157,598.95** in the S&P 500 (including dividends) by end of 2025
- vs **$2,578.30** in 3-month Treasury bills (cash-like)

Read it slowly.

That is the difference between:

- owning productive businesses
- and "playing safe" in cash forever

This is why I say in the New Wealth Order:

Cash is oxygen. Equity is growth.

One keeps you alive. The other builds your future.

4. THE INDIAN REALITY: EQUITY IS NO LONGER "RICH PEOPLE'S GAME"

India has entered a new phase of financial participation.

Look at the infrastructure growth:

- In January 2026 alone, CDSL reported **3,301,747 new BO accounts opened** during the month, and total **BO accounts at end of month 175,902,270** (about 17.59 crore).

(Yes—one person can have multiple demat accounts; still, this shows massive adoption.)

Look at mutual fund scale:

- AMFI reports the mutual fund industry AUM as on **January 31, 2026: ₹81,01,306 crore** and AAUM **₹82,01,175 crore**.

Look at where flows are going:

- AMFI's January 2026 monthly report shows **equity-oriented schemes net inflow ~₹24,028.59 crore** for the month.
- The same AMFI report shows passive funds (index funds/ETFs/gold ETFs/overseas FoFs in that table section) with net inflow **~₹39,954.63 crore** and passive AUM **₹15,41,350.31 crore**.

Look at SIP behavior:

- AMFI states: **"Total amount collected through during January 2026 was ₹31,002 crore."**

This is the big shift:

India is moving from "only gold + real estate" thinking into **market-linked ownership**.

But here is the painful part:

Participation has increased… but discipline has not increased at the same speed.

And that's where people get trapped.

5. THE BIGGEST CONFUSION: INVESTING VS TRADING

(And why most "stock market losses" are self-inflicted)

Let me be very direct, because I've seen families destroy years of progress with one wrong habit:

Most people don't lose money in equity investing.

They lose money in leveraged speculation wearing an "investor" mask.

And the data is not opinion.

SEBI's study on equity F&O (FY22–FY24) found:

- **93%** of over **1 crore** individual F&O traders incurred **average losses ~₹2 lakh per trader** (including transaction costs) over the three-year period
- Top 3.5% of loss-makers (4 lakh traders) averaged **₹28 lakh loss per person** over the same period
- Individuals collectively spent about **₹50,000 crore** in transaction costs over FY22–FY24, and in FY24 alone average transaction costs were **₹26,000 per person**
- Only **1%** of individual traders earned profits exceeding **₹1 lakh** after transaction costs
- A large share of participants were young; SEBI notes the proportion of traders below 30 rose to **43% in FY24**, and over **75%** had declared annual income below **₹5 lakh**

This is not a small warning.

This is a financial emergency.

So the New Wealth Order rule is:

If you are building wealth, treat F&O like fire.

Fire can cook your food… or burn your house down.

Most beginners don't need F&O at all.

They need a **boring equity ownership system.**

6. WHY STOCK PICKING HUMILIATES MOST PEOPLE (EVEN SMART PEOPLE)

Now I'm going to hit you with a fact that shocks new investors:

Most individual stocks do NOT outperform cash-like returns over their lifetimes.

That's not a motivational quote. That's academic research.

Hendrik Bessembinder's paper ("Do Stocks Outperform Treasury Bills?") shows that most individual U.S. common stocks had lifetime buy-and-hold returns that **fell short** of one-month Treasury bills, and broad market wealth creation comes from a **minority** of big winners.

And the global evidence says the same:

A large global study summary notes that across 1991–2020, the majority of U.S. and non-U.S. stocks underperform one-month U.S. T-bills, and the top-performing **2.4%** of firms accounted for essentially all net global wealth creation in that period.

So what's the New Wealth Order lesson?

If you are not a proven stock selector, the smartest move is broad diversification.

Because diversification gives you exposure to the winners you cannot predict in advance.

This is why index investing is not "lazy."

It is **mathematically intelligent**.

7. SPEAKER SINGH'S 3-LANE EQUITY FRAMEWORK

The only way most people should approach stocks

From my experience, the biggest mistake people make is mixing everything:

- long-term investing
- short-term trading
- tips
- memes
- and ego

And then they call the whole mess "my portfolio."

No.

In the New Wealth Order, your equity strategy has lanes.

Lane 1: Core Ownership (The Engine)

This is where your serious wealth is built.

It is diversified.

It is disciplined.

It is boring.

Typical examples:

- broad market index funds/ETFs
- diversified equity mutual funds
- a structured allocation approach

The objective: **capture the market's compounding**.

Nifty's own rolling return analysis shows something most people don't emotionally accept:

- Over the analysis period (June 30, 1999 to June 30, 2025), for the **Nifty 50 TR (INR)**, a **7-year or longer** investment horizon had **0% instances of negative returns** in their rolling analysis.

That is not a guarantee. It is a historical pattern that teaches one lesson:

Time reduces the probability of regret.

Lane 2: Satellite (The Enhancer)

These are controlled exposures:

- factor strategies (quality, value, low volatility)
- sectoral/thematic exposure (with strict limits)
- a small set of high-conviction ideas

Objective: **incremental returns**, not financial survival.

Lane 3: Speculation (The Casino Bucket)

This is where:

- penny stocks
- leverage

- options
- intraday
- "one trade will change my life"

lives.

If you insist on playing here, fine—but it must be:

- small
- capped
- and never allowed to destroy Lane 1

Because SEBI's data already tells you what happens to most people who treat speculation like income.

8. RISK MANAGEMENT IN EQUITIES (THE PART THAT SEPARATES RICH INVESTORS FROM BROKEN INVESTORS)

Let me say this in plain language:

The stock market is a beautiful wealth machine… but it is also a psychological torture chamber.

If you don't have a risk framework, you will do the classic mistakes:

- buy high when confidence is maximum
- sell low when fear is maximum
- keep switching strategies
- keep chasing "what's moving"
- and keep restarting compounding from zero

The UBS Yearbook summary reminds investors that equities have been rewarding long-term but the ride has not been smooth, and it highlights the importance of drawdowns and recovery time.

Now let me anchor this with a hard historical example:

During the Great Recession, the U.S. Federal Reserve history notes the S&P 500 fell **57%** from its October 2007 peak to its trough in March 2009.

That one number matters because it tells you the truth:

The market can cut your portfolio in half.

So if your plan cannot survive a 50% drawdown (emotionally and financially), your plan is fantasy.

9. THE 12 NEW WEALTH ORDER COMMANDMENTS FOR EQUITY INVESTING

(These are written for everyday investors—simple, but lethal when followed.)

1. **You are not buying "a stock." You are buying a business.**

   If you don't understand the business model, you are not investing. You are guessing.

2. **Never invest money needed in the next 12–24 months into volatile equities.**

   That's not courage. That's stupidity.

3. **Diversify unless you have proven edge.**

   Because most stocks underperform while a minority create most wealth.

4. **Time is your unfair advantage.**

   Nifty's rolling analysis shows long horizons historically reduced negative return instances dramatically.

5. **Don't confuse a bull market with skill.**

   Many people become "geniuses" in rising markets. Then markets turn… and reality collects fees.

6. **Stop checking your portfolio like a heartbeat monitor.**

   Daily price movement is noise. Wealth is built in years, not in notifications.

7. **Keep costs low and friction minimal.**

   Compounding hates leakage.

8. **Treat derivatives as a professional tool, not a middle-class lottery.**

   SEBI's numbers are not negotiable.

9. **Have a sell framework.**

   Not "I feel like selling."

   A real framework:

- business deterioration
- governance issues
- thesis broken
- valuation insanity
- better capital allocation elsewhere

10. **Rebalance when allocation drifts.**

    Not to predict markets—to control risk.

11. **Never anchor your identity to your portfolio.**

    If your ego is inside the stock, you can't exit rationally.

12. The goal is not to be right. The goal is to be rich.

Being rich requires consistency, not drama.

10. THE SPEAKER SINGH EQUITY STARTER PATH

"What should I do if I'm totally new?"

Let me make this easy for a beginner reader.

From my experience, most people don't need complexity. They need sequencing.

Step 1: Build your financial base first

- emergency fund
- insurance where appropriate
- toxic debt cleanup

Because otherwise the first market fall will force you to sell.

Step 2: Start with CORE ownership

If you want to build wealth without needing to become a full-time analyst, begin with diversified vehicles.

Why? Because the market's winners are hard to predict, and diversification captures them.

Step 3: Automate using SIP discipline

India's SIP culture is exploding for a reason—because it removes timing stress.

AMFI reports January 2026 SIP collections of **₹31,002 crore**.

That number is not just a statistic.

It is proof that disciplined investing is becoming a national behavior.

Step 4: Upgrade knowledge after you start

Most people say: "I'll start after I learn."

But learning never ends.

So they never start.

Start small. Start structured. Learn while compounding begins.

Step 5: Add satellite only after 12–18 months of consistent core investing

Because satellite exposure without core stability becomes emotional chaos.

Step 6: If you want direct stocks, earn that privilege

Direct stock investing is a skill.

You must learn:

- reading financial statements
- understanding business cycles
- valuation
- governance signals
- and capital allocation

If you can't do that, you don't need direct stocks. You need diversified ownership.

Step 7: Never mix investing with entertainment

Markets are not Netflix.

If you want entertainment, buy popcorn.

If you want wealth, buy ownership.

11. TWO STORIES FROM MY EXPERIENCE (ONE LOSS, ONE WIN)

Story 1: The "market victim" who wasn't a victim (loss story)

A young professional (details changed) opened a demat account, started watching reels, and began "investing."

But his behavior was pure speculation:

- concentrated bets
- rapid switching
- option trades "to recover losses"
- no emergency fund buffer
- high emotional involvement

He didn't lose because the market is bad.

He lost because he treated the market like a rescue helicopter.

SEBI's data shows how common this story is in derivatives.

The market didn't cheat him.

He entered the wrong game.

Story 2: The silent wealth builder (success story)

Another investor (details changed) did something boring:

- set a monthly SIP
- bought diversified equity exposure
- stepped up investments annually
- stayed invested through volatility
- never chased tips
- never used leverage
- gradually added knowledge and small satellite exposure

Years later, the portfolio became something powerful:

asset payroll—money that can fund life without begging a boss.

This is what equity investing is meant to do.

Not excitement.

Freedom.

12. HOW EQUITIES CONNECT TO REAL ESTATE (AND WHY DUBAI REMAINS PART OF THE NEW WEALTH ORDER)

Now let me connect this chapter to the broader Asset Framework of this book.

Equity and real estate are not enemies.

They are different weapons.

- **Equity** gives you liquidity, scalability, and compounding exposure to business growth.
- **Real estate** gives you tangible utility, potential inflation-linked rent dynamics, and leverage options (when used conservatively).

In the New Wealth Order, you do not choose one like a religion.

You allocate like a strategist.

That's why in later chapters, when we talk about Dubai real estate, the foundation remains the same:

- you don't buy emotion
- you buy math
- you buy cashflow logic

- you buy legal clarity
- you buy cycle awareness

Equity builds your **liquid compounding engine**.

Real estate can become your **inflation-linked income engine**.

Both are tools.

Only fools worship tools.

CLOSING: THE SENTENCE THAT DEFINES EQUITY INVESTING IN THE NEW WEALTH ORDER

Let me end this chapter with a truth I've seen in every wealth tier, in every country:

The middle class works for money.

The wealthy own what the middle class works for.

Equity is your chance—your legal, accessible, scalable chance—to own pieces of the economy.

But only if you approach it with:

- a framework
- a time horizon
- and risk discipline

Because in the market, intelligence without discipline is useless.

And discipline—executed for years—looks like magic to people who live month-to-month.

That magic is not magic.

It is ownership + compounding + patience.

Welcome to the New Wealth Order.

READER NOTE (IMPORTANT)

This chapter is educational and not personalized investment advice. Equity investing involves risk, including loss of principal, and markets can decline sharply. Derivatives and leverage can multiply losses. Always do your own due diligence and consult licensed professionals for decisions specific to your financial situation, residency, and tax profile.

Chapter 9

MUTUAL FUNDS & ETFS: THE SILENT CONVEYOR BELT TO WEALTH

Mutual Funds & ETFs: The Wealth Conveyor Belt (If You Stop Using It Like a Lottery)

Let me start with a confession from my journey.

When I began advising serious money—people with global businesses, family offices, and balance sheets most people can't imagine—I expected "complex strategies" to be the secret sauce.

What I found was almost insulting in its simplicity:

The wealthy don't win because they have secret investments.

They win because they have a system for owning assets—consistently, cheaply, and for a long time.

And for the modern middle class, there is one vehicle that can turn monthly income into lifelong ownership faster than anything else (without needing crores upfront):

Mutual funds and ETFs.

Not because they are magic.

Because they are a **machine.**

A machine that can either:

- quietly build you into an owner… **or**
- quietly bleed you with costs, bad choices, and emotional decisions.

This chapter is how you make sure it becomes your wealth machine—not your wealth leak.

1. THE "FUND" REVOLUTION IS NOT INDIAN. IT'S GLOBAL.

Before we go into what *you* should do, understand this:

Mutual funds and ETFs are not a "small investor product."

They are one of the largest wealth engines on Earth.

According to the Investment Company Institute (ICI), **worldwide regulated open-end fund assets** (which include mutual funds, ETFs, and institutional funds) were **$84.90 trillion** at the end of **Q3 2025**.

Now let's zoom into ETFs specifically.

ETFGI reported that **global ETF industry assets reached $19.85 trillion** at the end of **December 2025**, with **record net inflows of $2.37 trillion in 2025**, and **79 consecutive months of net inflows**.

Read that again.

79 consecutive months of people globally choosing a structure that is:

- transparent
- liquid

- diversified
- increasingly low-cost

This is not a trend. This is a **shift in how the world owns assets.**

2. INDIA'S MUTUAL FUND & ETF EXPLOSION (AND WHAT IT REVEALS)

Now, India.

AMFI's monthly industry report shows that as of **January 31, 2026**, India's mutual fund industry had:

- **Total net assets (AUM): ₹81,01,305.58 crore** (≈ ₹81.01 lakh crore)
- **Total folios: 26,63,13,561** (≈ **26.63 crore folios**)

That's not a "rich people product."

That's mass India stepping into ownership.

And here's the part most people missed:

AMFI data for January 2026 shows:

- **Equity-oriented schemes net inflow: ₹24,028.59 crore**
- **Passive category net inflow (Index funds + ETFs + FoF overseas): ₹39,954.63 crore**

Passive inflows were **bigger than equity active inflows.**

And within that passive bucket:

- **Gold ETFs net inflow: ₹24,039.96 crore**
- **Other ETFs net inflow: ₹15,005.87 crore**

This is a loud message from the market:

People are moving toward simple, transparent, "rule-based" ownership.

Also, AMFI's SIP page shows that **SIP collections during January 2026 were ₹31,002 crore**.

That is the sound of India shifting from "saving" to **systematic ownership**.

3. THE BRUTAL TRUTH: MUTUAL FUNDS & ETFS ARE NOT INVESTMENTS

They're Containers.

Most people talk like this:

"I invested in mutual funds."

"ETFs are good."

"Small-cap fund will make me rich."

No. That's like saying:

"I bought a bottle, so I must have bought good water."

Mutual funds and ETFs are vehicles.

What matters is:

- what's inside
- how much it costs
- how you behave while holding it

In my experience advising wealthy families, they don't ask:

"Which mutual fund is best?"

They ask:

"What job should this money do in the portfolio?"

"What risk is acceptable?"

"What is the cheapest clean exposure we can get?"

"What is the exit plan?"

That's how owners think.

4. MUTUAL FUND VS ETF (EXPLAINED LIKE YOU'RE NEW)

Let's make this simple and real.

Mutual Fund (Open-Ended)

- You buy units from the fund house (AMC) at **NAV**
- Transactions happen based on end-of-day NAV (for most schemes)
- Great for SIP discipline
- You don't need to think about market price vs NAV (usually)

ETF (Exchange Traded Fund)

- It trades on the stock exchange like a share
- You buy/sell during market hours
- Price is usually close to NAV, but can deviate
- You must consider:
- liquidity
- bid-ask spread
- brokerage
- tracking quality

And yes—**mispricing can happen**, which is why regulators pay attention. SEBI has proposed changes to ETF price band rules to curb significant price deviations from iNAV.

In short:

- Mutual funds are a *monthly discipline machine.*
- ETFs are a *market-trading instrument with index exposure.*

Both can build wealth. Both can harm you if used badly.

5. INDEX FUNDS & ETFS: THE SILENT "RICH PERSON MOVE"

Here's a sentence many people hate:

"Most investors don't need a 'smart' fund. They need a fund they can stick with."

Because wealth is not built by brilliance.

It's built by:

- time
- consistency
- avoiding disasters
- keeping costs low
- not panicking

That's why index funds and ETFs are growing so fast.

And it's not just "because they're cheap."

It's because **they reduce decision-making**—and decision-making is where most people destroy their own returns.

6. ACTIVE FUNDS VS PASSIVE FUNDS: THE SPIVA PUNCH IN THE FACE

Now let's talk about the uncomfortable data.

S&P's SPIVA reports have repeatedly shown that **many active funds underperform their benchmarks over longer periods**.

For example, SPIVA India Mid-Year 2025 reporting highlights large-cap underperformance rates rising to **66.7% (3-year), 89.7% (5-year), and 73.3% (10-year)** (category context: large-cap active vs benchmark).

And for ELSS (tax-saver funds), reporting summarized that underperformance rates were **35.9% (1-year), 52.6% (3-year), 68.3% (5-year), and 86.8% (10-year)**.

What does this mean in human language?

It means:

Paying higher fees does not guarantee higher returns.

And the longer the horizon, the more brutal the math becomes.

Now listen carefully—this is important:

I'm not saying "never buy active funds."

From my experience, active funds can add value:

- in certain segments
- with truly skilled managers
- with disciplined processes
- when you can stay invested long enough

But the default middle-class behaviour is this:

- buy last year's winner

- sell when it falls
- switch funds repeatedly
- pay regular plan commissions unknowingly

That behaviour makes active investing a wealth trap.

7. THE FEE MONSTER: THE RICH FEAR IT. THE MIDDLE CLASS IGNORES IT.

This is where my tone becomes aggressive, because this part decides your future:

Costs are guaranteed. Returns are not.

SEBI's investor education page gives a simple example:

If a mutual fund gives 10% gross return:

- Regular plan expense ratio 1.5% → effective return 8.5%
- Direct plan expense ratio 0.5% → effective return 9.5%

That 1% difference looks "small."

It isn't small.

The Speaker Singh Reality Check (Simple Math)

If you invest **₹10,000/month for 20 years**:

- At 12% annual return, you might reach **~₹98.9 lakh** (approx.)
- At 11% annual return, you might reach **~₹86.6 lakh** (approx.)

That's a **~₹12+ lakh difference** created by "only 1%".

And that's on a modest SIP.

Now imagine high-income earners investing ₹50,000/month for 25 years—**the gap becomes crores.**

This is why wealthy investors obsess over:

- expense ratio
- taxes
- trading friction
- unnecessary churn

Because they understand something most people don't:

The market doesn't have to defeat you. Your own fees can.

8. DIRECT PLAN VS REGULAR PLAN: THE "INVISIBLE SALARY CUT" YOU AGREED TO

Let me say this bluntly:

If you're buying regular plans without understanding it, you might be paying a lifelong commission with your future.

Yes—some people genuinely need guidance.

But here's what I've seen repeatedly in my journey:

- People don't pay advisors knowingly.
- They pay them invisibly through regular plans.
- And because it's invisible, they never question it.

In *The New Wealth Order*, we don't build wealth with invisible leaks.

We build wealth with visible systems.

So your rule should be:

- **If you're paying for advice, pay knowingly.**
- **If you're not getting real advice, don't pay anyway.**

9. ETFS: THE THREE HIDDEN RISKS NO ONE EXPLAINS

ETFs are powerful.

But beginners get hurt because they think ETF = "safe index."

No.

Here are the 3 hidden ETF risks:

1. **Liquidity & Spread Risk**

   An ETF might track Nifty—but if trading volume is low, you can lose money in the bid-ask spread.

2. **Price vs NAV Gap**

   ETF price can deviate from NAV/iNAV, especially in stressed markets or illiquid products—hence SEBI's focus on pricing controls.

3. **Tracking Quality**

   An ETF is only as good as how closely it tracks the index.

SEBI explains tracking error clearly:

Tracking error measures the **difference between fund returns and benchmark returns** and is essentially the deviation from the index.

If you're buying passive products, you must learn one phrase:

Tracking difference and tracking error are the "quality score" of passive investing.

10. THE DEBT FUND MYTH (AND THE FRANKLIN TEMPLETON LESSON)

Now we step into the area where many Indians make a dangerous assumption:

"Debt funds are safe like FD."

Debt funds are not FDs.

Debt funds carry:

- credit risk (issuer might default)
- liquidity risk (you may not be able to sell bonds quickly without loss)
- interest rate risk (bond prices move with rate changes)

A real-world reminder: in April 2020, Franklin Templeton India took the unprecedented step of winding up six yield-oriented debt schemes, citing severe liquidity issues.

The point is not to scare you.

The point is to upgrade you.

The New Wealth Order investor does not say "debt is safe."

He says: "Which debt? What quality? What liquidity? What duration?"

That's the difference between a saver and an allocator.

11. SPEAKER SINGH'S "CORE ENGINE" METHOD (USED BY REAL WEALTH)

Let me give you a framework I've seen again and again among serious money.

Step 1: Build the Core (Boring, Powerful, Non-Negotiable)

This is where most people should use:

- broad-market index funds/ETFs
- diversified large exposure
- high-quality debt/liquid exposure for stability

The core is meant to:

- participate in national growth
- avoid unnecessary complexity
- stay invested for years

Core rule:

If you can't hold it for 5–10 years, it doesn't belong in the core.

Step 2: Add Satellites (Where You "Try" for Extra Return)

This is where active funds *can* make sense:

- mid-cap/small-cap (carefully)
- sector/thematic (very limited)
- factor/smart beta (if you understand it)

Satellite rule:

Satellites should never be allowed to sink the ship.

Step 3: Create a Cash-Flow Buffer (So You Don't Panic Sell)

This is the piece most people miss.

In my experience, people don't sell because they are "stupid."

They sell because they are **forced**:

- job loss
- emergency
- EMI pressure
- medical event

So a liquid buffer prevents you from selling your future to survive the present.

12. HOW MOST PEOPLE STAY POOR USING MUTUAL FUNDS (YES, EVEN WHILE INVESTING)

I'm going to list the most common wealth-killers I've seen:

Wealth-Killer #1: Buying Funds Like Bollywood Hype

- NFO mania
- thematic fever
- "AI fund, PSU fund, defence fund" excitement

Excitement is expensive.

Wealth-Killer #2: Confusing Diversification With "More Funds"

Owning 12 funds is not diversification.

Often it's just *overlap* and confusion.

Wealth-Killer #3: Switching Too Much

Switching feels like action.

But action is not always progress.

Wealth-Killer #4: Investing Without Asset Allocation

If you don't know your equity/debt split, you don't have a portfolio.

You have a collection.

13. THE BEGINNER'S CHECKLIST (SIMPLE, PRACTICAL)

If you're new, you don't need complexity.

You need a checklist.

Mutual Fund Checklist

1. **Direct or Regular?** Know what you're paying.
2. **Category fit:** large-cap, flexi, hybrid, debt—what job is it doing?
3. **Risk level (Risk-o-meter):** SEBI requires product labeling via Risk-o-meter.
4. **Costs:** expense ratio
5. **Avoid performance chasing:** last year's winner is not a promise
6. **Hold long enough:** equity needs time

ETF Checklist

1. **Underlying index:** what exactly does it track?
2. **Trading volume & bid-ask spread:** don't ignore liquidity
3. **Tracking error:** how tightly does it follow the index?
4. **Price vs NAV discipline:** avoid illiquid ETFs where pricing can distort
5. **Brokerage & charges:** trading isn't free

14. TAXES: DON'T GUESS—KNOW THE RULE (BECAUSE RULES CHANGE)

One reason the wealthy stay wealthy is they don't guess tax rules. They verify them.

India's capital gains framework for equity-linked instruments has seen changes (including updated rates and thresholds effective after July 23, 2024).

The Income Tax Department's guidance indicates, for certain equity-linked gains:

- **LTCG (Section 112A):** 12.5% beyond ₹1.25 lakh (as reflected in official guidance)
- **STCG (Section 111A):** 20% for transfers after 23-07-2024 (per official tutorial)

I'm not giving you personal tax advice here—your situation matters.

But I am giving you a rule of survival in *The New Wealth Order*:

Never invest blindly without understanding the tax impact of:

- equity vs debt
- holding period
- exit timing
- turnover/switching frequency

Because taxes punish impatience.

15. WHERE REAL ESTATE FITS INTO THIS CHAPTER (AND WHY DUBAI KEEPS COMING UP)

Now let's connect this to your broader wealth path—especially real estate.

From my experience, real estate is where most people either:

- create generational wealth **or**
- create generational financial stress

And the biggest reason is simple:

Real estate is illiquid.

Mutual funds and ETFs are liquid.

So here is the strategy I've seen the smartest investors use (globally):

Use Mutual Funds/ETFs as the "Liquid Engine"

And use Real Estate as the "Hard Asset Anchor."

Meaning:

- Your funds/ETFs compound and stay accessible
- Your property (when chosen correctly) locks in inflation-linked scarcity and leverage

This is exactly why Dubai real estate becomes interesting in a global wealth conversation: it has positioned itself as a global capital magnet, and serious investors like environments where:

- rules are clearer
- transactions are smoother
- rental markets are structured
- global demand exists

But I will repeat what I said earlier in the book:

Real estate is not magic.

It is a system.

And your mutual fund/ETF portfolio is what gives you the power to:

- wait for the right deal
- avoid emotional buying
- avoid over-leveraging
- build the down payment without panic

In the next chapters, when we go deeper into real estate (including Dubai), you'll see why the strongest property investors are often the ones who already built a strong liquid portfolio first.

16. THE FINAL AGGRESSIVE TRUTH

Most people want a "hot tip."

But the wealthy want a "cold system."

Mutual funds and ETFs are that system—if you stop treating them like a casino.

Let me end with a line I tell clients (and I want you to hear it like it's spoken straight to your face):

If you can automate your spending, you can automate your wealth.

If you can pay EMIs, you can buy assets monthly.

If you can follow a boss's schedule, you can follow an investment system.

The New Wealth Order is ownership—repeated, disciplined, and protected.

And mutual funds + ETFs are your first mass-access weapon of ownership.

In the next chapter, we'll go deeper into selecting equity exposure the right way—**not based on hype, but based on roles inside your personal wealth architecture.**

Chapter 10

REAL ESTATE (RESIDENTIAL + COMMERCIAL)

The Most Misunderstood Asset on Earth, and the One That Can Make You Financially Unstoppable (If You Treat It Like a System)

*(From **The New Wealth Order** — by Speaker Singh)*

Let me speak with full clarity, from my journey and experience.

Real estate is the only asset class where **amateurs routinely behave like professionals**—because they live inside the product.

They sleep in it.
They marry in it.
They host relatives in it.
They fight in it.
They inherit it.
They get emotionally attached to it.

And then they call it an "investment."

Here's the uncomfortable truth:

MOST PEOPLE DON'T BUY REAL ESTATE AS AN ASSET.

They buy it as an emotion—and then they beg the market to reward their emotions.

Sometimes it does. That's why the myth survives.

But when it doesn't?

Real estate doesn't just disappoint you. It **traps** you.

Because unlike stocks, real estate is usually:

- **illiquid**
- **high transaction cost**
- **highly leveraged**
- **legally complex**
- **cyclical**
- and brutally unforgiving if you get the fundamentals wrong

This chapter is not about "property hype."

It's about **property truth**—residential and commercial—so you can build real wealth, not expensive stress.

1. THE REAL ESTATE RETURN FORMULA (SIMPLE, BUT MOST PEOPLE NEVER LEARN IT)

Most people think real estate return = price goes up.

That is childish thinking.

Real estate total return has **four engines**:

Total Return = (Net Cashflow) + (Equity Build-Up) + (Appreciation) - (Friction Costs)

Let me translate that into human language:

1. **Net Cashflow** = rent minus all costs (maintenance, vacancy, taxes, society charges, repairs, management)
2. **Equity Build-Up** = if you have a loan, EMI pays down principal over time (tenant + you together are building your ownership)
3. **Appreciation** = market value rise (the sexy part)
4. **Friction Costs** = stamp duty, registration, brokerage, loan fees, vacancy losses, renovations, opportunity cost, and sometimes legal mess

If you ignore friction costs, you will **hallucinate profits**.

And in my experience, that is the #1 reason people say, "Real estate made me money," while their bank account says, "No, it didn't."

2. REAL ESTATE IS NOT "ONE MARKET." IT'S THOUSANDS OF MICRO-MARKETS.

A city is not one market.

A sector is not one market.

A building is not one market.

Even two towers in the same society can perform differently.

That's why broad indexes help you understand direction—but never replace local underwriting.

In India, RBI's House Price Index (HPI) showed an **all-India annual increase of 3.1% in Q4 FY25**—but city performance varied widely. So if someone tells you "India property always goes up," they're speaking emotionally, not analytically.

Globally, BIS data showed that **inflation-adjusted ("real") house prices fell year-on-year** in aggregated global data in **Q2 2025**—and noted multi-year stretches of real price declines worldwide.

Translation:

Real estate is cyclical.

Inflation is persistent.

Your job is to buy assets that can survive cycles and benefit from persistence.

3. RESIDENTIAL VS COMMERCIAL: UNDERSTAND THE GAME BEFORE YOU PLAY IT

Residential property (the "people" business)

Residential works when:

- you buy in locations where **income growth and population growth** support rental demand
- supply is controlled or naturally constrained
- the unit type matches the tenant market
- you keep leverage conservative
- you treat it like a cashflow system, not a trophy

Residential fails when:

- you buy because your relatives told you
- you buy because "prices were rising"
- you buy bigger than your affordability

- you ignore maintenance + vacancy + legal clarity
- you assume rent will cover EMI without stress-testing

Residential is easier to understand.

But yields are often lower and emotions are higher.

Recent market reporting highlighted that in major Indian cities, **gross rental yields** were around the ~4% range in several markets (example: Chennai ~4.16% reported) and showed signs of yield compression when capital values rise faster than rents.

And rental inflation can swing:

- reports noted India's residential rents moderated to **~7–9%** in H1 2025, after much sharper increases in 2021–2024 in many metros
- a Reuters poll of housing experts expected Indian home prices to rise around **6.5%** in 2025 and rents to rise **7–10%**—faster than inflation—highlighting affordability pressure and the "renter nation" shift

So residential is not "safe."

Residential is **a business whose customer is the tenant.**

Commercial property (the "cashflow contract" business)

Commercial real estate is closer to buying a **bond backed by a building**:

- long leases
- escalation clauses
- tenant credit matters
- location and building quality matter
- vacancy can be expensive
- lease structure determines your stability

Commercial can offer higher yields when done right—but the due diligence is more serious.

A Knight Frank guide (older, 2014) gave a simple rule-of-thumb: residential yields often **2–4%**, while commercial can be **~8–11%**, depending on asset quality and lease terms. I'm citing it not as "today's guarantee," but as a long-standing way professionals think about the yield gap.

More recent industry analysis in India also describes commercial returns as generally higher than residential, especially for Grade-A assets, while noting residential tends to sit in the ~3–4% range in many scenarios.

Commercial is not "better."

Commercial is **sharper**.

It rewards structure—and punishes laziness.

4. THE MACRO TRUTH: WHY REAL ESTATE BECOMES POWERFUL IN THE "NEW WEALTH ORDER"

From my journey managing wealth across different markets, the wealthiest families don't ask:

"Should I buy property?"

They ask:

"What role should property play in the portfolio—growth, cashflow, hedge, or optionality?"

Here's the macro logic:

A. Limited land + rising replacement costs

Over time, materials, labour, compliance costs rise. Replacement cost rises.

B. Rent is a form of inflation transmission

In functioning markets, rent tends to move with income growth and demand pressure.

C. Leverage is the accelerant

A home loan is one of the few ways normal people can borrow at scale.

Leverage can create generational wealth.

Leverage can also create generational trauma.

5. THE MOST IMPORTANT REAL ESTATE SKILL: UNDERWRITING

Let me be aggressive here, because soft talk destroys people:

If you can't underwrite, you are not investing.

You are shopping—with debt.

Underwriting means: you write the story in numbers before the market writes it for you in pain.

6. RESIDENTIAL UNDERWRITING: THE "5 FILTERS" OF SPEAKER SINGH

Filter 1: Location logic (not location hype)

Location logic is:

- job hubs/transport lines/universities/hospitals
- ability to rent quickly
- tenant pool quality
- future supply pipeline (will your area be flooded with new inventory?)

Filter 2: Unit liquidity (exit matters)

Ask:

- If I need to sell in 90 days, who buys this?
- Is this unit type common or niche?
- Is this ticket size affordable for many buyers or only a few?

Filter 3: Cashflow realism (the truth)

Don't ask "What is rent today?"

Ask "What is rent after reality?"

Reality includes:

- vacancy
- maintenance
- repairs
- broker fees
- insurance (if applicable)

- property tax
- society charges

Filter 4: Legal clarity (the wealth killer)

Most property losses are not "market losses."

They are **document losses**.

Basic principle:

- no clean title, no deal
- no approvals, no deal
- no verified seller identity, no deal

Filter 5: Leverage discipline (the survival rule)

A property is only an asset if it doesn't force you into panic.

If EMI is so high that one job shock breaks you, the property owns you.

7. COMMERCIAL UNDERWRITING: THE "LEASE IS THE ASSET"

Commercial is not about the building first.

Commercial is about the **lease contract** first.

Commercial Terms You Must Understand (simple explanations)

- **NOI (Net Operating Income):** rent minus operating expenses
- **Cap Rate:** NOI ÷ property price. It is a one-year yield snapshot.
- **Escalation Clause:** rent increases periodically (e.g., 5% yearly or 15% every 3 years)
- **Lock-in:** tenant cannot leave easily during lock-in period

- **Vacancy Risk:** empty property can burn cash (maintenance + taxes continue)
- **Tenant Credit:** how reliable is this tenant's ability to pay?
- **Fit-out & Capex:** who pays to build/upgrade interior or building systems?

Cap rates matter even more when interest rates move; professional investors compare cap rates to bond yields and spreads.

Commercial can win when:

- tenant is strong
- lease is long
- escalations are clear
- asset is Grade-A quality
- location has durable demand

Commercial can destroy you when:

- you buy a "cheap" unit with no tenant
- you underestimate vacancy time
- you don't understand local demand
- you buy in a dying micro-market
- you ignore building obsolescence

8. INDIA'S COMMERCIAL REALITY: WHY IT'S BECOMING INSTITUTIONAL

India's office market has been scaling hard.

JLL reported India's **gross office leasing hit 83.3 million sq ft in 2025,** with Q4 hitting an all-time quarterly high.

That is a structural signal: demand is not dead—quality demand is rising.

Crisil (as reported) projected Grade-A office vacancy in India could decline by about 50 bps to **~15.5–16.0%** by fiscal year end, reflecting demand-supply dynamics.

Retail is also active: CBRE reporting cited **record retail leasing of ~8.9 million sq ft in 2025** across major cities.

And Colliers reporting (via coverage) noted India accounted for **68% of APAC office leasing** in 2025 across major markets, showing regional dominance.

So commercial in India is not just "shops."

It's a maturing ecosystem—offices, retail, logistics, data centres—where institutional money cares about:

- yield stability
- tenant strength
- building quality
- governance

This is exactly why REIT's emerged as a mainstream bridge for investors to access commercial cashflow—REIT's are required to distribute a large portion of cash flows to unitholders (90% NDCF distribution requirement is embedded in the framework).

(We go deeper into REIT's later, but I want you to understand: commercial real estate is becoming **systematic**, not just "buy a shop.")

9. GLOBAL REAL ESTATE: THE CYCLE HUMILITY EVERY INVESTOR NEEDS

If you want to be a serious investor or HNWI, you must have one trait:

Cycle humility.

Because the world gives you periods where everything feels brilliant… and then it reminds you who is boss.

BIS data has repeatedly shown house prices behave very differently across countries and that "real" house prices can rise or fall depending on policy and cycle.

And long-run research on returns shows something many people don't expect:

A major long-run study on asset returns (including housing) across advanced economies found that **long-run returns on housing and equities can look remarkably similar**, while housing tends to be less volatile in some frameworks.

Translation:

Real estate isn't "low return."

Real estate is "behaviorally survivable" for many—IF you buy it right.

But survivable does not mean guaranteed.

It means: **structure matters more than optimism.**

10. DUBAI: THE POSITIVES (AND THE REALITY CHECKS) — THE NEW WEALTH CORRIDOR

You asked me to keep global markets in mind and bring focus to the positivity of Dubai. I will do that—without selling dreams.

Dubai's structural strengths (why investors watch it)

Dubai's government communications reported that in **2025**, Dubai recorded:

- **270,000+ transactions**
- **AED 917 billion** in transaction value
- about **20% year-on-year growth** in value

That is scale. That is liquidity. That is global capital.

Yield profile (why cashflow investors like it)

REIDIN's UAE Residential Property Price Report (Nov 2025) reported:

- Dubai residential **gross rental yields ~6.55%**
- Dubai apartment gross yields around **~7.03%**

Savills' World Cities Prime Residential Index (World Cities 2025) noted Dubai prime yields around **5.3%** in that research context—high relative to many prime global cities.

Appreciation momentum (what the cycle has recently delivered)

ValuStrat reported Dubai residential capital values showing **~19.8% annual appreciation** around late 2025/early 2026 in its index commentary (with villas outperforming apartments).

Now, stop. Breathe.

This is where amateurs become fools: they see recent numbers and assume it's permanent.

Professionals do the opposite:

They treat strong years as proof of demand—and then they stress test the downside.

The reality checks (why you must underwrite Dubai like a professional)

UBS' Global Real Estate Bubble Index 2025 placed Dubai in an **"elevated risk"** category and noted it had one of the strongest risk increases versus the prior edition.

Reuters reported Fitch's view that Dubai property prices could face a **moderate correction of up to ~15%** in late 2025 into 2026 due to a large supply pipeline.

So the message is not "Dubai is perfect."

The message is:

Dubai is powerful because it is liquid, globally demanded, and yield-rich—but it is still a cycle-driven property market. You must buy with a system.

Dubai due diligence tools (this is why I respect Dubai's framework)

Dubai Land Department (DLD) provides a **Rental Index** tool to check rental benchmarks and rent increase guidance. DLD also provides a **Service Charge Index** to check approved service fees for jointly owned properties.

This matters because service charges can quietly destroy your net yield.

Transaction friction (budget correctly)

Dubai transaction fees are real and must be modeled.

DLD materials and service pages indicate:

- a **4% fee** is part of sale registration processes (examples referenced by DLD communications and transaction service guidance)
- mortgage fee (if any) **0.25% of mortgage value** is listed in DLD service fee breakdowns

And currency regime matters for global investors:

The Central Bank of the UAE describes operations to maintain the stability of the dirham peg to the US dollar.

If you're an India-resident investor considering global property, you must also understand compliance (clean money is non-negotiable). RBI's Liberalised Remittance Scheme (LRS) FAQs describe permissible remittances and conditions relevant to overseas transactions (always follow FEMA rules and bank compliance).

11. SPEAKER SINGH'S "TWO-TRACK PROPERTY STRATEGY" (HOW WEALTHY PEOPLE THINK)

From my journey, wealthy families don't treat property as one thing. They separate it into two tracks:

Track 1: Lifestyle property

Home you live in.

This is not automatically an "investment." It's a life decision.

Track 2: Investment property

Property bought to produce cashflow and/or strategic appreciation.

Problems happen when people confuse Track 1 and Track 2.

They buy a luxury home and call it an asset.

Then they struggle to pay EMIs.

Then they become "property rich, cash poor."

Real estate should reduce stress, not increase it.

12. CASE STUDIES (COMPOSITE, BUT REAL PATTERNS)

Case Study A: The Residential Trap — "Appreciation Will Save Me"

A young professional buys an under-construction apartment in a "future hotspot."

- EMI starts
- possession delays happen
- rent doesn't start
- resale is illiquid
- stress rises

What killed him wasn't the market.

It was his assumption that **time risk doesn't matter**.

Lesson: A delayed asset is not an asset. It's a liability in disguise.

Case Study B: The Commercial Win — "Lease Quality = Sleep Quality"

Another investor buys a pre-leased commercial asset with:

- strong tenant
- lease lock-in
- escalation clause
- conservative purchase price (cap rate makes sense)

He didn't get emotional returns.

He got contractual returns.

Lesson: In commercial real estate, you're not buying a shop. You're buying a contract.

Case Study C: Dubai Done Right — "Math First, Emotion Never"

An investor targets Dubai for diversification and cashflow.

He uses:

- DLD Rental Index for rent sanity checks
- DLD Service Charge Index to model expenses
- conservative vacancy assumptions
- realistic transaction costs (including 4% fee and mortgage fee where applicable)

He buys only when net yield survives stress tests.

Lesson: Dubai rewards underwriting. It punishes fantasy.

Case Study D: Dubai Done Wrong — "The Flipper Who Confused a Cycle for Skill"

A buyer flips off-plan because the market is hot.

Then supply surges, sentiment cools, buyers disappear.

Warnings exist for this reason:

- UBS flags elevated risk dynamics
- Fitch (via Reuters) expected correction pressures due to supply

Lesson: If your plan depends on uninterrupted appreciation, you didn't buy an asset—you bought a prayer.

13. THE "12-POINT REAL ESTATE CHECKLIST" (RESIDENTIAL + COMMERCIAL)

If you do nothing else, use this.

A. Asset & Market

1. **Micro-market demand**: who is the tenant/buyer?
2. **Supply pipeline**: how many competing units are coming?
3. **Replacement cost trend**: is construction cost rising here?

B. Cashflow

4. **Net yield** (after costs, not before)
5. **Vacancy stress test** (2–6 months)
6. **Repair reserve** (properties age; budget it)

C. Leverage

7. **Conservative LTV** (don't max out)
8. **EMI survivability** (job shock scenario)
9. **Interest-rate risk** (can you handle higher rates?)

D. Legal & Governance

10. **Title + approvals** (no clean docs, no deal)

11. **Developer/tenant quality** (track record matters)
12. **Exit liquidity** (who buys this from you?)

14. WHERE MOST PEOPLE GO WRONG (AND HOW YOU DON'T)

Mistake 1: They calculate returns like children

They ignore transaction costs and vacancy.

Mistake 2: They buy what they can't exit

Illiquid trophy assets are wealth traps.

Mistake 3: They over-leverage

Over-leverage is not courage. It's slow self-destruction.

Mistake 4: They confuse residential and commercial

Residential = tenant behavior + local demand

Commercial = lease contract + tenant quality + asset obsolescence

Mistake 5: They treat Dubai (or any global market) as a one-way road

Professional investors treat every market as a cycle—because it is.

15. THE NEW WEALTH ORDER REAL ESTATE PRINCIPLE

Let me end this chapter with the principle I want stamped into your brain:

Real estate is not a shortcut to wealth.

Real estate is a system to store value, build cashflow, and amplify capital—IF you underwrite correctly.

If you buy real estate as emotion, inflation will punish you.

If you buy real estate as a system—cashflow, location logic, legal clarity, conservative leverage—then inflation can become your ally.

In Part 4 of this book, we go deeper into property strategy:

- rental yield vs appreciation
- cashflow strategy
- global markets
- and the playbooks that turn property into generational wealth

But if you learn nothing else from Part 3, learn this:

In real estate, the deal is made at purchase—not at sale.

Buy right, and time becomes your partner.

Buy wrong, and time becomes your enemy.

READER NOTE

This chapter is for education and strategic thinking. It is not individualized financial advice or a solicitation. Real estate involves market risk, liquidity risk, legal risk, tenant risk, and leverage risk. Regulations and taxes vary by jurisdiction and can change. Always consult qualified legal, tax, and financial professionals before executing real estate transactions—especially cross-border.

Chapter 11

RENTAL INCOME SYSTEMS

How to Build "Asset Payroll" From Property Without Becoming a Full-Time Landlord

*(Narrated in the voice of Speaker Singh — **The New Wealth Order**)*

Let me say this with full clarity, from my journey.

Rental income is one of the most misunderstood wealth tools on Earth.

People think rent is "passive."

People think rent is "guaranteed."

People think one property = financial freedom.

People think "rent will pay the EMI."

And then reality arrives—late rent, vacancy, repairs, tenant drama, maintenance bills, legal headaches, service charges, taxes, and the worst enemy of all:

bad math.

So here's the New Wealth Order definition:

Rental income is not a return. It's a system.

A system has inputs, controls, reserves, rules, and discipline. If you don't build it like a system, it will behave like a gamble.

And I'll be blunt:

Most people don't fail in real estate because real estate is bad.

They fail because they buy property like an emotion, then expect it to behave like a spreadsheet.

This chapter will turn you into a rental-income operator—not a rental-income dreamer.

1. THE REAL PURPOSE OF RENTAL INCOME

Why the wealthy love it (and why amateurs get punished)

In private wealth rooms, rental income is respected for one reason:

It builds Asset Payroll.

Asset payroll is money that comes in because you own something—not because you wake up and go to work.

But here's the part that separates the wealthy from the middle class:

The wealthy don't buy "a house for rent."

They build a **rental business model**.

They ask:

- Who is my tenant?
- What's the demand engine here?
- What's the vacancy risk?

- What are the true operating costs?
- What's the legal system?
- What's the rent reversion ability?
- What's the exit plan?

The middle class asks:

- "Will the price go up?"
- "Is it a good area?"
- "My friend said buy here."

That's not investing. That's hope.

2. THE BIG LIE: "RENTAL INCOME IS PASSIVE"

Rental income is only passive **after** you build operations.

Until then, rental income is:

- tenant selection
- legal paperwork
- maintenance scheduling
- vendor management
- rent collection follow-ups
- renewal negotiations
- vacancy marketing
- accounting & compliance

So the New Wealth Order rule is:

Rental income is passive only when your systems are active.

You either:

- build systems
- or you become the system

And if you become the system, you become a stressed landlord—not a wealth builder.

3. THE RENTAL INCOME EQUATION

The five numbers that decide whether you become rich or regretful

If you remember nothing else from this chapter, remember this:

Rental property returns are not one number. They are a stack.

A. Gross Rental Yield

Gross yield = Annual rent ÷ Property price

This is the number developers love to shout on billboards because it's the prettiest.

But gross yield is not what you keep.

B. Net Rental Yield

Net yield = (Annual rent – Operating expenses) ÷ Property price

Operating expenses include:

- maintenance/repairs
- society or service charges
- insurance
- property taxes (where applicable)

- vacancy allowance
- property management fees
- furnishings replacement (if furnished)

Dubai example: service charges can be significant, which is why Dubai Land Department provides a **Service Charge Index** through RERA to check approved service fees for joint ownership properties.

C. Cash-on-Cash Return

This is what serious investors care about if they use loans.

Cash-on-cash = Annual net cashflow ÷ Cash invested

Because if you invest ₹20 lakh down payment and you earn ₹2 lakh net cashflow per year, that's 10% cash-on-cash.

D. Debt Service Coverage (DSCR)

Can your rent comfortably pay your EMI?

If rent barely covers EMI, one vacancy month will punch you in the face.

E. Total Return

Total return = Net cashflow + Principal paydown + Appreciation (or depreciation)

Most amateurs obsess over appreciation.

Owners obsess over **total return with survivability**.

4. THE GLOBAL REALITY: PROPERTY PRICES CAN FALL WHILE RENTS BEHAVE DIFFERENTLY

Why rental systems matter in cycles

Property is cyclical. Policy-driven. Credit-driven.

The Bank for International Settlements reported that in **Q2 2025**, aggregated global house prices **adjusted for consumer prices declined 0.8% year-on-year**, marking the third consecutive year of falling real prices globally.

Read that carefully.

Even when the world is "growing," real house prices can fall.

That is why rental income matters:

- It can provide cashflow even when capital values stagnate.
- It reduces forced selling risk.
- It turns property from "speculation" into "business."

At the same time, rents in many places keep rising—often steadily.

For example, Eurostat reported that in the **EU**, in **Q1 2025**, rents rose **3.2%** year-on-year, and between **2010 and Q1 2025**, EU rents increased **27.8%**.

This is the lesson:

Capital values are moody. Rental demand is structural.

Your job is to build a system that can survive both.

5. WHY RENTAL SYSTEMS FAIL (THE FIVE KILLERS)

Let me expose the killers, aggressively, because these are the reasons people stay stuck.

Killer 1: Buying the wrong asset for the wrong tenant

A luxury apartment in a weak rental zone is not "premium."

It's a vacancy machine.

Killer 2: Over-leverage

People use maximum loan because they can.

Then one vacancy month turns "investment" into panic.

Killer 3: Underestimating operating costs

Service charges. Repairs. Painting. AC replacement. Plumbing. Lift upgrades. Society major works.

If you don't model operating costs, your yield is fiction.

Killer 4: No vacancy reserve

Vacancy is not an accident. It's part of the business.

Killer 5: No rent revision power

If your market has weak rent growth or rent controls without strategy, your income stagnates while costs rise.

This is why regulation tools matter, especially in places like Dubai where rent adjustments tie into official indices.

Dubai Land Department provides a **Rental Index** service (often referred to as the RERA rental index/calculator) that can be used to evaluate rent levels for renewals.

6. THE NEW WEALTH ORDER RENTAL BLUEPRINT

Build rental income like a CEO, not like a buyer

Here is the blueprint I use conceptually when advising serious money—translated into beginner language.

STEP 1: Decide the job of the property

Every property must have a job:

- **Cashflow engine** (income first)
- **Growth engine** (appreciation + rent later)
- **Hybrid** (balanced)

If you don't define the job, you'll buy random assets.

STEP 2: Underwrite like a banker, not like a dreamer

Your underwriting must include:

- realistic rent (not broker fantasy)
- vacancy assumption (I prefer conservative)
- maintenance assumption
- legal costs buffer
- insurance
- management fees
- service charges/society costs

In Dubai, you can literally check service fees via the official DLD **Service Charge Index**.

STEP 3: Create an operations plan

Who will:

- find tenants?
- manage maintenance?

- handle contracts?
- handle disputes?
- handle renewals?

Dubai Land Department's **Dubai REST** app describes services including rental index and service charge index and other property transactions—this matters because strong infrastructure reduces friction for landlords.

STEP 4: Protect the downside

Downside protection is not negativity. It is professionalism.

You need:

- vacancy reserve
- repair reserve
- insurance
- conservative leverage
- legal clarity
- tenant screening discipline

STEP 5: Scale only after stability

Most people try to scale too early.

First build:

- one stable cashflow property
- one stable process
- one stable vendor network

Then scale.

Not before.

7. THE RENTAL YIELD TRUTH: STOP BELIEVING "10% GUARANTEED"

Let me attack one dangerous lie:

"Guaranteed 10% rental return."

In real markets, consistent 10% rental yields are rare unless you are taking hidden risks (location, quality, tenant reliability, maintenance burden, or fake projections).

A Reidin report examining Dubai's rental market since 2015 explicitly notes that **10% net yields** are largely absent from the data and appear only a few times in a decade—suggesting many claims are based on gross yields or optimistic assumptions.

So my rule is:

If someone promises you 10% as "normal," demand audited reality.

If they can't show reality, they are selling excitement—not income.

8. GLOBAL YIELD COMPARISON

Why Dubai stands out for income-focused investors (when done right)

Now we go global—because The New Wealth Order is not local-only thinking.

Across major world cities, yields can be surprisingly low—especially in prime areas.

Savills reported that across an average of world cities, **prime gross yields** moved slightly in 2024, and the average was around **3.15%**.

That's why in many "prestige cities," real estate becomes more of:

- capital preservation
- lifestyle asset
- long-term appreciation play

than a strong cashflow play.

Dubai's difference: the income story is stronger

Reidin's **UAE Residential Property Price Report (Nov 2025)** shows:

- Dubai residential market **gross rental yields around 6.55%** (market level, month shown in chart).
- Dubai apartment gross rental yields around **7.03%** (in the apartments section chart).

It also reports Dubai rent index growth **+6.14% YoY** in Nov 2025.

So compared to the world-city prime yield average (~3.15%), Dubai's gross yield profile can look meaningfully stronger.

Now, don't misread this:

Higher yield does not mean "no risk."

It means Dubai can be more attractive for investors who want **income + liquidity + global demand**, provided you underwrite correctly.

Rental growth momentum matters too

- Savills highlighted Dubai as a standout in 2024, with prime rents growing **23.5%** and capital values up **6.8%** (prime segment).
- ValuStrat noted rental growth in value-driven neighborhoods where affordable apartment rents rose **more than 20% in 2025**, supported by population growth and inward migration.

This is a powerful combination for landlords:

- higher starting yields
- plus rent growth engine
- plus global capital interest

9. WHY DUBAI KEEPS ATTRACTING INVESTORS

Regulation, scale, tools, and the "friction advantage"

Serious investors don't just look at yields.

They look at **friction**.

Friction is:

- how hard it is to buy
- how hard it is to rent
- how hard it is to enforce contracts
- how hard it is to exit

Dubai's market has scaled massively.

A Government of Dubai press release (Dubai Media Office / DMO platform) states that Dubai's real estate sector achieved record performance in **2025** with **over 270,000 transactions worth AED 917 billion**, up **20% year-on-year**.

That scale matters because:

- liquidity tends to be stronger in active markets
- services mature

- transparency tools improve
- professional property management ecosystems develop

Dubai also emphasizes regulatory tools for rental fairness:

- DLD Rental Index service exists for rent level referencing.
- DLD Service Charge Index exists to inquire about approved service fees for joint ownership properties.
- Dubai REST app lists these services and more in one ecosystem.

In my experience, this "ecosystem maturity" is what separates:

- markets where landlords behave like operators from
- markets where landlords behave like victims

10. TAX REALITY: "TAX-FREE" IS POWERFUL, BUT DON'T BE NAÏVE

Dubai's appeal is amplified by taxation.

The Official UAE Government platform states clearly that the UAE **does not levy income tax on individuals** (while also noting VAT at 5% on goods and services).

For rental income, this can be significant **locally**.

But here's the New Wealth Order discipline:

Your home-country tax rules still matter.

If you're an Indian resident for tax purposes, global income reporting rules may apply depending on residency and structure.

So the correct mindset is:

- Dubai can be tax-advantaged locally.
- But your personal situation must be structured properly with qualified advisors.

We don't do fantasies in this book.

11. RESIDENCY ANGLE: RENTAL INCOME + LIFESTYLE OPTIONALITY

Many investors also consider residency optionality.

Dubai Land Department provides a **Golden Visa (Investor) request service** describing a 10-year residency permit workflow and lists fee components, with a total shown (AED 9,884.75 in the page excerpt).

For requirements, the UAE government's Golden Residency service notes documentation including proof of property ownership valued at ≥ **AED 2 million** (as described in the service requirements).

DLD also has an **Investor Residence Application (Taskeen)** service for property investors owning property with purchase value ≥ **AED 750,000** at time of purchase for a renewable residence permit (2 years described).

I'm not saying "buy property for visa."

I'm saying: the ecosystem creates **global demand**, and demand supports rental markets.

12. THE RISK SECTION (BECAUSE REAL PROFESSIONALS TALK RISK)

Now I'm going to do what most property marketers won't do.

I'll talk risk openly.

Dubai risk: supply cycles and price corrections

Reuters reported that Fitch forecast Dubai real estate prices could face a **double-digit decline (up to ~15%)** in the latter half of 2025 and into 2026, driven by a large expected increase in housing supply (210,000 units projected).

This matters.

Because the New Wealth Order approach is not "Dubai is always up."

The approach is:

Dubai is attractive—so underwrite conservatively and prepare for cycles.

If you buy with:

- conservative leverage
- real rental assumptions
- service-charge clarity
- cash reserves

then even if prices soften, your rental system can survive.

But if you buy with:

- maximum loan
- minimum down payment
- "guaranteed yield" fantasies

then a correction will expose you.

13. INDIA RENTAL INCOME REALITY (AND WHY MANY INDIAN LANDLORDS FEEL DISAPPOINTED)

Let's talk India—because most Indian families still emotionally trust property.

India's rental dynamics vary hugely by city and micro-market.

- Economic Times reported that India's residential rental inflation cooled to **7%–9%** in H1 2025 across major cities (per the cited NoBroker analysis), after higher hikes in earlier years.
- A Reuters poll reported India home prices were forecast to rise **6.3% in 2025** and **7.0% in 2026**, and noted urban rents forecast to rise **5%–8%** (higher than inflation).

Now yields.

Rental yields in India are often discussed as "low," especially in high-value prime metros.

Knight Frank (in an official LinkedIn post) stated that residential rental yields typically range between **2%–4%**.

At the same time, listing-based datasets sometimes show higher national averages depending on sample, segment, and city mix. For example, Global Property Guide reported an average gross rental yield in India around **5.09% (Q4 2025)**, noting it is calculated using median prices and rents sourced from local listings.

So here's the honest interpretation:

India can give you rental income—

but many people buy in high-ticket areas where:

- prices are high
- rents don't rise proportionally
- net yields shrink after maintenance and taxes

That's why Indian landlords often feel:

"Property is valuable, but the rent doesn't feel like income."

It's because they bought appreciation assets and expected cashflow behavior.

Different job. Different outcome.

14. THE RENTAL INCOME SYSTEM MODEL

A complete operating system you can run anywhere (India, Dubai, or global)

Now we build the actual system.

SYSTEM LAYER 1: Acquisition (Buy right or suffer later)

The Three Filters:

1. **Tenant demand filter**
    - Who rents here and why?
    - What events can reduce demand?

2. **Supply filter**
   - Is massive new supply coming?
   - Is it a tenant's market or landlord's market?
3. **Quality filter**
   - Building quality reduces maintenance surprises
   - Bad quality destroys net yield quietly

Speaker Singh rule:

If you cannot explain your tenant in one sentence, don't buy.

SYSTEM LAYER 2: Legal and regulatory (Clarity is cashflow)

In Dubai, there are official tools and structures that matter:

- Rental Index service (RERA rent referencing).
- Service Charge Index for approved service fees.
- Dubai REST app integrates major services.

These reduce ambiguity.

In any market (India included), your legal checklist should cover:

- title clarity
- encumbrances
- society rules
- rental contract enforceability
- local compliance requirements

Because a property with legal uncertainty is not an asset.

It's a liability wearing a suit.

SYSTEM LAYER 3: Finance (Leverage is a weapon, not a lifestyle)

Leverage can amplify outcomes—good or bad.

Your loan rules must include:

- conservative EMI coverage
- buffers for vacancy
- buffers for rate changes (if variable)
- a rule for maximum leverage percentage

Speaker Singh rule:

Never structure a rental deal where one vacancy month creates panic.

If you do, you didn't buy an investment.

You bought a stress subscription.

SYSTEM LAYER 4: Operations (This is where amateurs lose)

Here is the professional landlord checklist:

Tenant selection:

- stable income verification
- references where appropriate
- deposit discipline
- clear contract terms

Property management:

- documented inspections
- scheduled maintenance calendar
- emergency vendor list
- rent collection automation
- renewal system 90 days before lease expiry

Dubai landlords often use the Rental Index referencing during renewal conversations to keep negotiations grounded.

Repairs & reserves:

- monthly reserve set aside
- annual repainting / deep maintenance budget
- large replacements planning (AC, plumbing, appliances)

SYSTEM LAYER 5: Optimization (This is how rental systems become wealth engines)

Optimization levers include:

- raising rent strategically (within legal framework)
- reducing vacancy via better tenant experience
- improving furnishing strategy (where it increases net yield)
- renegotiating service contracts
- refinancing only when it improves total return, not ego

15. THREE REAL STORIES (SUCCESS, FAILURE, AND DUBAI CLARITY)

Story A: The failure — "One property, infinite assumptions"

A client (details changed) bought a "premium" unit because it sounded impressive.

The gross yield looked okay on paper.

But the system was missing:

- vacancy budget
- service charge understanding
- maintenance reserve
- tenant screening

Within two years:

- the unit had multiple vacancy gaps
- repairs hit unexpectedly
- net yield collapsed
- and the investor emotionally blamed "real estate"

But the real culprit was not the asset.

It was the absence of a system.

Story B: The success — "Boring property, powerful process"

Another investor (details changed) did something unsexy:

- chose a demand-heavy tenant zone
- targeted stable mid-market tenants
- hired professional property management
- kept conservative leverage
- built reserves

The property didn't become a "viral success."

It became something far more valuable:

predictable cashflow + psychological peace.

That is wealth.

Story C: The Dubai lesson — "Tools reduce friction"

One reason investors like Dubai is the operational infrastructure:

- Rental Index referencing exists.
- Service charge checks exist.
- The ecosystem is active and liquid at scale (record AED 917B transactions in 2025).

That doesn't eliminate risk—Fitch's warning on supply cycles still stands.

But it can reduce friction and improve professional execution.

16. DIRECT RENTAL INCOME VS REIT-STYLE RENTAL INCOME

"I want rental yield, but I don't want tenant headaches"

This chapter is about rental income systems, so I must say this:

Not everyone should be a landlord.

If you want exposure to rental income-like cashflows without directly operating property, REIT's can be an alternative (depending on jurisdiction).

In India, Times of India reported that Indian REIT's have been delivering average yields of **6%–7.5%**, citing a CREDAI and ANAROCK Capital report and projecting market cap growth.

Again: not a promise, not advice—just a structural option.

New Wealth Order principle:

- If you can't operate the system, use a vehicle where someone else operates it.

17. SPEAKER SINGH'S HARD RULES FOR RENTAL INCOME SYSTEMS

(Print these in your head.)

Rule 1: Never buy property for rent without knowing net yield

Gross yield is marketing.

Net yield is reality.

Rule 2: Service charges can destroy your deal

In Dubai, check the official Service Charge Index.

Rule 3: Vacancy is part of the model

Budget it. Or it will budget you.

Rule 4: Leverage must be survivable

If EMI depends on perfect occupancy, you're not investing—you're praying.

Rule 5: 10% "guaranteed yield" is a red flag

Even market research has called out how rare consistent 10% net yields are.

Rule 6: Rent revision power matters

Dubai's rental index framework is a tool; learn it.

Rule 7: Don't confuse a boom with intelligence

Dubai has had massive momentum, but even rating agencies warn of possible corrections as supply rises.

Rule 8: Your goal is not property ownership

Your goal is **income stability + total return + exit flexibility**.

CLOSING: THE SENTENCE THAT ENDS THE FANTASY AND BEGINS THE SYSTEM

Let me end the chapter the way I want you to remember it:

Rental income is not "monthly rent."

Rental income is a business model built on demand, discipline, and systems.

If you build it correctly, it becomes one of the most powerful forms of asset payroll on the planet—especially in markets where yields are structurally higher and rental tools are stronger, which is why Dubai keeps showing up in global investor conversations.

If you build it emotionally, inflation and vacancy will punish you.

In the next chapters, we will go deeper into:

- **Dubai vs global market selection logic**
- **how to underwrite property like a professional**
- **how to combine equity portfolios + rental systems into one wealth architecture**

That combination—liquid compounding + hard-asset cashflow—is a serious New Wealth Order strategy.

READER NOTE

This chapter is educational and not personal financial, legal, tax, or investment advice. Real estate involves market risk, liquidity risk, legal risk, tenant risk, and leverage risk. Regulations and taxes vary by country and personal residency status. Consult qualified professionals before acting. Recent reports and news referenced for rental market context.

Chapter 12

LEVERAGE DONE RIGHT

The Most Powerful Wealth Tool… and the Fastest Way to Ruin If You're Emotional

*(Narrated in the voice of Speaker Singh — **The New Wealth Order**)*

Let me begin with a statement that will make some people uncomfortable:

Most people are not financially stuck because they don't earn enough.

They're stuck because they keep using debt like a lifestyle… instead of using leverage like a weapon.

And yes—debt and leverage are related, but they are not the same in outcome.

Debt is what the majority uses to **consume**.

Leverage is what the wealthy uses to **control assets**.

Same instrument. Completely different intelligence.

From my journey—working with millionaires and billionaires across multiple markets—I've watched the same tool do two opposite things:

- **Leverage has built empires.**
- **Leverage has erased family wealth in one bad quarter.**

So if you're reading this as a beginner, here's what I want you to understand in simple language:

Leverage is not wealth. Leverage is a magnifier.

It magnifies:

- your profits
- your losses
- your mistakes
- your stress
- your timeline

If you don't have a system, leverage doesn't "help you get rich."

It helps you get exposed.

1. THE HONEST DEFINITION OF LEVERAGE

Control more assets than your cash alone would allow

Leverage is any structure that lets you control an asset using:

- borrowed money (loan, mortgage)
- borrowed exposure (derivatives, swaps)
- borrowed time (buy now, pay later, EMIs)
- borrowed confidence (guarantees, co-signing)

But financially, leverage usually means this:

You borrow money at a cost, to buy an asset you believe will outperform that cost.

That's the theory.

Reality is harsher:

You borrow money at a cost you must pay on time, even when life goes wrong.

That's why leverage is not "math only."

Leverage is **behavior + cashflow + risk control.**

2. THE TWO TYPES OF LEVERAGE

Productive leverage vs destructive leverage

I'm going to simplify the world for you:

A Destructive leverage (what keeps the middle class stuck)

This is borrowing to buy things that:

- don't produce cashflow
- don't grow in value reliably
- don't improve your earning power

Examples:

- credit card revolving debt
- personal loan for lifestyle
- car loan that stretches your budget

- "EMI mindset" purchases
- trading leverage without risk control

When destructive leverage enters your life, your future income becomes a servant.

B. Productive leverage (what builds wealth)

This is borrowing to buy or build things that:

- produce cashflow
- have durable demand
- have collateral value
- have an exit path

Examples:

- a mortgage on a cashflow-positive rental asset (when done right)
- business debt used for expansion with predictable revenue
- working capital financing for a profitable operation
- conservative real estate leverage in regulated markets

Same debt. Different brain.

3. WHY LEVERAGE IS SO DANGEROUS

Because repayment is not "optional"

Let me say it aggressively, because you need it:

The market can be wrong longer than you can remain solvent.

If you buy an asset with your own cash, and the price falls—painful, but survivable.

If you buy the same asset with leverage, and the price falls—your lender doesn't care about your hopes.

They want:

- EMIs on time
- margin calls met
- covenants respected
- paperwork compliant

Your emotions don't matter.

This is why leverage destroys people:

They think leverage is a "shortcut."

But leverage is not a shortcut.

Leverage is **pressure**.

And pressure reveals character.

4. WHY REGULATORS PUT LIMITS ON LEVERAGE

Because leverage can destroy a whole economy

If leverage was harmless, central banks wouldn't regulate it so tightly.

Look at the UAE as an example of a system that clearly understands leverage risk:

The Central Bank of the UAE (CBUAE) applies borrower-based controls to mortgages, including:

- **Loan-to-Value (LTV) caps** (how much the bank can finance)
- **Debt-burden ratio (DBR)** limits

- caps on maximum financing amount in years of income
- a **maximum mortgage tenor of 25 years**

Specifically, the CBUAE Financial Stability Report (FSR) states:

- DBR max **50%** of gross monthly income for expatriates and **60%** for nationals
- max financing amount capped at up to **7 years of annual income for expatriates** and **8 years for nationals**
- max tenor **25 years**

And for LTV rules (owner-occupier):

- **Expatriates**: up to **80%** LTV for property value ≤ AED 5 million; **70%** if > AED 5 million
- subsequent property: max **60%**
- off-plan schemes: max **50%**

When a central bank sets rules like this, it is essentially saying:

"Leverage is powerful, so we will not allow you to destroy yourself and the banking system."

That is the voice of experience—at national scale.

5. THE "LEVERAGE TRAP" IN THE REAL WORLD

People don't get trapped by poverty—people get trapped by repayments

Let's bring this home to India.

India's household debt has risen, and a key problem is **where the debt is going**.

Reuters, citing the RBI's Financial Stability Report, noted household debt at **41.9% of GDP**, with **non-housing retail loans** forming over half of household debt and **25.7% of disposable income**, and warned about rising delinquencies in segments like credit cards, personal loans and microfinance.

Read that again.

Not housing. Not business.

Consumption-oriented debt.

This is exactly why people feel stuck even when their salary rises:

- income rises slowly
- repayments rise fast
- lifestyle expands
- cashflow collapses
- savings become a joke
- investing becomes "next month" forever

So here is a New Wealth Order definition:

Financial freedom is not about income. It's about removing compulsory repayments from your life—or converting them into productive repayments.

6. LEVERAGE DONE WRONG: THE "TRADING SHORTCUT" THAT DESTROYS RETAIL INVESTORS

Leverage without skill is not investing—it's self-harm (financially)

Now I'm going to hit a national nerve.

A huge number of people—especially new investors—try to use leverage through trading because they want fast money.

SEBI's official study found that **93% of individual traders** incurred losses in equity F&O between FY22 and FY24, with **aggregate losses exceeding ₹1.8 lakh crore** over three years.

That is not "small loss."

That is a national leak of capital.

Why does this matter in a chapter on leverage?

Because derivatives are often **embedded leverage**.

And embedded leverage punishes beginners faster than any other weapon.

This is why in my work, when someone says, "I want to do options," my first response is:

Options are not an investment plan. Options are a skill profession.

And if you don't have the skill, you are donating money to the market.

Leverage is not your friend when your knowledge is weak.

7. THE GLOBAL WARNING: LEVERAGE CREATES HISTORIC COLLAPSES

Three case studies every serious investor must know

If you want to become "New Wealth Order" intelligent, you must study how leverage kills.

Case Study 1: The Great Recession

The U.S. Federal Reserve's history essay notes that home prices fell about **30%** on average from mid-2006 peak to mid-2009, and the S&P 500 fell **57%** from the October 2007 peak to the March 2009 trough.

This was not just "market volatility."

This was leverage exploding:

- over-borrowing
- weak underwriting
- fragile borrowers
- complex financial structures
- refinancing dependency

Leverage doesn't just "increase returns."

Leverage increases **systemic fragility**.

Case Study 2: Long-Term Capital Management (LTCM)

The U.S. Treasury's 1999 report on hedge funds and leverage explicitly warns that excessive leverage can greatly magnify negative shocks and highlights LTCM as a near-collapse event.

LTCM is the story of intelligence without humility.

Brilliant models. Massive leverage.

Then the market did something the model didn't price.

Leverage doesn't forgive arrogance.

Case Study 3: Archegos

Credit Suisse's report states it incurred about **$5.5 billion** in losses after the March 2021 default of Archegos.

Reuters reported Archegos amassed roughly **$160 billion** in stock exposure using total return swaps before margin calls triggered a collapse.

This is the key lesson:

Leverage hides size.

Swaps hid exposure.

Prime brokers couldn't see full concentration across the street.

Then the margin calls came like a guillotine.

If you don't understand how leverage works, you can die without even seeing the blade.

8. LEVERAGE DONE RIGHT: THE 5 NON-NEGOTIABLE RULES

Speaker Singh's "Leverage Protocol"

Now we shift from fear to power.

Here is the system.

RULE 1: Only use leverage on assets with a job

Your borrowed money must buy something that does at least one of these:

- generates **cashflow**
- generates **productive growth**
- increases your earning power
- improves your balance sheet strength

If the asset has no job, the debt becomes your new boss.

RULE 2: Leverage must be survivable under stress

In my experience, this is where people fail.

They calculate returns in a perfect world.

But wealth is not built in a perfect world.

Wealth is built by surviving ugly periods.

So you must stress test:

- vacancy
- interest rate rise
- income disruption
- medical emergency
- market correction
- currency movement (if investing internationally)

If your leverage breaks under stress, it is not leverage—it is a trap.

RULE 3: Always calculate net returns, not fantasy returns

Leverage makes people lie to themselves.

They ignore:

- transaction fees
- registration costs
- taxes
- maintenance
- insurance
- vacancy
- refinancing fees
- currency costs

- service charges

And then they say, "My ROI is 18%."

No. Your imagination is 18%.

Your **net** may be 6%.

RULE 4: Liquidity is not optional

If you have leverage, you must have liquidity.

Liquidity means:

- emergency fund
- repair reserve
- EMI reserve
- buffer for rate changes
- buffer for vacancy

No buffer = one shock = forced selling.

RULE 5: Exit strategy before entry

Before you take leverage, ask:

- If I need to sell quickly, can I?
- What is the liquidity of this asset?
- Who is the next buyer?
- What is my timeline?
- What happens if prices drop 10–15%?

If you don't have an exit plan, you don't have a strategy.

You have a prayer.

9. REAL ESTATE LEVERAGE DONE RIGHT

The "asset-backed leverage" that can build long-term wealth

Real estate is the most common leverage vehicle on earth because:

- it has collateral
- banks understand it
- it can cashflow
- it can be long duration

But real estate leverage is only powerful when you respect the rules.

(A) Understand the three real estate leverage numbers

1. **LTV (Loan-to-Value)**

   Higher LTV = higher risk = lower safety.

2. **DSCR (Debt Service Coverage Ratio)**

   Can your rental cashflow cover your EMI with comfort?

3. **Cash-on-Cash Return**

   How much cash return do you generate on the cash you invested?

If you don't understand these three, you should not take real estate leverage.

10. DUBAI AS A LEVERAGE CASE STUDY

Why Dubai attracts global investors—and why leverage discipline matters even more there

Dubai deserves its own section because it's becoming a serious global capital magnet—and that changes the leverage landscape.

But let me be clear:

Dubai is not magical.

Dubai is a market—cyclical, supply-driven, sentiment-driven.

The "positives" Dubai offers for leverage users

1. **Clear mortgage macroprudential rules (structured borrowing limits)**

   CBUAE sets LTV caps and DBR caps—this forces discipline.

2. **Transparent fee framework (know your true costs)**

   Dubai Land Department's investor guide lists examples of registration fees, including:

   - **Sale and Purchase Contract registration: 4% of purchase price** (split between seller and purchaser unless agreed otherwise)
   - **Mortgage Contract registration: 0.25% of the mortgage value (loan)**

   This matters because fees affect your effective leverage and your break-even.

3. **Currency stability mechanics**

   The UAE runs a long-standing USD/AED peg mechanism; the Central Bank lists intervention rates around **USD/AED 3.672 (buying USD)** and **3.673 (selling USD)**.

For international investors, currency stability can reduce one layer of uncertainty (though your home-country currency exposure still matters).

Now the discipline part: Dubai is still cyclical

Reuters reported Fitch's view that Dubai real estate prices could face a **double-digit decline**, potentially up to **~15%**, in the latter half of 2025 and into 2026, driven by a sharp rise in expected housing supply deliveries.

This is exactly why leverage must be handled like a system.

Because here is the brutal math:

If you buy a property for AED 2,000,000 with 80% LTV (AED 1,600,000 loan), your equity is roughly AED 400,000 (before fees).

A 15% price drop is AED 300,000.

That means **most of your equity can get crushed**, even though the property "only" fell 15%.

That is leverage.

Dubai Example: The True Cost of Leverage (simple numbers)

Property price: AED 2,000,000

Loan (80% LTV): AED 1,600,000

Down payment: AED 400,000

Now fees (minimum framework examples):

- DLD sale contract registration example: 4% of purchase price = AED 80,000
- DLD mortgage registration example: 0.25% of loan value = AED 4,000

So your "cash invested" is not just AED 400,000.

It's **AED 484,000** (and that's before other practical costs).

This is why amateurs struggle:

They calculate returns on down payment only.

Professionals calculate returns on **total cash deployed.**

11. THE MOST IMPORTANT LEVERAGE PRINCIPLE IN REAL ESTATE

"Rent must pay the loan" is not enough

A rookie says:

"Rent covers EMI, so I'm safe."

No.

A professional asks:

- Does rent cover EMI **and** service charges **and** maintenance **and** vacancy buffer?
- Can I survive 3 months vacancy?
- What if interest rates rise?
- What if rents fall?
- What if the property needs a major repair?

This is why the wealthy don't buy property as "one unit."

They buy it as a **cashflow machine.**

12. PORTFOLIO LEVERAGE: THE SILENT WEALTH KILLER

Margin loans, leverage products, and emotional trading

If you are a beginner investor, let me say this with authority:

Do not touch portfolio leverage until you have discipline and cash reserves.

Because portfolios are volatile by nature.

The Great Recession example is enough to humble anybody:

S&P fell **57%** peak-to-trough.

Now imagine you were leveraged.

You wouldn't just lose money.

You would be margin-called at the worst moment—when prices are low and fear is high.

Leverage doesn't wait for recovery.

Leverage forces liquidation.

That is the opposite of compounding.

13. SPEAKER SINGH'S 12 RULES OF LEVERAGE DONE RIGHT

(Write these down. These are survival rules.)

1. **Never use leverage to impress people.**
2. **Never use leverage on an asset you don't understand.**
3. **Never use leverage without reserves.**
4. **Never use leverage with no exit plan.**
5. **Never accept "guaranteed returns" to justify borrowing.**
6. **Keep repayments below your pain threshold** (regulators do this with DBR limits for a reason).

7. **Prefer collateral-backed leverage** over unsecured leverage (unsecured debt is usually the highest stress).
8. **Match the duration**: long-term asset + short-term loan = danger.
9. **Calculate net return after all fees** (DLD 4% registration and 0.25% mortgage registration are real examples of cost layers).
10. **Stress test price drops** (Dubai's cycle warnings show why).
11. **Don't confuse liquidity with value**—you may be right long-term and still be forced to sell short-term.
12. **Leverage is earned**: you use it after building financial habits, not before.

14. THE NEW WEALTH ORDER LEVERAGE LADDER

What I prefer, in sequence (simple and practical)

From my experience, the safest progression looks like this:

Level 1: No leverage — build discipline

- emergency fund
- insurance
- basic investing habit
- low risk of wipeout

Level 2: Low leverage on productive assets

- conservative mortgage
- conservative business expansion
- repayments that don't choke you

Level 3: Moderate leverage with systems

- professional underwriting
- management systems
- liquidity reserves
- diversification of income

Level 4: Advanced leverage (only for experts)

- portfolio leverage
- derivatives
- structured products
- concentrated bets

Most people skip Level 1 and Level 2... and jump into Level 4.

Then they call the market "scam" when the market simply followed mathematics.

15. CLOSING: THE SENTENCE THAT ENDS THE CONFUSION

Leverage is not good. Leverage is not bad.

Leverage is truth serum.

It exposes:

- whether your cashflow is real
- whether your discipline is real
- whether your planning is real
- whether your risk management is real

If you use leverage emotionally, you will eventually pay for it.

If you use leverage as a system—conservatively, with buffers, with underwriting, with exits—then leverage can accelerate your path into asset ownership and long-term wealth.

That is "Leverage Done Right."

And in the next chapters, we'll connect this leverage framework to:

- **Dubai real estate strategy** (how to underwrite cycles, not hype)
- **equity portfolios** (liquid compounding alongside hard-asset leverage)
- and the full **New Wealth Order** capital architecture.

READER NOTE

This chapter is for education and storytelling, not personal financial, legal, tax, or investment advice. Markets carry risk. Debt increases risk. Regulations and tax treatment vary by jurisdiction and residency. Consult qualified professionals for your situation.

Chapter 13

REIT's & GLOBAL INVESTING

Own Real Estate Like the Wealthy… Without Becoming a Landlord

*(Narrated in the voice of Speaker Singh — **The New Wealth Order**)*

Let me speak to you plainly, from my journey.

Most people want real estate wealth.

But they don't want real estate pain.

They want:

- rental income
- appreciation
- inflation protection
- "something tangible"
- respect in society
- a feeling of security

But they don't want:

- tenants

- vacancy
- repairs
- legal battles
- broker lies
- illiquidity
- society charges
- builder delays
- the "I'm stuck with this property" anxiety

So they end up in the worst place:

They keep dreaming about real estate... and never own real estate properly.

This is where **REIT's** come in.

REIT's are one of the most powerful wealth tools of the modern financial system because they do something very rare:

They turn real estate into a liquid, scalable, investable "asset payroll" machine.

But—and this is important—REIT's are also one of the most misunderstood products on Earth, because people treat them like fixed deposits.

They see "high yield" and their brain shuts down.

They forget:

- interest rates move
- property cycles move
- sectors behave differently
- leverage exists

- taxes matter
- currency matters
- global rules matter

So in this chapter, I'm going to do what The New Wealth Order demands:

No fantasies. No blind optimism. Only systems.

1. WHAT A REIT REALLY IS

Real Estate Investment Trust = rental business packaged like a stock

A REIT is essentially a structure that allows you to own units/ shares in a pool of income-generating real estate—offices, apartments, malls, warehouses, data centers, hospitals—without buying the building yourself.

SEBI's own REIT FAQ explains it simply: a REIT is a trust registered with SEBI that raises funds by issuing units and invests primarily in real estate sector assets (directly or via structures).

Now here's the key reason REIT's became powerful:

REIT's are designed to push income back to investors.

In the U.S., regulators require REIT's to distribute at least **90% of taxable income** to shareholders (to maintain the REIT tax status).

In India, SEBI's REIT framework similarly requires REIT's to distribute at least **90% of net distributable cash flows (NDCF)** to unitholders, subject to applicable laws.

So the New Wealth Order translation is:

REIT's are built to behave like "rental income systems," not like growth-only stocks.

2. WHY REIT's BELONG IN THE NEW WEALTH ORDER

Because most people can't scale direct property safely

Direct property has advantages:

- control
- leverage flexibility
- "I can touch it" comfort
- value-add possibilities

But direct property also has brutal limitations:

- large ticket size
- concentration risk (one asset, one location)
- illiquidity (selling takes time)
- management burden
- legal risk
- emotional decision-making

A REIT solves many of these:

- you can start small
- you get instant diversification (multiple assets/tenants)
- it trades (liquidity)
- professional management runs operations
- distributions can be regular

That's why I call REIT's:

"Real estate ownership for people who want freedom, not landlord duty."

But you must accept one truth:

If you want liquidity, you must accept volatility.

A REIT trades like a stock because it is priced every day by the market.

So REIT's are not "safe."

They are **transparent**.

And transparency can feel painful to people who prefer illusions.

3. HOW REIT RETURNS ACTUALLY WORK

The 3 engines of a REIT (easy breakdown)

REIT total returns usually come from three sources:

Engine 1: Rental income → distributions

Tenants pay rent.

Costs are paid (maintenance, interest, management).

What remains gets distributed (based on rules and policy).

Nareit highlights that REIT's must distribute at least 90% of taxable income and that a large share of long-term REIT returns historically comes from dividends.

Engine 2: Rent growth

If rents rise over time, the income stream rises.

That can raise distributions and valuations.

Engine 3: Asset value re-rating

If cap rates compress (or interest rates fall), REIT valuations can expand.

If cap rates expand (or interest rates rise), REIT valuations can compress.

This is why REIT's can fall even when rents are fine—because markets reprice discount rates.

4. THE BIG MYTH: "REIT = GUARANTEED HIGH YIELD"

Yield is not a gift. Yield is a message.

When you see a high yield, it can mean:

- the REIT truly generates strong stable cashflow
- OR the price has fallen (yield rises mathematically)
- OR the payout is not sustainable
- OR risk has increased
- OR the sector is under pressure

Yield is not free money. Yield is a signal.

That's why in The New Wealth Order, we don't chase yield.

We chase **sustainable cashflow.**

5. INDIA REIT's: THE REAL OPPORTUNITY (AND THE REAL DISCIPLINE)

India is building a listed real estate culture—slowly, but seriously

India's REIT market is still young compared to the U.S., Singapore, or Japan.

But it's growing, and the structures are becoming more sophisticated.

The key Indian REIT rule you must remember

- **Minimum distribution:** at least **90% of NDCF**.
- **Borrowing cap:** maximum borrowing permitted is **49% of the REIT's asset value** (with additional governance requirements beyond thresholds).

This matters because leverage is where real estate can either:

- become a compounding machine

or

- become a bankruptcy engine

The cap forces discipline.

India REIT yields (what the data shows, not what the broker screams)

A 2025 ANAROCK report shows trailing twelve-month distribution yields for India's major REIT's around the ~5–6% zone (example values shown: Embassy 5.7%, Mindspace 5.1%, Brookfield India 6.0%, Nexus 5.2%, Knowledge 5.4%, as per the report's snapshot).

Now listen carefully:

Those are not "promises."

Those are **observed distribution yields** at that time based on market price and distributions.

India's listed REIT ecosystem is becoming index-visible

Nifty has a "REIT's & InvITs" index factsheet that shows major constituents like Embassy Office Parks REIT, Brookfield India RE Trust, Nexus Select Trust, Mindspace Business Parks REIT, etc.

This matters because index inclusion is how "big money" begins to allocate systematically.

The institutional money signal (why this is maturing)

You're seeing REIT's raise longer-duration debt and ESG-linked bonds. For example, Mindspace REIT raising sustainability-linked bonds with IFC was reported publicly.

And here's a major policy signal you should not ignore:

Reuters reported (February 2026) that the RBI proposed guidelines allowing banks to lend to REIT's with guardrails—like a 10% exposure cap for banks and limits tied to REIT asset value—showing regulators are thinking seriously about REIT financing channels while managing risk.

That is not "small news."

That is the plumbing of a future market.

6. GLOBAL REIT's: THIS IS WHERE THE REAL SCALE IS

The world has already built what India is beginning

Globally, REIT's are not a niche product.

Nareit's global investing page notes **1,021 listed REIT's** worldwide with combined equity market capitalization of about **$2.04 trillion (as of 2024)**.

That's a serious universe.

Global listed real estate performance is regionally different (and that's the point)

Nareit's market commentary reported that the **FTSE EPRA Nareit Developed Index returned 10.7% in 2025**, while performance diverged across regions (Asia/Europe stronger, North America lagging).

And in the U.S. specifically:

Nareit reports the **FTSE Nareit All Equity REIT's Index finished 2025 with a total return of 2.3%** (after a weak December).

This is a huge lesson:

Global investing is not about "best country."

It's about different cycles at different times.

7. THE REIT TRUTH WALL: INTEREST RATES MATTER

REIT's are income assets… and income assets get repriced when rates move

When interest rates rise:

- borrowing costs rise
- cap rates expand
- property values can cool
- yield alternatives (bonds) become attractive
- REIT prices can face pressure

When interest rates fall:

- discount rates fall

- refinancing becomes easier
- valuations often improve

So a REIT investor must be emotionally mature.

If you panic-sell every time rates move, you don't need REIT's.

You need therapy.

8. SECTOR SELECTION: REIT's ARE NOT ONE MARKET

Office is not data centers. Retail is not warehouses.

This is where amateurs get punished.

They buy "a REIT" like it's one product.

No.

REIT's are a **collection of property businesses**, and businesses perform differently.

A Nareit/FTSE index snapshot (as of **Feb 13, 2026**) shows massive differences across U.S. REIT property sectors in recent performance:

- **Data Centers:** strong 1-year total return (shown as 21.55% in that snapshot)
- **Office:** negative 1-year total return (shown as -7.91% in that snapshot)

Same "REIT label." Completely different reality.

This is the New Wealth Order rule:

Don't invest by label. Invest by cashflow engine + demand engine.

Demand engines that have been structurally strong globally:

- logistics/warehouses (e-commerce)
- data centers (cloud + AI compute)
- well-located residential rentals in supply-constrained cities
- certain healthcare categories (demographics)

Sectors that can be cyclical or disrupted:

- office (work patterns, supply, location quality)
- some retail formats (depends on experience vs commodity shopping)
- hotels (travel cycle sensitive)

The point isn't fear.

The point is intelligence.

9. THE "DIVIDEND + COMPOUNDING" REALITY (THE BORING MAGIC)

The best REIT strategy is often not exciting

If you want excitement, go to casinos.

If you want wealth, you want:

- steady distributions
- reinvestment discipline
- long runway
- diversification
- risk control

Nareit index data (Feb 13, 2026 snapshot) shows dividend yields around:

- **FTSE Nareit All Equity REIT's: ~3.74% dividend yield** (as of that report date)

And the same snapshot shows long-period annualized total return figures for U.S. REIT indexes (e.g., 25–40 year compound annual total returns in the ~8–10% zone depending on the index category).

Again: not a promise.

But it shows why REIT's became a core institutional asset class.

10. GLOBAL INVESTING FOR INDIANS: THE REAL ROADMAP

The world is your opportunity... but you must follow rules

Now let's get practical for Indian readers.

Route A: Buy Indian listed REIT's

This is the simplest operationally.

You get:

- rupee exposure
- local regulation
- familiar market hours
- simpler compliance

Route B: Buy global REIT's/global REIT ETFs

This gives:

- currency diversification

- access to sectors India doesn't have listed at scale (like large data center REIT's)
- country cycle diversification

But you must respect remittance rules.

The RBI's LRS FAQ states resident individuals can remit up to **USD 250,000 per financial year** for permissible current or capital account transactions.

The same RBI FAQ also explicitly mentions that remittances for acquiring **immovable property outside India** may be consolidated for relatives (subject to conditions), which confirms that overseas property acquisition can be within LRS permissibility (subject to compliance).

It also lists prohibited items like remittances for margins/margin calls to overseas exchanges and trading in foreign exchange abroad.

So the New Wealth Order mindset is:

- global investing is allowed
- but it is regulated
- and you must operate cleanly

Route C: International FoFs/global real estate securities funds via Indian mutual funds

This can be convenient for many investors.

But these funds are constrained by industry-wide overseas investment limits and operational caps at times.

For example, Economic Times (Feb 2026) reported PGIM India MF reopening subscriptions in international funds with daily investor caps.

This is why I teach this:

Global investing is not one door. It's multiple doors.

Choose the one that fits your compliance comfort and your risk maturity.

11. TAXES & FRICTION: THE PART PEOPLE IGNORE… THEN REGRET

The rich respect friction. The poor ignore friction.

When you invest globally, friction comes from:

- withholding taxes
- dividend taxation
- capital gains rules
- reporting requirements
- currency conversion costs
- remittance charges
- "paperwork fatigue"

If you ignore friction, your returns get quietly eaten.

Indian REIT taxation (high-level reality)

REIT distributions in India can include different components (like interest/dividend/rental), and taxation differs based on the component and investor category; ClearTax summarizes that REIT/InvIT distribution streams are taxed and TDS applies on certain income streams (subject to prevailing law and specifics).

I'm not going to drown you in tax sections inside a chapter.

But I will give you the New Wealth Order rule:

Never buy an income asset without understanding the tax character of the income.

TCS and remittances (don't get shocked)

India's outward remittances under LRS can attract Tax Collected at Source (TCS) beyond thresholds depending on purpose and latest budget rules.

Economic Times reported that Budget 2026 reduced TCS on LRS remittances for education and medical treatment to **2%** (effective timeline as per the budget coverage).

This chapter is not telling you what to do.

It's telling you what smart people check **before** they move money.

12. DUBAI: THE GLOBAL REIT STORY INDIANS SHOULD UNDERSTAND

Dubai has moved from "property market" to "capital market real estate"

Now we come to a region that has become impossible to ignore in global wealth conversations: **Dubai.**

Dubai is doing something that matters for investors:

It's converting real estate into investable market instruments.

The landmark example: Dubai Residential REIT

Reuters reported that Dubai Holding launched the IPO of **Dubai Residential REIT** in May 2025, valuing it up to about **$3.9 billion,** and it was expected to distribute at least **AED 1.1 billion** in dividends for 2025.

Dubai Holding's own release states the units were expected to list on DFM and notes the listing under the symbol expectations and timeline (May 2025 announcement).

A later Dubai Holding release confirms Dubai Residential REIT debuted on DFM (May 28, 2025) under symbol "DUBAIRESI".

And here is the real "income investor" detail:

Dubai Holding stated that the offer price range implied a **gross dividend yield of ~7.7%–7.9% for 2025** (depending on price), and reiterated the intent to distribute at least **80% of profit** (before fair value changes) for FY 2026 and thereafter (subject to approvals).

Dubai Residential REIT's investor relations page states it distributed an interim cash dividend of **AED 550 million for H1 2025** (paid September 2025) and follows a semi-annual dividend policy.

And most importantly—this is very recent and very "deep research":

Dubai's official media office reported (Feb 3, 2026) Dubai Residential REIT delivered revenue of AED 1.95 billion in 2025 and that the board proposed a dividend of **AED 550 million for H2** and **total dividends of AED 1.10 billion for 2025**.

So what does this mean in New Wealth Order language?

Dubai is building "rental yield assets" that are tradable, regulated, and scale-friendly.

That is exactly the kind of infrastructure global capital loves.

But Speaker Singh's discipline: Dubai is not immune to cycles

Reuters reported Fitch's view that Dubai real estate prices could face a potential decline (up to ~15%) in the latter half of 2025 and into 2026 due to a large supply pipeline.

So here is the intelligent investor stance:

- Dubai has strong income-focused vehicles and high investor interest.
- Dubai also has cycles and supply waves.
- Therefore, Dubai is attractive **when you invest with underwriting and risk control,** not with hype.

That is how you win in global markets:

You respect both the upside and the cycle.

13. NON-TRADED REIT's & PRIVATE FUNDS: THE LIQUIDITY TRAP

"It looks stable"... because they don't mark it daily

Now I'm going to protect you from a common global trap.

Some investors prefer **non-traded REIT's** or private real estate funds because the price doesn't bounce daily like a stock.

But that "stability" can be cosmetic.

When liquidity stress hits, some private funds restrict withdrawals.

A Wall Street Journal report described Blackstone's Real Estate Income Trust (BREIT) having faced heavy redemption pressure in prior years and highlighted fund performance dynamics and withdrawal limits during stress periods.

The New Wealth Order rule is:

If you choose private real estate, you must understand redemption rules before you invest.

Liquidity is not a marketing line. It's a contract term.

14. SPEAKER SINGH'S GLOBAL REIT DUE-DILIGENCE CHECKLIST

The system I want you to run before you buy any REIT

Here's what I teach beginners because it keeps them alive.

A. Cashflow quality

- What percentage of income is contracted (leases)?
- How strong is occupancy?
- Is rent growing?

B. Balance sheet discipline

- How much debt relative to assets?
- When does debt mature?
- Fixed vs floating rates?
- Interest coverage?

(India's REIT leverage cap structure exists for a reason.)

C. Payout sustainability

- Is distribution covered by recurring cashflow, or by one-off gains?
- Is the REIT funding distributions by selling assets repeatedly?

D. Sector reality

- Office ≠ data centers ≠ residential
- Demand engines are different (and the Nareit sector data shows how returns diverge).

E. Country & currency layer (for global REIT's)

- Are you taking USD exposure? AED exposure? SGD exposure?
- What happens if INR moves against that currency?

F. Tax character

- What is your expected post-tax yield?
- Does withholding tax apply?

G. The most important: your holding period

If you plan to exit in 6 months, REIT's can hurt you.

If you plan to hold for years and reinvest intelligently, REIT's can become asset payroll.

15. THE PORTFOLIO FRAMEWORK (SIMPLE, READABLE, REALISTIC)

How REIT's fit into a normal investor's wealth architecture

Let me be very direct:

A REIT is not meant to replace everything.

It's meant to solve one problem:

"How do I own income-producing real estate while keeping liquidity and diversification?"

So a practical framework looks like this:

1. **Emergency reserves (cash safety)**
2. **Core compounding (equity/index funds)**
3. **Income engines (REIT's + high-quality cashflow assets)**
4. **Hard-asset exposure (direct property only if you can operate it as a system)**

In The New Wealth Order, the goal is not "own property."

The goal is:

Own systems that pay you—across geographies, across currencies, across cycles.

CLOSING: THE NEW WEALTH ORDER VERDICT ON REIT's & GLOBAL INVESTING

Let me end this chapter with a statement that should reset your financial identity:

If your wealth is trapped in one country, one currency, and one income source—you are not secure. You are exposed.

REIT's are a bridge:

- between real estate and markets
- between rental income and liquidity
- between local comfort and global scale

Use them correctly, and they become a powerful part of your Asset Framework.

Use them emotionally—chasing yield, ignoring cycles, ignoring taxes—and they will punish you.

That's the New Wealth Order promise:

The system will always reward discipline.

The system will always punish fantasy.

READER NOTE

This chapter is educational and not personal financial, legal, or tax advice. Investing involves risk, including loss of capital. Rules and tax treatment vary by jurisdiction and may change. Consult qualified professionals for your specific situation. **PART 4 — THE POWER OF PROPERTY**

PART 4

THE POWER OF PROPERTY

Chapter 14

WHY REAL ESTATE BUILDS GENERATIONAL WEALTH

The Asset That Survives You — If You Stop Treating It Like an Emotion

(Narrated in the voice of Speaker Singh — ***The New Wealth Order****)*

Let me start with a sentence that will offend the financially lazy:

Most people don't build generational wealth because they never own anything that outlives their salary.

They work for 30 years.

They save.

They sacrifice.

They run a respectable life.

And still—one illness, one job loss, one bad business decision, one family dispute—and the entire financial structure shakes.

Why?

Because **income is temporary**.

But **assets are permanent**—when chosen and held correctly.

And among all assets, property has a unique power:

it can turn time into equity, inflation into advantage, and discipline into inheritance.

But only when it's done right.

From my journey—working with wealthy families across markets—I've learned something the middle class is rarely told honestly:

Real estate is not "get rich quick."

Real estate is "stay rich long."

And staying rich is the real game.

1. WHAT "GENERATIONAL WEALTH" ACTUALLY MEANS

Let's keep it simple for readers new to this concept.

Generational wealth is not Instagram wealth.

It's not a luxury car.

It's not a one-time jackpot.

Generational wealth means:

- Your family has assets that **keep paying** even if one person stops earning
- The next generation starts with **options**, not pressure
- A crisis becomes an inconvenience—not a collapse
- The family has **time** (the most expensive currency)

Now here's the uncomfortable truth:

The average family is one shock away from financial decline.

And the wealthy are shock-resistant because they build **asset systems**.

Real estate—when structured properly—becomes one of the strongest asset systems ever invented.

2. WHY PROPERTY SITS AT THE CENTER OF NATIONAL WEALTH

This is not my opinion. This is how economies work.

A major long-run study on returns across asset classes notes that **housing wealth is on average roughly one half of national wealth in a typical economy**.

That's not "one sector."

That's the core of the balance sheet of society.

And when you look at household wealth data, the pattern repeats:

- In Great Britain, the ONS reports **net property wealth was the largest component of household wealth (40%)** in April 2020–March 2022.
- In India (AIDIS, as summarized in a government press release), **land and buildings together held 91% of asset value in rural India**, and in urban India land ~49% and buildings ~38%.

Let that sink in.

In India—where people argue daily about "stocks vs gold vs FD"—the biggest wealth reality is already visible:

Indians are already property-heavy… but many are property-inefficient.

Meaning: they own property emotionally, without systems, without cashflow logic, without legal discipline.

And that's why some families build dynasties… while others build disputes.

3. THE CORE REASON REAL ESTATE BUILDS GENERATIONAL WEALTH

Property has three embedded wealth engines

Most assets don't have all three.

Engine 1: A place in the real world

Property is physical.

It has utility.

People need shelter, office space, warehouses, retail, land.

This makes property a "needs-based asset," not purely a sentiment asset.

Engine 2: Inflation linkage

Over long periods, property values and rents often move with the real economy and replacement costs—materials, labor, approvals, land.

Eurostat notes that between 2010 and Q1 2025, **EU house prices rose 57.9% and rents rose 27.8%**.

That doesn't mean "property always goes up."

It means property tends to have a **structural relationship** with long-run price levels and income growth.

Engine 3: Leverage (the legal kind)

Real estate is one of the few assets where:

- banks are comfortable lending against it
- loans are long duration
- the asset itself is collateral

This allows average people to control a large asset with a smaller initial capital base—something that's far harder in many other asset classes.

This is also why real estate can create wealth fast **or destroy it brutally**.

4. THE PROPERTY TRUTH THAT CREATES DYNASTIES

"Debt turns into equity" if you survive long enough

Here's the wealth formula the wealthy understand:

When you buy a property with conservative leverage and stable cashflow:

- every EMI has two parts: interest + principal
- the principal portion reduces your loan balance
- that means your **net ownership increases** over time
- and inflation can quietly reduce the *real burden* of a fixed payment (not always, but often, depending on your loan type and rate environment)

This is why property has built families:

It forces ownership accumulation for people who wouldn't otherwise invest consistently.

A salary earner might skip investing in equities in a tough year.

But they won't skip the home EMI unless life becomes extreme.

So property becomes a *forced ownership machine.*

But I will warn you:

If the property is wrong—location, price, legal status, leverage—then the same EMI becomes a forced suffering machine.

5. THE GLOBAL REALITY: PROPERTY CAN MAKE YOU RICH... OR BREAK YOU

Let me destroy the biggest myth right now:

"Real estate always goes up."

No.

Real estate is cyclical. Inflation is persistent.

The BIS reported that in Q2 2025, **global house prices adjusted for consumer prices fell 0.8% year-on-year**, marking the third consecutive year of falling property prices globally in real terms.

And history has been brutal when leverage is reckless:

The Federal Reserve's history of the Great Recession notes:

- home prices fell about **30%** from mid-2006 peak to mid-2009
- the S&P 500 fell **57%** from Oct 2007 peak to March 2009 trough

- US household net worth fell from about **$69T (2007)** to **$55T (2009)**

That was not "bad luck."

That was property + leverage + weak underwriting = collapse.

And right now, you can see multi-year property pain in major economies:

Reuters reported China's property weakness continued into January 2026, with new home prices down **3.1% year-on-year** (steepest decline in seven months), despite policy easing.

So here is the New Wealth Order rule:

Property builds generational wealth only when you build it as a system—not as a belief.

6. WHY PROPERTY IS THE "WEALTH DIVIDER" BETWEEN FAMILIES

Let's speak plainly.

In most societies, people don't become wealthy because they're smarter.

They become wealthy because they **get positioned** early into assets that inflate.

In the UK, property wealth is literally the largest slice of household wealth (40%).

In India, land and buildings dominate household asset value.

Globally, housing is roughly half of national wealth in a typical economy.

Now add inheritance.

Property is:

- easy to understand
- culturally respected
- commonly transferred
- politically sensitive (often protected)
- usable as collateral

So it becomes the default inheritance machine.

And global wealth trends show inheritance is only becoming more important. A UBS-related report covered by The Guardian described record numbers becoming billionaires through inheritance and cited expectations of trillions transferring hands in coming years.

Property is often the bridge between "earned wealth" and "inherited wealth."

7. THE HIDDEN REASON PROPERTY CREATES GENERATIONAL WEALTH

It changes family psychology

This is not talked about in finance textbooks, but it's real in the real world:

A family with property has:

- stability (a base)
- confidence (collateral)
- patience (less panic)

- bargaining power (options)

A family without assets experiences:

- urgency
- dependence on employers
- fear-driven decisions
- forced compromises

A home is not just shelter.

A property portfolio is not just investment.

It's autonomy.

And autonomy is what creates multi-decade compounding.

8. LONG-RUN RETURNS: WHAT THE DATA SAYS ABOUT HOUSING VS EQUITY

Now let's step into "serious research."

A landmark long-run dataset (16 advanced economies, 1870–2015) compared returns across equities, housing, bonds, and bills.

In that study's table of real returns, average annual **real returns on equity and housing were remarkably close** over the long run. For the GDP-weighted average, housing and equity real returns in the full sample are reported around **6–7% range**, with equity ~7.0% and housing ~6.7% (and excluding world wars, both rise further).

This matters because it destroys another myth:

"Property is always inferior to stocks."

No.

In many countries, housing has been a powerful long-run wealth engine—especially because it combines:

returns + usability + leverage + inheritance

But (and this is a big "but"):

Those are **index-level academic returns**, not your personal return after:

- bad purchase price
- poor tenant selection
- maintenance neglect
- legal disputes
- broker manipulation
- emotional upgrades
- overleverage

Your real estate returns are not decided by the market alone.

They're decided by your **discipline**.

9. INDIA REALITY CHECK: PROPERTY GROWTH IS NOT UNIFORM

In India, people speak about property like it's one national market.

It's not.

It's micro-markets.

The RBI's All-India House Price Index showed an annual increase of **3.1% in Q4 FY25** (Jan–Mar 2024–25).

That number is not "bad."

It's not "great."

It's real.

And it proves something important:

Property wealth is often built over long timeframes, not quick flips—unless you're in a hot micro-cycle.

India property can create generational wealth… but only when you:

- buy right
- hold long
- manage well
- document legally
- control leverage

Otherwise, you don't build wealth.

You build a headache.

10. ENTER DUBAI: A MODERN WEALTH MARKET BUILT AROUND PROPERTY

Now I'm going to bring the global lens in sharply—because the New Wealth Order is not limited to one country.

Dubai has become one of the world's most watched property markets for one reason:

It has built a property ecosystem designed for global capital.

Dubai's official media office reported that in **2025**, Dubai's real estate sector recorded **over 270,000 transactions worth AED 917 billion**, up 20% year on year.

That number matters because liquidity matters.

Generational wealth is not just "buy."

Generational wealth is also "sell when you must, refinance when you should, restructure when cycles shift."

Liquidity gives you options.

Dubai's yield conversation (why global investors pay attention)

Globally, prime residential yields are often low in major "trophy" cities.

Savills reported that across an average of world cities, prime gross yields moved to **3.15%** in 2024, and noted yields moved out fastest in Dubai to **~5.3%**.

Now look at Dubai's broader residential rental yields as tracked by REIDIN:

- Dubai residential market gross rental yields around **6.55%** (Nov 2025)
- apartment gross rental yields around **7.03%** (Nov 2025)

These are not guaranteed returns.

But they explain the attention:

When a global city offers stronger yields, rising rental indices, and high transaction activity, capital will look.

REIDIN also reported Dubai rents rising (e.g., rent price index changes and year-on-year increases in their November 2025 report).

Dubai is also institutionalizing rental income

Dubai Residential REIT reported very high occupancy and strong operating performance:

- 2025 revenue **AED 1.95 billion**
- occupancy **98.3%**

And it confirms it distributed an interim cash dividend of **AED 550 million for H1 2025**.

This matters for generational wealth because it shows something powerful:

Dubai isn't only "buy property."

It's building listed, scalable rental-income platforms too.

That is what mature wealth ecosystems look like.

But Speaker Singh's warning: Dubai is still cyclical

Fitch (reported by Reuters) forecast a potential **double-digit decline** in Dubai real estate prices, possibly up to **15%**, due to a large supply pipeline (210,000 units projected to be delivered).

And UBS's 2025 Global Real Estate Bubble Index notes **elevated risk** in cities including Dubai, and that Dubai recorded one of the strongest risk increases from the prior edition.

So Dubai is not a fantasy land.

Dubai is a market.

A powerful market. A liquid market. A globally attractive market.

And a market that will punish emotional buyers.

This is exactly why, in The New Wealth Order, Dubai is not presented as "hype."

Dubai is presented as:

A case study in how a modern property market rewards systems and punishes improvisation.

11. THE 7 PILLARS OF GENERATIONAL PROPERTY WEALTH

Now I'll give you the framework I want you to remember for life.

Pillar 1: Scarcity + location logic

Land in prime zones is limited.

And demand concentrates where jobs, infrastructure, schools, safety, and connectivity concentrate.

Bad location = dead wealth.

Good location = durable wealth.

Pillar 2: Inflation + replacement cost

When construction costs rise (materials, labor), replacement becomes expensive.

That can support property values over time.

Eurostat's long-run rise in both rents and house prices shows how housing costs can trend upward over long periods.

Pillar 3: Rent = the "cashflow engine"

Appreciation is hope.

Rent is evidence.

Rent is what keeps a family stable through cycles.

Pillar 4: Leverage = controlled acceleration

Leverage magnifies outcomes.

Used conservatively, it accelerates equity build-up.

Used aggressively, it creates forced selling and generational trauma.

Pillar 5: Tax + legal structure (varies by jurisdiction)

Every country has different treatment, but wealthy families globally share one behavior:

They treat property as a **structured holding**, not a casual purchase.

Pillar 6: Collateral power

Property can unlock capital for:

- education
- business
- expansion
- emergency
- reinvestment

This collateral ability is one reason property is deeply embedded into wealth systems worldwide.

Pillar 7: Transferability (inheritance)

Property is one of the most commonly transferred assets because it is:

- visible
- culturally valued
- easy to explain across generations
- often held for decades

That's why property becomes a dynasty tool.

12. THE DARK SIDE: HOW PROPERTY DESTROYS GENERATIONAL WEALTH

Now I'm going to be aggressive again, because I don't want readers to be fooled.

Property destroys families when:

1. **They buy emotionally** (status, ego, "society pressure")
2. **They overleverage** (EMIs that depend on perfect life conditions)
3. **They ignore legal clarity** (title issues, approvals, disputes)
4. **They underestimate illiquidity** (can't exit quickly)
5. **They forget cycles exist** (China's multi-year decline is a living reminder).
6. **They confuse boom markets with permanent markets** (Dubai's correction warnings prove cycles matter).
7. **They treat property like FD** (property is a business; it requires management)

The Great Recession proved what happens when property is treated as "risk-free."

13. SPEAKER SINGH'S PROPERTY CODE

The rules I want in every reader's head before they buy anything

From my experience, these rules separate builders from victims:

1. **Cashflow first. Appreciation second.**
2. **Buy location logic, not builder marketing.**

3. **Never let one property become your entire net worth.**
4. **Use leverage conservatively. Always keep buffers.**
5. **Legal clarity is not paperwork — it's survival.**
6. **Rent should cover risk, not just EMI.**
7. **Assume vacancy will happen. Budget for it.**
8. **Assume rates can rise. Plan for it.**
9. **Assume you may need to sell. Buy with exit liquidity in mind.**
10. **If a deal looks "too easy," it's designed to trap beginners.**

14. THREE REAL STORIES (COMPOSITE, FROM PATTERNS I'VE SEEN)

(I'm using composite stories to protect privacy, but every pattern is real.)

Story 1: The family that built a dynasty with one boring rental

A middle-class father bought a small, simple property near a growing job corridor. No luxury. No ego.

He rented it. He maintained it. He raised rent slowly, respectfully, and kept tenants long.

Thirty years later, that one property:

- paid for children's education
- funded a small business
- created stability during job transitions
- became collateral for expansion
- became an inheritance with clear title

No dramatic "flip."

Just relentless, disciplined ownership.

That's how dynasties are built: **boring, consistent, legal, cashflow-based.**

Story 2: The family that "bought prestige" and bought stress

Another family bought a high-EMI luxury apartment because they wanted to look rich.

The EMI depended on one job. Then the job changed, income dipped, and expenses rose.

They didn't lose money only.

They lost:

- peace
- health
- family harmony
- decision-making power

Eventually, they sold under pressure.

The market didn't "cheat" them.

Their structure cheated them.

Story 3: The investor who used Dubai like a system

A client treated Dubai like a market, not a miracle.

They focused on:

- rental demand
- service charges
- vacancy assumptions
- conservative leverage

- exit liquidity
- cycle awareness

They liked Dubai because:

- transaction activity is high (liquidity)
- yields can be structurally stronger than many global prime cities
- the ecosystem is institutionalizing (REIT's, professional rental platforms)

But they also respected:

- correction risk due to supply cycles
- bubble risk measures that demand caution

Result: no panic, no hype, no fear.

Just system-based investing.

That is the New Wealth Order way.

15. A SIMPLE PROPERTY WEALTH BLUEPRINT FOR THE INDIAN READER

If you're a beginner, I want this to feel doable.

Step 1: Build a survival base first

- emergency fund
- basic insurance
- clean credit behavior

If you can't survive shocks, property leverage will crush you.

Step 2: Buy only after you can hold

Property wealth is not created by buying.

It's created by **holding through cycles**.

Step 3: Your first property should reduce stress, not increase it

If it's self-use, keep it within a safe EMI range.

If it's investment, demand cashflow logic.

Step 4: Your second property is where generational wealth starts

Because now you have:

- home stability
- rental income
- expanding collateral
- diversification in income streams

Step 5: Add global exposure when your systems mature

Global investing is not for ego.

It's for diversification and opportunity.

Dubai becomes relevant here because it's a global capital magnet with strong property infrastructure—**but only for disciplined investors.**

CLOSING: THE FINAL TRUTH OF PROPERTY WEALTH

Let me end this chapter with the line I want readers to remember:

Salaries die with time. Property can survive time.

But only if you stop treating property like:

- emotion
- status
- speculation
- social proof

And start treating it like:

- a cashflow system
- a legal structure
- a disciplined balance sheet decision
- a multi-cycle strategy

That is why real estate builds generational wealth.

Not because it is "magic."

Because it is **structured ownership**—and structured ownership is the real wealth religion of the world.

READER NOTE

This chapter is for education and storytelling and does not constitute financial, legal, tax, or investment advice. Real estate involves risk, including loss of capital, illiquidity, leverage risk, legal/title risk, and market cycles. Always consult qualified professionals and verify regulations applicable to your residency and the property's jurisdiction.

Chapter 15

RENTAL YIELD VS APPRECIATION

The Two Engines of Real Estate Wealth — And Why Most People Pick the Wrong One

*(Narrated in the voice of Speaker Singh — **The New Wealth Order**)*

Let me be very direct, from my journey.

When most people say, "I want to invest in property," what they really mean is:

"I want the price to go up."

They don't talk about rent.

They don't talk about vacancy.

They don't talk about net yield after expenses.

They don't talk about service charges, repairs, taxes, tenant turnover, legal costs.

They talk about one thing only:

Appreciation.

And this is why so many people get stuck in real estate for years—owning a "valuable asset" that doesn't improve their life.

Because there are only **two ways** property makes you money:

1. **Rental yield (cashflow)** — money you receive while you hold the asset
2. **Appreciation (capital gain)** — money you may receive when you sell the asset

Everything else is noise.

So in this chapter, I'm going to give you the New Wealth Order truth:

Rental yield is your paycheck. Appreciation is your bonus.

And if you build your entire financial plan on "bonus," you deserve the stress you get.

1. FIRST, DEFINITIONS IN HUMAN LANGUAGE

Because most people lose money in real estate due to confusion, not bad luck.

Rental yield

Rental yield answers: **"How much income does this property generate compared to its price?"**

- **Gross rental yield** = Annual rent ÷ Property price
- **Net rental yield** = (Annual rent - All operating costs) ÷ Property price

Operating costs include:

- maintenance & repairs
- vacancy periods
- service charges/society charges
- insurance
- property management fees
- furnishing replacement (if furnished)
- taxes (depending on jurisdiction)

Appreciation

Appreciation answers: **"How much did the property's value rise?"**

- Appreciation % = (New price – Purchase price) ÷ Purchase price

Total return

Total return is the **real** scorecard:

Total return = Income return + Capital growth

This is not "my framework." It's how professional real estate performance is measured: total return is commonly broken into **income return** and **capital growth** components.

Now here is the sentence that changes how you invest forever:

If rent is weak, you are forced to depend on appreciation.

And appreciation is the part you control the least.

2. THE MOST IMPORTANT PROPERTY TRUTH MOST PEOPLE NEVER LEARN

Yield and appreciation often move in opposite directions

Let me show you a simple reality.

When property prices run faster than rents, yields get crushed.

Why?

Because yield is a fraction:

Yield = Net Operating Income ÷ Property Value

That concept is the foundation of cap rates in property valuation: cap rate is commonly calculated as net operating income divided by asset value.

So if:

- rent stays the same
- but the price doubles

Your yield gets cut in half.

This is exactly why people in expensive "hot" cities often experience this strange frustration:

"My property is worth a lot, but the rent feels useless."

That's not bad luck. That's math.

3. THE CAP RATE MIRROR

Why interest rates decide whether appreciation is easy or painful

This is where I want beginners to stop guessing and start understanding.

A large part of real estate pricing is driven by the relationship between:

- **income (NOI/rent)**
- and **required returns** (cap rates/discount rates)

In plain terms:

- When interest rates are low, investors accept lower cap rates → prices can rise
- When interest rates rise, cap rates often expand → prices can come under pressure

You don't need to memorize theory. Just remember this:

When money is expensive, appreciation becomes harder. When money is cheap, appreciation becomes easier.

This is why property cycles exist.

And this is why the New Wealth Order investor never buys property on the sentence:

"It will always go up."

Because global data shows it doesn't.

The BIS reported that in **Q2 2025**, global house prices **declined in real terms by 0.8% year-on-year**.

So if you are depending only on appreciation, you are depending on something that can disappear for years.

Cashflow doesn't make you invincible.

But it makes you survivable.

4. WHAT THE WORLD'S DATA QUIETLY REVEALS

Rents rise steadily. Prices rise violently.

Look at the European Union trend as an easy-to-understand example:

Between **2010 and Q1 2025**, EU **house prices increased 57.9%** while **rents increased 27.8%**.

What does that tell you?

- Rents: slower, steadier, more "economic"
- Prices: faster, more volatile, more "financial"

Eurostat also reported that in **Q3 2025**, EU house prices were up **5.5%** year-on-year while rents rose **3.1%**.

So here is the New Wealth Order conclusion:

Appreciation is a market story. Yield is an economic story.

If you want stability, you need the economic story in your portfolio.

5. THE ACADEMIC TRUTH: PROPERTY RETURNS ARE TWO ENGINES

And they don't always cooperate

A powerful study on U.S. single-family rentals found something that should permanently humble every "property guru":

- Total returns are about **8.5%** on average
- And **net rental yields** and **house price appreciation** each contribute about **half** of total returns, on average
- But they are **negatively correlated** across cities (cities with high yields often have lower appreciation, and vice versa)

Read that again because it's one of the most important lines in this chapter:

**High-yield markets and high-appreciation markets are often not the same markets. **

This is why amateurs get confused:

They want:

- high yield
- and high appreciation
- and zero vacancy
- and perfect tenants
- and no repairs
- and instant liquidity

That is not investing. That is a children's fantasy.

6. THE INSTITUTIONAL INVESTOR LENS

Why professionals respect yield more than retail buyers do

Retail buyers chase "profit" (appreciation).

Professionals build "return streams" (income + appreciation).

Look at how professional U.S. commercial real estate performance is presented by NCREIF:

For **Q4 2025**, NCREIF's Property Index Expanded showed:

- **Total: 1.14%**
- **Income: 1.15%**

- Appreciation: -0.01%

So in that quarter, appreciation did nothing—income carried the return.

And over a longer horizon, a Nareit analysis (using NCREIF index history) noted that over 25 years (1992Q3–2017Q2), the NCREIF Property Index showed income averaging about **+5.25% per year** (compounded) after fees/expenses that were charged against income.

That's not "motivation." That's how institutions think:

Income is not a side benefit. Income is the foundation.

7. THE MIDDLE-CLASS PROPERTY TRAP

"Negative cashflow today, hoping for appreciation tomorrow"

Let me describe the most common trap I've seen in my journey:

Someone buys a property with:

- low yield (sometimes 2–4%)
- high EMI
- high maintenance
- and then says: "I'll cover the gap from my salary."

That person is not investing.

That person is slowly bleeding.

Because they are funding a property every month like it's a charity—hoping appreciation will rescue them later.

And when appreciation slows, they panic.

When a vacancy hits, they break.

When an emergency comes, they sell under pressure.

This is how people "own" property but stay financially stuck.

8. INDIA: RENTAL YIELD VS APPRECIATION — THE REAL REALITY

Let's talk India with clean eyes.

A. Appreciation reality

India's all-India House Price Index (HPI) increased **3.1% year-on-year in Q4 FY25** (Jan–Mar 2024–25), as reported based on RBI data.

That's not "bad." It's not "amazing."

It's reality—and it shows why betting everything on appreciation can be slow and frustrating.

B. Yield reality

Residential yields in India have historically been described as modest.

- A Knight Frank investment guide stated (in its context) that yields from residential properties are **between 2–4%**, while commercial can be higher.
- A later Economic Times article also described residential yields hovering around **2–4%** (in the context of comparing residential to commercial).

At the same time, listing-based datasets can show higher averages depending on city mix and segment.

Global Property Guide reported an average gross rental yield in India around **5.09% (Q4 2025)**, noting the yields are calculated using median prices and rents sourced from local listings.

So what's the honest interpretation?

India is not "one yield." India is many yields.

- Prime, high-ticket residential often has lower yields
- Certain demand-heavy micro-markets can show better yields
- Commercial is a different game entirely

C. Rent growth matters (and is very real)

In India, rents can rise meaningfully in some periods and micro-markets.

Economic Times reported residential rental inflation cooled to **7–9%** in H1 2025 across major cities, after much higher hikes in earlier years.

So here is the New Wealth Order India lesson:

India can give you appreciation. India can also give you rent growth.

But if you buy the wrong asset in the wrong micro-market at the wrong price, you'll get neither.

D. A powerful micro-market reminder

A Times of India report (Feb 3, 2026) citing NHB RESIDEX data said Bhubaneswar delivered **148.3% appreciation** over the 10-year period Sept 2015–Sept 2025, while also citing rental yields around **2–3%** in that context.

Whether or not you care about that specific city, the point is universal:

Returns are local, not national.

9. DUBAI: THE MARKET WHERE YIELD AND APPRECIATION HAVE BOTH BEEN LOUD

Now we go global—and yes, we talk Dubai.

Because Dubai has become one of the world's most watched property markets precisely due to the yield + growth conversation.

A. Dubai in global context: yields

Savills reported that prime yields across world cities moved out slightly in 2024 to around **3.15%** on average.

In the same Savills coverage, Dubai was highlighted as a standout, with prime yields moving out fastest to **5.3%** (and record rental growth in 2024).

That difference is not small.

It's one reason Dubai keeps attracting income-focused investors: it can offer higher yields than many "trophy" global cities.

B. Dubai in local data: yields + rents + prices

REIDIN's UAE Residential Property Price Report (Nov 2025) shows:

- Dubai residential market gross rental yield around **6.55%**
- Dubai apartment gross rental yield around **7.03%**
- Dubai residential rent price index up **6.14% year-on-year** (Nov 2025)
- Dubai sales price index up **12.62% year-on-year** (Nov 2025)

Again: not guarantees. But this is exactly what investors watch:

- yield
- rent growth

- capital growth
- in one place.

C. Dubai appreciation momentum (recent)

ValuStrat reported that Dubai's ValuStrat Price Index reached **240.4 points**, with **19.8% annual appreciation** (12 months) as of Jan 2026 reporting.

So Dubai's story (recently) has been:

- yield that is globally competitive
- and appreciation that has been strong in the cycle

This is why I tell readers of *The New Wealth Order*:

Dubai is not "magic." Dubai is a system market.

And system markets reward system investors.

10. THE REAL BATTLE: YIELD INVESTOR VS APPRECIATION INVESTOR

In my journey, I've noticed property investors fall into two mindsets:

Type 1: The Yield Investor

This person asks:

- "How much cashflow do I keep after expenses?"
- "How stable is demand here?"
- "What is vacancy risk?"
- "What's the rent revision potential?"
- "How fast can I rent it again if a tenant leaves?"

This person builds:

- safety
- holding power
- long-term compounding

Type 2: The Appreciation Investor

This person asks:

- "What will this be worth in 3 years?"
- "Which area will become next big hotspot?"
- "Which project will explode?"

This person can win big—**but only if timing is right.**

And when timing is wrong, they don't just lose returns.

They lose confidence.

New Wealth Order conclusion

Yield makes you patient. Appreciation tempts you to gamble.

If you are a beginner, you need patience more than gambling.

11. THE PRICE-TO-RENT RATIO: THE "TRUTH METER" MOST BUYERS IGNORE

If I had to choose one metric for beginners to understand the yield vs appreciation relationship, it's this:

Price-to-rent ratio

Price-to-rent ratio = Property price ÷ Annual rent

Higher ratio = lower yield.

Lower ratio = higher yield.

Global Property Guide gives a simple interpretation framework:

- below 16: generally cheaper to buy than rent
- 17–20: roughly comparable
- above 21: generally cheaper to rent than buy

You don't have to use those thresholds blindly, but the mindset is powerful:

If price-to-rent is extremely high, appreciation must work hard to justify the purchase.

If price-to-rent is reasonable, yield carries more of the return.

This is why, in many "expensive prestige zones," buyers end up with emotional ownership and low income.

12. THREE STORIES (COMPOSITE) THAT TEACH THE REAL LESSON

(Details changed to protect privacy. Patterns are real.)

Story 1: The "Appreciation Only" investor who got stuck

A professional (details changed) bought a high-status apartment in a premium neighborhood.

The rent was fine, but the yield was weak after:

- society charges
- maintenance
- periodic vacancy
- agent fees

They were negative cashflow and told themselves:

"It's okay, the price will rise."

Then the cycle slowed.

Not crashed. Just slowed.

In that slow period:

- EMI kept going
- repairs kept coming
- vacancy hit once
- job stress increased

And the investor realized a brutal truth:

"I didn't buy an asset. I bought a liability with a fancy address."

That property didn't destroy them.

But it delayed their wealth by years.

Story 2: The "Yield First" investor who built stability

Another investor (details changed) bought a boring property in a strong rental corridor.

Not luxury. Not ego.

Just:

- tenant demand
- transport access
- realistic rent
- conservative leverage
- reserves

The rent wasn't "amazing."

But it was **reliable**.

And reliability changes a human being.

Because when your property pays you, you stop begging the market for appreciation.

Story 3: The "Dubai system buyer" who treated it like a business

This investor approached Dubai with discipline:

- underwriting rents using real market evidence
- factoring operating costs
- stress-testing vacancy
- avoiding emotional purchases

They liked Dubai because:

- prime yields are high by global city standards (Savills noted ~5.3% in that context)
- broader residential gross yields were shown around mid-6% to ~7% in REIDIN's November 2025 dataset
- and appreciation had been strong in the cycle (ValuStrat's ~19.8% annual appreciation figure at that time)

But they didn't buy because "Dubai is hot."

They bought because the numbers worked with buffers.

That's the New Wealth Order method:

If you can't hold it through a cycle, you don't own it. The bank owns you.

13. THE TRUTH NOBODY LIKES: APPRECIATION IS OFTEN PSYCHOLOGICAL

Rent feels small month-to-month.

Price changes feel massive in headlines.

So people get addicted to appreciation stories because:

- it sounds faster
- it feels smarter
- it gives bragging rights

But in actual wealth building, appreciation has a dark secret:

Appreciation is only real when you can sell or refinance without pain.

If:

- the market is illiquid
- buyers disappear
- regulations change
- transaction costs are high

then your "paper profit" is not wealth.

It's a screenshot.

Yield is harder to fake.

14. THE NEW WEALTH ORDER PROPERTY DECISION MATRIX

If you want a simple system, here it is.

Quadrant A: High Yield + Moderate Appreciation

Best for: building stability, asset payroll, survivability

Risk: tenant/vacancy/operations must be managed

Mindset: "This is a cashflow business."

Quadrant B: Low Yield + High Appreciation

Best for: long-term capital growth if you can hold for years

Risk: you may bleed cashflow and panic-sell at the worst time

Mindset: "This is a long game."

Quadrant C: Low Yield + Low Appreciation

Best for: almost nobody (except pure end-use lifestyle reasons)

Risk: wealth stagnation

Mindset: "This is emotional ownership."

Quadrant D: "Hope-Based Investing"

This is where people buy:

- under construction without safeguards
- speculative far locations with no real demand
- overpriced assets with "guaranteed returns" talk

Best for: brokers, not investors.

15. SPEAKER SINGH'S RULES: HOW TO CHOOSE YIELD VS APPRECIATION (WITHOUT CONFUSING YOURSELF)

Rule 1: Decide your objective first

If you need monthly support, you need yield.

If you don't need monthly support and can hold long, you can afford appreciation plays.

Rule 2: Never compare gross yield. Compare net yield

Gross yield is what people use to impress you.

Net yield is what feeds you.

Rule 3: If you're leveraged, yield matters more

Because debt doesn't wait for appreciation.

Rule 4: Appreciation is a cycle; yield is a system

Cycle = timing.

System = repeatability.

Choose repeatability if you want generational wealth.

Rule 5: Respect the global cycle reality

Global prices can fall in real terms (BIS reported global real decline of 0.8% YoY in Q2 2025).

So a yield-backed strategy is your survival engine in "flat years."

Rule 6: Your market matters

Dubai's recent cycle has shown strong rent and price performance (REIDIN, ValuStrat), but it is still a market—so you must underwrite and manage.

Rule 7: If yield is weak, demand a stronger margin of safety on price

Because you're betting on appreciation.

So you must buy with discipline, not with excitement.

16. WHAT I WANT YOU TO REMEMBER FOREVER

Let me end this chapter with the sentence that separates the wealthy from the trapped:

Rental yield keeps you alive. Appreciation makes you rich.

But you cannot become rich if you don't stay alive financially.

That is why the New Wealth Order investor builds property wealth like this:

1. **First**: survivable cashflow systems
2. **Then**: disciplined appreciation exposure
3. **Always**: buffers, legal clarity, location logic, and exit planning

In the next chapters, I will go deeper into:

- how to identify **yield zones vs appreciation zones**
- how to read **rent cycles** and **supply waves**
- and why Dubai's ecosystem (when approached with discipline) can be positioned as a serious global chapter in your wealth architecture—without falling into hype.

Because the truth is simple:

Property doesn't reward dreams.

Property rewards systems.

READER NOTE

This chapter is educational and does not constitute financial, legal, tax, or investment advice. Real estate involves risk including illiquidity, leverage risk, vacancy risk, legal/title risk, and market cycles. Rules and taxes vary by jurisdiction and may change. Consult qualified professionals for your specific situation.

Chapter 16

GLOBAL PROPERTY MARKETS

Real Estate Is Local. Wealth Is Global. And The New Wealth Order Belongs to People Who Understand Both.

*(Narrated in the voice of Speaker Singh — **The New Wealth Order**)*

Let me start this chapter with a truth that will irritate anyone who still thinks like the old middle-class rulebook:

If your entire net worth is trapped inside one country, one currency, and one set of government rules… you are not "safe." You are concentrated.

And concentrated wealth is fragile wealth.

In my journey—advising wealthy families, entrepreneurs, and global investors—I've seen something very consistent:

- The poor fight for income.
- The middle class fights for stability.
- The wealthy fight for **positioning**.

And property is positioning.

But here's the catch:

Most people treat real estate as a "local" story—*my city, my builder, my society, my area.*

The New Wealth Order investor treats property as a **global map of opportunity and risk.**

Because in 2026, money moves faster than ever. People migrate. Work goes remote. Governments change laws. Taxes shift. Interest rates cycle.

So this chapter is not just about "global property prices."

It's about something more important:

How global property markets actually work—so you stop investing like a tourist and start investing like a strategist.

1. THE BIG ILLUSION: "PROPERTY IS ALWAYS SAFE"

Property is not "always safe."

Property is **always real.**

And those are not the same thing.

A real thing can still be a real loss.

The BIS (Bank for International Settlements) reported that in **Q2 2025**, global house prices **adjusted for consumer prices fell 0.8% year-on-year**, marking the **third consecutive year** of falling global property prices in real terms.

Read that again.

Not one year. Not one country.

Three years. Globally. In real terms.

So the New Wealth Order rule is:

Property is not "safe." Property is "cyclical."

If you don't respect cycles, property will educate you with pain.

2. THE 5 FORCES THAT MOVE EVERY PROPERTY MARKET ON EARTH

You don't need to memorize 50 countries.

You need to understand 5 forces.

Force 1: Interest rates and credit availability

When money is cheap, property becomes easier to finance → prices can rise.

When money is expensive, buyers weaken → prices can stall or drop.

Force 2: Local incomes and job growth

Rents and demand ultimately depend on incomes and employment.

Force 3: Supply pipeline

Property crashes are often not demand problems.

They are **oversupply + leverage** problems.

Force 4: Government policy

Taxes, foreign buyer rules, lending restrictions, and visa programs can change the game overnight.

Force 5: Population flows

Migration, expat inflows, students, corporate expansions—these are rent engines.

Now let's apply this to real markets, with real data.

3. THE GLOBAL PROPERTY SCOREBOARD: A 2025–EARLY 2026 SNAPSHOT

This is not a "who is best" beauty contest.

This is a strategic map:

- which markets are cooling
- which are stabilizing
- which are recovering
- which are running hot
- and which are structurally changing

A. NORTH AMERICA — Big Markets, Big Liquidity, Big Sensitivity to Rates

4. THE UNITED STATES: THE "FROZEN" MARKET THAT STILL HAS A PULSE

The US housing market has been in what I call a "transaction freeze" period:

buyers hesitate, sellers hesitate, everyone watches interest rates.

As per S&P Cotality Case-Shiller, the **U.S. National Home Price NSA Index posted a 1.4% annual increase in November 2025**.

That number is not explosive.

But it's not collapse either.

This is what many mature markets look like when affordability is tight:

prices don't die—volume dies first.

Speaker Singh's insight from experience:

When markets freeze, amateurs complain. Professionals negotiate.

Because low volume often creates mispricing—meaning disciplined buyers can find better entry points than during hype cycles.

5. CANADA: POLICY-HEAVY, COOLING PRICES, AND RESTRICTIONS THAT MATTER

Canada is a perfect example of how **policy** becomes a market force.

Foreign buyer restrictions

Canada extended the ban on foreign ownership of Canadian housing to **January 1, 2027** (announced Feb 4, 2024).

This is exactly the kind of rule that can shift demand composition.

Price signals

Canada's official **New Housing Price Index** showed month-to-month movements in December 2025 (e.g., Canada overall down **0.2%** in the NHPI monthly change).

For resale pricing trends, Scotiabank's housing news flash noted that in the 12 months to **December 2025**, the **national MLS HPI declined about 4%**, with declines across unit types.

New Wealth Order takeaway:

Canada proves a brutal truth—property markets are not only driven by economics. They're driven by politics and affordability pressure.

B. EUROPE — High Regulation, High Taxes in Some Places, and Strong Rental Fundamentals

6. THE UNITED KINGDOM: FLAT GROWTH, REGIONAL DIVERGENCE, AND LONDON FATIGUE

UK property is teaching a lesson many global investors are learning:

"Prime cities don't always outperform forever."

Nationwide reported that **UK annual house price growth slowed to 0.6% in December 2025**, with prices falling **0.4% month-on-month** (seasonally adjusted).

Inside the UK, performance isn't uniform. It's "two-speed."

The Financial Times reported that as of October 2025, prices fell in **18 out of 33 London boroughs**, showing divergence even within one city.

Speaker Singh's rule:

If your strategy depends on "London will always rise," you are not investing—you are worshipping history.

7. GERMANY: THE RECOVERY CASE STUDY

Germany is one of the best examples of why sophisticated investors track cycles and recovery phases.

Reuters reported that Germany's residential property prices rose for the **fourth consecutive quarter** in Q3 2025, up **3.3% year-on-year**, and +1.0% quarter-on-quarter.

Reuters also cited analysts forecasting residential prices rising around **3.5% in 2025, 3.4% in 2026, 3.2% in 2027**—a recovery path after a downturn.

And Destatis (Germany's statistical office) shows the context:

- 2023: house price index –8.4%
- 2024: house price index –1.5%

This is why I tell readers:

Generational wealth is not built by entering only in "good years."

It is built by understanding *when* an asset is repricing and *why*.

C. ASIA — The Most Policy-Controlled Property Region on Earth

8. SINGAPORE: A MASTERCLASS IN "POLICY AS A MARKET WEAPON"

Singapore is not a free-for-all market.

Singapore is a controlled market, and it controls speculation aggressively.

Price + rent performance

URA reported that in **Q4 2025**, Singapore's private residential price index rose **0.6%**, and for **2025 overall**, prices rose **3.3%** (modest).

URA also reported the private residential **rental index fell 0.5% in Q4 2025**, the first decline since Q2 2024; and for 2025 overall, rentals rose **1.9%**.

Foreign buyer friction

Singapore's IRAS (tax authority) shows a clear example: a **foreigner buying residential property can face ABSD of 60%** (example calculation shown).

That is not a small "fee."

That is a demand filter.

Speaker Singh's takeaway:

Singapore teaches the world something important: **the government can choose who is allowed to speculate.**

So if you're a global investor, your return is not only about "location."

It's also about **whether you are welcome capital—or punished capital**.

9. CHINA: THE GLOBAL WARNING LABEL

China is not just a China story.

It's a global wealth psychology story.

Reuters reported that China's new home prices fell **3.1% year-on-year in January 2026** (and 0.4% month-on-month), the steepest annual decline in seven months, with price drops in 62 of 70 cities.

Reuters also reported state firms buying foreclosed properties at discounts (often **19%–43%**) in efforts to slow the downturn—while oversupply remains a major issue.

New Wealth Order lesson:

Property can stay "down" longer than your emotions can survive—especially when a leverage era ends.

China is the clearest reminder that "real estate always goes up" is not a law.

It's a belief. And beliefs are expensive.

D. AUSTRALIA — Strong Growth, Affordability Pressure, Cyclical Momentum

10. AUSTRALIA: A STRONG 2025, BUT NOT A PROMISE OF FOREVER

Australia's market has been resilient in recent data.

Cotality's Home Value Index commentary noted that the index surged **8.6% higher in 2025**, adding roughly **$71,400** to the national median dwelling value, and described it as the strongest calendar year gain since 2021.

They also noted that all capital cities and rest-of-state regions recorded increases, with big variation across places.

Speaker Singh's warning:

Strong markets create lazy underwriting. Lazy underwriting creates future pain.

When growth feels easy, people stop checking fundamentals—yield, vacancy, buffers, and exit liquidity.

That's when a market becomes dangerous for beginners.

E. MIDDLE EAST — THE MODERN CAPITAL MAGNET STORY

11. DUBAI: THE GLOBAL CASE STUDY EVERY SERIOUS INVESTOR MUST UNDERSTAND

Now we come to Dubai—because in the New Wealth Order, Dubai is not "a destination."

Dubai is a **global property system**:

- global demand
- global capital
- visa-driven migration
- infrastructure growth
- strong transaction liquidity
- and very visible cycles

The numbers that explain global attention

Dubai Media Office reported that Dubai's real estate sector recorded **over 270,000 transactions worth AED 917 billion in 2025**, up **20% year-on-year**—a historic milestone.

ValuStrat reported that Dubai's ValuStrat Price Index (VPI) reached **240.4 points**, with **19.8% annual appreciation** (12 months) reported in early January 2026.

This is not "marketing."

This is why global investors keep watching Dubai.

Dubai's yield advantage (one of the biggest reasons it stands out)

Savills' world cities prime residential research reported that prime yields across world cities averaged about **3.15%** in 2024, and noted Dubai as a standout with capital values up **6.8%** and rents up **23.5%** in 2024.

Savills also highlighted that yields moved out fastest in Dubai, to about **5.3%** (prime context).

And REIDIN's UAE Residential Property Price Report (Nov 2025) showed Dubai gross rental yields around **6.55%** for the residential market, and **~7.03%** for apartments (report context).

So what does that mean in plain language?

Dubai has recently offered a rare combination:

- meaningful yields (income)
- strong rent growth in prior periods
- strong capital growth in the cycle
- and high transaction activity (liquidity)

That combination is exactly what global money searches for.

But Dubai is not a fantasy. Dubai is a cycle.

Fitch (reported by Reuters) warned Dubai prices could face a **double-digit fall** (possibly up to **15%**) driven by a major supply pipeline (210,000 units projected) in late 2025 into 2026.

UBS's Global Real Estate Bubble Index 2025 also categorized Dubai as **"elevated risk"** and noted Dubai recorded the **strongest risk increase** from the prior edition (along with Madrid).

This is the New Wealth Order truth:

Dubai rewards system investors. Dubai punishes emotional investors.

You don't go into Dubai with blind confidence.

You go into Dubai with disciplined underwriting.

And that's why I keep bringing Dubai into this book:

because it is one of the clearest examples of how modern property wealth works globally.

Currency stability matters (especially for Indian investors thinking globally)

The Central Bank of the UAE describes intervention rates around **USD/AED 3.672–3.673** in its domestic market operations (reflecting the peg mechanism).

That peg link is one reason UAE rates often mirror U.S. rate moves (a practical reality investors feel through mortgages and liquidity).

12. "GLOBAL MARKETS" ARE NOT COUNTRIES — THEY ARE ARCHETYPES

Most beginners ask:

"Which country is best?"

That question is childish.

The real question is:

"Which market archetype matches my objective, my risk tolerance, and my holding power?"

Here are the archetypes I use.

Archetype 1: Yield-and-cashflow hubs

You want income that helps you hold through cycles.

Dubai has been a major conversation in this category because yields have been higher than many global prime cities in recent datasets.

Archetype 2: Policy-cooled, capital-preservation cities

Places like Singapore are intentionally engineered to slow speculation with heavy buyer taxes (ABSD 60% for foreigners).

They may still rise, but they don't allow "easy flipping."

Archetype 3: Recovery markets

Germany is a classic recovery narrative—down hard, then stabilizing, then recovering (recent quarters positive).

Archetype 4: Distress/deleveraging markets

China is the obvious warning label: oversupply and a deleveraging sector can create long pain even with policy support.

Archetype 5: Mature slow-growth markets

The UK's 0.6% annual growth in late 2025 shows what "mature + affordability pressure" can look like.

The New Wealth Order investor chooses archetypes intentionally—like a chess player.

Not like a gambler.

13. THE ONLY HONEST WAY TO COMPARE GLOBAL PROPERTY RETURNS

Let me simplify "global ROI" without confusing the beginner reader.

Your real return has 4 layers:

Layer 1: Property return (local currency)

- rental yield (net, not gross)
- plus appreciation

Layer 2: Currency return (your home currency vs that currency)

If you earn in INR but your asset is in AED, USD, GBP, SGD—currency movement can boost or destroy your INR return.

Layer 3: Friction costs

- stamp duty/transfer fees
- brokerage
- maintenance/service charges
- vacancy
- repairs
- management fees
- taxes

Layer 4: Exit reality

A market can look good on paper, but if you can't sell easily, your return becomes theoretical.

This is why high transaction activity matters—liquidity is oxygen.

Dubai's 2025 transaction volume and value show why it's viewed as liquid compared with many markets.

14. THE GLOBAL POLICY REALITY: GOVERNMENTS ARE NOW "ACTIVE PLAYERS"

In the old world, people thought the market alone decides prices.

In the new world, governments actively shape:

- who can buy
- how much they can borrow
- how much tax they pay
- and sometimes whether foreigners are welcome at all

Examples that prove this isn't theory:

- **Canada** extended a foreign ownership ban to **Jan 1, 2027**.
- **Singapore** imposes ABSD reaching **60%** for foreigners in its official guidance.
- **New Zealand** introduced a foreign buyer ban in 2018 and later carved out limited exceptions (e.g., golden visa luxury home permission under conditions, reported in 2025).

Speaker Singh's blunt conclusion:

When you invest globally, you are not only investing in buildings. You are investing in governance.

15. INDIA'SPOSITIONINTHEGLOBALPROPERTYCONVERSATION

I'm writing this book with the Indian reader in mind—because India is where most people still think:

"One home. One city. One lifetime."

But the New Wealth Order is different:

1. **Indian families are becoming globally mobile**

   Kids study abroad. People work abroad. Businesses expand abroad.

2. **Indian capital is becoming globally curious**

   Not because India is bad—because diversification is intelligent.

3. **Access is becoming structurally easier**

   Under RBI's Liberalised Remittance Scheme (LRS), a resident individual can remit up to **USD 250,000 per financial year** for permissible transactions (within FEMA rules).

That doesn't mean "go and buy foreign property tomorrow."

It means the old wall is not as high as it used to be.

16. STORIES FROM MY JOURNEY (COMPOSITE) — HOW GLOBAL PROPERTY BUILDS OR BREAKS WEALTH

I will keep these stories anonymous and composite—because privacy matters.

But the patterns are real.

Story 1: The "passport investor" who bought pride, not profit

A client family wanted a "London address" because it sounded powerful.

They didn't look at:

- yield
- local taxes
- the fact that London itself can be "two speed"
- and the reality that UK annual growth had slowed to around 0.6% late 2025

Result: the asset didn't collapse.

But it underperformed expectations and tied up capital.

Their mistake wasn't London.

Their mistake was **buying reputation instead of return logic**.

Story 2: The "recovery buyer" who built wealth by buying when others were scared

Another investor entered a European market after a clear correction, when:

- prices had already taken pain (Germany's prior declines are visible in Destatis history)
- and recovery signals began showing up (Germany Q3 2025 up 3.3% YoY).

This wasn't luck.

This was cycle awareness + patience + conservative leverage.

Story 3: The Dubai system buyer who treated it like a business

This client didn't buy Dubai because it was "hot."

They bought only after underwriting:

- net yield using conservative assumptions (REIDIN yields are one input, not a promise)
- liquidity and transaction depth (Dubai 2025 milestone)
- the cycle risk (Fitch warning about supply and potential declines)
- and market heat indicators (UBS "elevated risk")

They built buffers.

They planned for vacancy.

They had an exit strategy.

That's the New Wealth Order approach:

In global property, enthusiasm is not strategy. Underwriting is strategy.

17. SPEAKER SINGH'S GLOBAL PROPERTY FRAMEWORK

If you read only one section in this chapter, read this.

When I evaluate global property, I use 10 questions:

1. **What is the net yield after all costs?**
2. **What is the real demand engine—jobs, tourism, students, migration?**
3. **What is the supply pipeline and delivery risk?** (Dubai's supply discussion is a live example)
4. **Is this market policy-friendly or policy-hostile to my buyer type?** (Singapore ABSD 60% for foreigners is a direct example)
5. **Is the market liquid enough to exit without begging buyers?** (Dubai transaction scale is one liquidity indicator)
6. **What does bubble-risk research say?** (UBS flags elevated risk in Dubai and high risk in certain cities)
7. **What is my currency exposure—and can I emotionally handle it?** (AED peg mechanics matter here)
8. **What's the tenant reality—quality, legal enforcement, churn?**
9. **Can I hold this asset through a 2–3 year flat period?** (BIS shows multi-year real declines globally)
10. **Is this asset part of a system—or is it a trophy?**

Trophy assets impress people.

System assets feed families.

Generational wealth is built by systems.

18. THE NEW WEALTH ORDER CONCLUSION: HOW TO THINK GLOBALLY WITHOUT LOSING YOUR MIND

Let me close this chapter with full clarity.

Global property is not about chasing the "best country."

It is about:

- choosing the right archetype
- entering at a sensible point in the cycle
- understanding policy risk
- managing currency exposure
- and building holding power through yield and buffers

And this is why Dubai keeps showing up in this book:

Because it's one of the clearest modern examples of a global capital city where:

- transaction liquidity is massive
- yields have been competitive in recent datasets
- the cycle has been strong (recent appreciation data)
- and yet the market still demands respect for supply, overheating risk, and correction possibility

That combination makes it perfect for teaching the New Wealth Order mindset:

You don't invest where you feel excited. You invest where the numbers survive stress.

In the next chapters, we will go deeper into:

- building property portfolios as "income machines"
- using leverage intelligently across cycles
- and how to structure real estate holdings so they don't become family conflicts—but family legacies

Because in the New Wealth Order, the end goal is not just wealth.

The goal is wealth that survives time.

READER NOTE

This chapter is educational and for storytelling. It is not financial, legal, tax, or investment advice. Property markets are cyclical and involve risk (illiquidity, leverage risk, vacancy risk, currency risk, policy risk, legal/title risk). Laws, taxes, and foreign ownership rules vary by jurisdiction and can change. Consult qualified professionals before acting.

Chapter 17

CASHFLOW STRATEGY

If Your Property Doesn't Pay You, You Don't Own an Asset — You Own a Stress Machine

*(Narrated in the voice of Speaker Singh — **The New Wealth Order**)*

Let me say this with full clarity, from my journey:

Most people don't buy property.

They buy a **dream**… and then spend the next 10 years paying EMIs to keep that dream alive.

They call it "investment."

But the bank statement calls it **outflow**.

And here is the brutal truth that separates the financially free from the financially stuck:

Real estate only becomes "wealth" when it becomes cashflow.

Not gossip. Not hope. Not appreciation screenshots.

Cashflow.

Because cashflow is the only thing that does all three jobs at once:

1. **It pays your lifestyle.**
2. **It protects you through cycles.**
3. **It gives you holding power** — and holding power is what turns time into wealth.

In this chapter, I'm going to teach you the New Wealth Order cashflow strategy the way professionals think — but in language a beginner can understand.

And yes, I'm going to be aggressive, because soft advice keeps people broke.

1. THE FIRST RULE OF PROPERTY CASHFLOW

Rent is proof. Appreciation is opinion.

Markets can lie to you.

Builders can lie to you.

Even your relatives can lie to you.

But rent is hard to fake — because it has to land in your account every month.

If you want to live in the New Wealth Order, burn this into your mind:

A property that doesn't generate reliable net income is not an investment. It is a speculative bet wearing a suit.

And global data backs the deeper idea behind this: rents tend to move steadily while house prices move in waves.

Eurostat showed that between **2010 and Q1 2025**, EU house prices rose **57.9%** while rents rose **27.8%**, with rents increasing steadily and prices being more variable.

That one paragraph contains a lifetime lesson:

- **Rents** usually behave like economics (steady demand, household formation, wages).
- **Prices** behave like finance (credit cycles, sentiment, rate changes).

If you build your entire plan on "prices will go up," you've built your house on fog.

2. HOW INSTITUTIONS MEASURE REAL ESTATE RETURNS

Most retail investors talk like this:

"Bro, how much appreciation?"

Professionals talk like this:

"What's the total return — income return + capital growth?"

That is not my opinion. That is how real estate performance is widely measured.

MSCI's property index methodology explicitly frames performance as **total return** and its **income and capital components**.

Even more blunt: sometimes **income carries everything**.

NCREIF's **NPI Expanded** showed **4Q 2025** returns as:

- Total **1.14%**

- Income **1.15%**
- Appreciation -0.01%

Do you understand what that means?

In that period, appreciation did nothing.

Income did the heavy lifting.

So if your "strategy" has no income component, you are not investing the way serious money invests.

3. THE CASHFLOW WATERFALL

This is the real math — simple, but most people never do it

Let's simplify property cashflow into a clean waterfall.

Step 1: Gross Rent

What the tenant pays (on paper).

Step 2: Minus Vacancy + Collection Loss

No property is occupied 365 days forever.

Even with great tenants, you'll face:

- vacancy weeks
- tenant turnover
- negotiation gaps
- occasional delays

Step 3: Effective Gross Income (EGI)

Gross rent after reality hits.

Step 4: Minus Operating Expenses

This is where amateurs die.

Operating expenses include:

- service charges/society maintenance
- repairs & replacements
- insurance
- property management fees
- periodic painting/AC/plumbing
- municipal costs (varies by jurisdiction)
- furnishing replacement (if furnished)

Step 5: Net Operating Income (NOI)

NOI is the pure income power of the asset.

Step 6: Minus Debt Service

Your EMI: principal + interest.

This is why DSCR matters (I'll explain it in one minute).

Step 7: Minus Capital Reserves

The hidden killer.

If you don't reserve for:

- major repairs
- tenant refresh
- unexpected costs

then your cashflow is fake.

Step 8: Net Free Cashflow

This is the number that decides if your property is:

- an income machine

or

- a monthly burden

4. THE THREE NUMBERS THAT DECIDE EVERYTHING

If I could force every beginner to learn only three metrics, it would be these.

Metric A: Cap Rate (Income Yield)

Cap rate is typically calculated as:

Cap Rate = NOI ÷ Property Value

This is a standard definition used in real estate finance.

Cap rate answers:

"What is the income yield of this asset if bought with cash?"

Metric B: DSCR (Debt Safety)

DSCR is commonly defined as:

DSCR = NOI ÷ Debt Service

Lenders use it to assess whether the income covers the loan payments.

DSCR answers:

"Will this property pay for its own debt — or will my salary have to rescue it?"

Metric C: Cash-on-Cash Return

Cash-on-cash answers:

"On the actual cash I invested, how much cash do I receive per year?"

It forces honesty because it includes leverage impact.

5. THE CASHFLOW TRAPS THAT DESTROY INVESTORS

From my experience, most investors don't lose money because the market is evil.

They lose money because their underwriting is childish.

Here are the classic traps:

Trap 1: "My property is premium, so it will always be rented"

Premium properties can stay vacant too — especially when supply rises.

Trap 2: Ignoring service charges and ongoing fees

In Dubai, for example, service charges can materially change net yield — which is why Dubai Land Department provides a **Service Charge Index** inquiry tool to check approved fees for jointly owned properties (via RERA).

If you don't check service charges, you're calculating returns blind.

Trap 3: Not using official rent reference tools

Dubai Land Department also provides a **Rental Index** service that allows users to calculate rental increase/market averages by entering area details.

Serious investors don't guess rent.

They verify.

Trap 4: Confusing gross yield with net yield

Gross yield is what people use to sell you a dream.

Net yield is what feeds you.

Trap 5: Overleveraging because "rent will cover the EMI"

That sentence has destroyed more middle-class wealth than any stock market crash.

If rent doesn't cover the EMI + reserves, your strategy is not investing.

It's survival.

6. WHY CASHFLOW STRATEGY WINS IN THE NEW WEALTH ORDER

Cashflow gives you power that appreciation can't.

Power 1: Holding power through cycles

When markets soften, weak hands sell.

Cashflow investors hold.

And global property markets do soften — even Dubai has cycle warnings.

Fitch (reported by Reuters) warned of a potential **moderate correction** in Dubai prices (possibly up to **15%**) due to a large supply pipeline (210,000 units projected).

Do you see why cashflow matters?

If prices correct but your net income is solid, you can survive and even expand.

If prices correct and your property is negative cashflow, panic arrives fast.

Power 2: Cashflow lets you reinvest without begging banks

Cashflow is internal capital.

And internal capital is freedom.

Power 3: Cashflow reduces emotional decision-making

Investors who depend on appreciation become anxious.

Anxious people make stupid decisions.

7. THE TRUTH ABOUT YIELD VS APPRECIATION (GLOBAL EVIDENCE)

There is an important global insight here:

High-yield markets and high-appreciation markets are often not the same markets.

An NBER working paper on U.S. single-family rentals found that total returns across cities were roughly equalized (~**8.5%**), with net rental yields and house price appreciation each contributing about half **on average**, but they were **negatively correlated across cities**.

Translation in plain language:

- Some places pay you through rent.
- Some places reward you through price growth.

- Trying to force both often makes you overpay.

The New Wealth Order investor doesn't chase "perfect."

They choose the return engine intentionally.

8. THE SPEAKER SINGH CASHFLOW STRATEGY

The system I want you to copy

Here is the framework I teach:

Stage 1: Build the "Cashflow Base"

Goal: stable, boring, reliable income.

Characteristics:

- strong rental demand corridor
- reasonable price-to-rent relationship
- manageable service charges
- legal clarity
- conservative leverage
- professional property management

Stage 2: Add "Cashflow Growth"

Goal: increase NOI without gambling.

Methods:

- renovate smartly (rent uplift > cost)
- improve tenant profile
- furnish if it materially lifts rent (and still stays net positive)

- reduce vacancy through better marketing and leasing process
- optimize service provider costs (management, maintenance)

Stage 3: Add "Cashflow Scaling"

Goal: repeat, refine, diversify.

Scaling tools:

- recycle equity (sell underperformers, buy better yield)
- refinance responsibly when interest rates and valuations allow
- diversify across markets/currencies where appropriate

9. DUBAI AS A CASHFLOW CASE STUDY

Now let's talk Dubai — because Dubai is one of the clearest modern examples of a market where cashflow strategy can be executed with **systems**, not just emotion.

Why Dubai stands out for income-focused investors

A. Gross yields have been competitive

REIDIN's November 2025 report showed Dubai's residential market gross rental yields around **6.55%**, and apartment gross rental yields around **7.03%** (report context).

B. Rent growth has been visible

In the same REIDIN dataset, Dubai rents were reported up **6.14% year-on-year** (Nov 2025).

Savills also highlighted that across world cities, average prime gross yields moved to about **3.15%** in 2024, and that yields moved out fastest in **Dubai to 5.3%**, supported by strong rental growth.

So Dubai's income narrative has been "globally noticeable" in recent research.

C. Fee transparency tools exist

Dubai Land Department provides:

- a **Service Charge Index** lookup
- a **Rental Index** tool for rental calculations/benchmarking

That transparency matters because cashflow dies in hidden costs.

D. Liquidity and market activity have been high

Dubai Media Office reported that Dubai's real estate market recorded **over 270,000 transactions worth AED 917 billion in 2025**, up **20% YoY**.

Liquidity doesn't guarantee profits — but it improves your ability to exit or rebalance when needed.

10. A REAL CASHFLOW UNDERWRITING EXAMPLE (DUBAI-STYLE, SIMPLIFIED)

Let's do a simple example to show you how professionals think.

Purchase price: AED 1,500,000

Annual rent (market): AED 110,000

Gross yield: 110,000 ÷ 1,500,000 = **7.33%**

Now reality:

Vacancy/turnover assumption (5%): -AED 5,500

Effective rent: AED 104,500

Operating costs (example):

- Service charges: AED 18,000 *(check DLD Service Charge Index before buying)*
- Maintenance reserve: AED 4,000
- Property management (5%): AED 5,225
- Insurance/other: AED 1,500

Total OpEx: AED 28,725

NOI: 104,500 - 28,725 = **AED 75,775**

Net yield (NOI yield): 75,775 ÷ 1,500,000 = **5.05%**

Now leverage:

If debt service is AED 60,000/year, then:

DSCR: 75,775 ÷ 60,000 = **1.26x**

That is the type of buffer lenders and serious investors like, because DSCR measures the relationship between NOI and debt service.

This is not "Dubai math."

This is **real estate math**.

And now you understand why I'm strict about it:

If you buy based on gross yield, you can get fooled.

If you buy based on net yield + DSCR + reserves, you protect yourself.

11. "BUT SPEAKER SINGH... WHAT ABOUT DUBAI CYCLE RISK?"

Good. You're learning to think like a professional.

Dubai has had strong activity, but it's still cyclical.

Fitch's warning about possible price correction tied to supply is exactly why cashflow strategy matters — you want income strength, not only price dependence.

And this is the New Wealth Order rule for Dubai:

Don't buy Dubai because you want Dubai. Buy Dubai because the numbers survive stress.

That means:

- use the official rental and service charge tools
- avoid emotional off-plan hype unless your buffers are real
- treat supply pipeline like weather: it changes conditions

12. THE "INDIRECT CASHFLOW" OPTION: REIT's (DUBAI EXAMPLE)

Many people want property cashflow but don't want:

- tenant headaches
- maintenance chaos
- vacancy management

This is where REIT's can play a role (not a replacement for all property, but a tool).

Dubai Residential REIT (as a public/structured vehicle) has been presented as an income-oriented exposure.

Dubai Media Office reported Dubai Residential REIT delivered **AED 1.95 billion revenue in 2025**, with average occupancy **98.3%.**

Reuters also reported (during the IPO process) expectations that the REIT would distribute at least **1.1 billion dirhams** in dividends in 2025 (as per IPO reporting context).

Again: not a guarantee of future returns.

But it shows the ecosystem is actively building **income products,** not just speculative flips.

13. INDIA: THE CASHFLOW REALITY INDIAN FAMILIES MUST ACCEPT

Now let's bring this home for Indian readers.

India is emotional about property — because property represents security, status, and family pride.

But security without cashflow can become a trap.

Rent growth exists — but it's uneven

Economic Times (citing NoBroker analysis) reported that rental inflation cooled to **7–9% in H1 2025** across major metros, after steeper hikes in earlier years.

At the same time, headlines also show certain segments saw sharp rental jumps — for example, Times of India reported rents surged about **25%** in prime Indian cities in 2025 (context: driven by multiple factors including return-to-office and demand).

New Wealth Order conclusion:

India is not "one rental market." India is micro-markets.

Cashflow strategy in India requires local precision:

- not just city selection
- but corridor selection, tenant selection, and entry price discipline

Residential yields can be modest in many Indian contexts

Knight Frank (in an older investment guide) noted residential yields between **2–4%**, while commercial yields were higher (context-specific and time-specific).

I'm not quoting that as a timeless law — I'm using it to hammer one point:

If your yield is low, your discipline must be high.

Because a low-yield property gives you less margin for error.

14. WHY CASHFLOW INVESTORS BEAT "FAST MONEY" TRADERS

Let me be harsh for a moment because India needs it.

Millions of people are being psychologically pushed into "fast profit" culture — trading, speculation, leverage without understanding.

SEBI reported that **93% of individual traders** incurred losses in equity F&O between FY22 and FY24, with aggregate losses exceeding **₹1.8 lakh crores**.

That's the dangerous temptation: quick gains, big losses, emotional damage.

Property cashflow is not "sexy."

But it is closer to what wealthy families actually build:

- controlled leverage
- durable demand
- income streams
- time compounding

In the New Wealth Order, boring is beautiful — **if boring pays.**

15. THE SPEAKER SINGH CASHFLOW PLAYBOOK

Here is the step-by-step strategy I want you to follow.

Step 1: Decide your cashflow objective

Are you building:

- lifestyle income (replace salary)?
- reinvestment income (build portfolio)?
- defensive income (inflation shield)?

Be honest.

Step 2: Set your minimum thresholds

My conservative baseline (example mindset, not universal advice):

- Target net yield (after expenses)
- Target DSCR buffer (income must exceed debt payment)
- Target vacancy assumptions

Step 3: Underwrite like a CFO, not like a dreamer

Checklist:

- rent comparables
- vacancy assumptions
- operating expenses
- service charges/HOA
- taxes and fees
- repair reserves
- tenant profile stability
- legal/title clarity
- exit liquidity

In Dubai specifically, use official DLD tools:

- Rental Index
- Service Charge Index

Step 4: Don't ignore friction costs

Fees matter more than amateurs understand.

In Dubai, even mortgage-related registration costs exist — Dubai Land Department pages list a **mortgage fee of 0.25% of the mortgage value** (plus admin items) in certain transaction contexts.

Small percentages become big numbers on big assets.

Step 5: Build a reserve fund before you buy

If you buy property with zero reserves, you are not investing.

You are walking into a storm without shoes.

Step 6: Stabilize first, optimize later

Your first goal is not "maximum rent."

Your first goal is:

- stable tenant
- stable payments
- stable operations

Then you optimize.

Step 7: Increase NOI, not stress

The professional game is to increase NOI through:

- small upgrades that create rent uplift
- tenant retention strategies
- faster leasing turnaround
- cost control

Not through gambling.

Step 8: Scale only when your system is repeatable

If your property success depends on luck or your constant presence, it's not a system.

The New Wealth Order requires systems.

16. THREE REALISTIC STORIES (COMPOSITE) FROM MY JOURNEY

(Details changed. Patterns are real.)

Story 1: The "negative cashflow pride purchase"

An investor bought a premium property because it looked successful.

The rent was decent — but the costs were heavy, and the EMI was heavier.

Every month, salary filled the gap.

Then a vacancy happened.

The investor didn't lose "money" first.

They lost peace first.

Eventually, they sold under pressure — not because the asset was worthless, but because the strategy was weak.

Lesson: If your property needs your salary to survive, your salary is the real asset — not the property.

Story 2: The "boring corridor cashflow winner"

Another investor bought a boring unit near consistent demand.

No ego location.

Just logic.

The rent wasn't glamorous — but it was reliable.

They reserved for repairs, used a manager, tracked DSCR, and kept leverage conservative.

In five years, they didn't just build equity.

They built **financial breathing space**.

Story 3: The "Dubai income system builder"

This investor liked Dubai because:

- yields were visible in recent datasets
- official tools existed for service charges and rental benchmarking
- market liquidity and activity were strong

But they still respected cycle risk (supply and correction warnings).

They bought only when the net yield survived stress tests.

That's the difference between a tourist and an investor.

17. THE FINAL TRUTH OF THIS CHAPTER

Let me end with the most important sentence of this entire chapter:

Cashflow is not a feature of real estate. Cashflow is the purpose of investment real estate.

If you want generational wealth, stop buying property to impress people.

Start buying property to build **income architecture**.

Because in the New Wealth Order:

- Appreciation is the bonus.
- Cashflow is the paycheck.
- Systems are the legacy.

READER NOTE

This chapter is educational and does not constitute financial, legal, tax, or investment advice. Property markets involve risk (illiquidity, leverage risk, vacancy risk, policy risk, legal/title risk, currency risk). Always verify local regulations and consult qualified professionals for your situation.

PART 5

BUILDING YOUR WEALTH EMPIRE

Chapter 18

THE 5-YEAR ASSET ROADMAP

A Practical, Punjabi-Youth Proof Plan to Go From "Paise Aayenge Kab?" to "Paise Kaam Kar Rahe Hain."

*(Narrated in the voice of Speaker Singh — **The New Wealth Order**)*

Let me speak with full honesty, from my journey.

Punjab's youth is not lazy. Punjab's youth is **restless**. Ambitious. Hungry. Proud.

But the system around them often pushes two dangerous extremes:

1. **"Sarkari naukri nahi mili to life over."**
2. **"Fast money chahiye — trading, betting, shortcut, agent."**

And both extremes can keep you financially stuck for a decade.

Here's the truth that nobody says out loud:

You don't need a "perfect job" to build wealth. You need a perfect system.

Why am I being so aggressive about it?

Because the numbers are not comforting.

Recent PLFS-based reporting showed Punjab's youth unemployment (15–29 years) at **19.3%** in Oct–Dec 2025, higher than the national average reported in that coverage, with rural youth unemployment even higher.

And when young people feel stuck, the most common next step is not "planning."

It's **panic**.

Panic leads to:

- credit card debt
- personal loans
- "bro told me this stock/option will double"
- illegal or shady agents promising overseas jobs
- buying cars on EMI to look successful while cashflow collapses

And Punjab has been a hotspot for the overseas-dream ecosystem—both genuine and fraudulent. Reporting citing Ministry of External Affairs data noted Punjab accounted for **53% of complaints** in the region (2023–2025) against illegal recruiting agents; it also mentioned a big spike in 2025 and that the eMigrate portal listed **3,505 unregistered agents** by Jan 2026.

So this chapter is not motivation.

This chapter is a **weapon**.

A weapon to build a real wealth empire in **5 years**—practical, doable, and designed for Punjab's youth whether you live in:

- Chandigarh/Mohali
- Ludhiana/Jalandhar/Amritsar
- Moga/Bathinda/Patiala

- a village with land in the family
- or you're planning to move abroad

I will give you:

- a **Year-by-Year Roadmap**
- a simple **asset framework**
- "what to do Monday morning" style steps
- real pitfalls (and how people lose money)
- and how to build a reputation of disciplined wealth, not loud lifestyle

1. THE NEW WEALTH ORDER RULEBOOK

Before the roadmap, you need the rules. Without rules, the plan becomes Instagram.

Rule #1: Your first goal is not "rich." Your first goal is unbreakable.

Most people don't fail because returns were low.

They fail because one shock (health, job loss, family emergency) breaks the entire structure.

Rule #2: Income builds your engine. Assets build your empire.

A salary is a tap. It can close.

An asset is a spring. It can keep flowing.

Rule #3: Cashflow > bragging rights

If you're earning ₹30,000/month and your EMI lifestyle is ₹28,000/month, you are not "settled."

You are **one delay away from collapse.**

Rule #4: Punjab-specific reality — avoid "agent debt"

Borrowing huge money for "going abroad" through the wrong channel can destroy families. Punjab has seen high complaint volumes about illegal recruiting agents.

Rule #5: Never build wealth using tools designed to transfer wealth from beginners to professionals

If you think I'm exaggerating, read this slowly:

SEBI reported that **93% of individual traders** incurred losses in equity F&O between FY22–FY24; aggregate losses exceeded **₹1.8 lakh crore.**

Reuters' coverage of the same study noted **43%** of retail derivatives traders were under 30 and many were in lower income groups.

So yes—"fast money" is fast, but usually fast in the wrong direction.

2. THE PUNJAB YOUTH WEALTH REALITY

I want to anchor this roadmap in the real world.

Punjab has income, but the pressure is real

Punjab's per capita income in 2023–24 was estimated at **₹1,95,621** (current prices) in a PRS budget analysis.

That sounds decent on paper. But per-capita is not your salary. It hides inequality and employment gaps.

Debt pressure is also real—especially in agriculture families

Reporting noted Punjab's outstanding Kisan Credit Card (KCC) debt at **₹57,536 crore** (March 2025), rising over four years while KCC accounts declined—meaning the burden per borrower increased.

The bigger India context is also dangerous: consumption debt is rising

RBI's Financial Stability Report (as covered by Reuters) noted household debt at **41.9% of GDP** and highlighted that non-housing retail loans form over half of household debt and about **25.7% of disposable income** (as of March 2024 in that reporting).

So the environment is clear:

- youth stress + unemployment
- debt temptation
- "fast money" traps
- overseas dreams with both opportunity and fraud risk

Now the question becomes:

How do you win anyway?

Answer: **You build a 5-year asset roadmap that forces discipline.**

3. YOUR ASSET BUCKETS

This is the foundation of the roadmap.

Bucket A — Survival Assets (0–12 months)

Purpose: keep you alive in shocks.

- emergency fund
- basic insurance (health + term if needed)
- zero high-interest debt

Bucket B — Compounding Assets (Year 1–5)

Purpose: long-run growth.

- diversified equity mutual funds/index funds/ETFs (through SIP discipline)

SIP isn't "for rich people." AMFI notes SIP instalments can be as small as **₹500/month**, and even **₹250/month** under "Chhoti SIP."

Also note: SIP culture is already massive in India—AMFI data reported SIP inflows around **₹31,000 crore** in Jan 2026 (and similar in Dec 2025).

Bucket C — Cashflow Assets (Year 2–5)

Purpose: income that reduces dependence on salary.

- rental income systems (India/Dubai later if appropriate)
- REIT's (for those who want property cashflow without landlord headaches)
- business cashflow

Bucket D — Optional Global Diversification (Year 3–5)

Purpose: reduce single-country risk.

If you become eligible and compliant, RBI's LRS allows resident individuals to remit up to **USD 250,000 per financial year** for permissible transactions.

(This bucket is optional. You don't start here. You earn your way here.)

THE 5-YEAR ROADMAP

(Read this like a training program. Wealth is trained.)

YEAR 1 – "BASE CAMP" (STABILITY BEFORE SPEED)

If you skip Year 1, your Year 3 will collapse. I've seen it too many times.

Goal of Year 1

1. Stop financial bleeding
2. Build emergency reserves
3. Start compounding
4. Upgrade income skill

Month 1: The Financial Audit (Non-negotiable)

Do this in one notebook or one Google Sheet:

- monthly income (all sources)
- fixed expenses (rent, travel, phone, EMI)
- variable expenses (food, shopping)
- debts (amount, interest rate, EMI, due date)
- assets (cash, FD, gold, investments)

Then compute your **Net Wealth Score**:

Net Worth = Assets - Liabilities

Most Punjabi youth I meet (composite, from my experience) are shocked because they "feel okay" but net worth is negative due to:

- bike/car EMI
- credit card
- personal loan
- informal borrowing

Month 1–3: Kill the High-Interest Snake

If you have:

- credit card revolving
- BNPL
- personal loan at high rate

Your "investment plan" is fake until this is controlled.

Aggressive rule:

Pay off the highest interest debt first (avalanche method), while maintaining minimums on others.

Month 1–6: Build Emergency Fund (Your Anti-Panic Asset)

Target: **3 months of expenses** first.

Then move to **6 months**.

Why? Because when the emergency fund exists:

- you don't borrow for emergencies
- you don't sell investments in panic
- you don't fall for fast-money scams

Month 2–12: Start SIP (Even Small)

AMFI states SIP can start at **₹500/month** (and ₹250 for Chhoti SIP).

Your job is not "pick perfect fund."

Your job is **start**, and then **step up**.

And you're not alone—SIP inflows around **₹31,000 crore** in Jan 2026 show millions are building this habit.

Income Upgrade (Punjab-specific practical track)

Punjab youth often has either:

- strong communication + hustle (business mindset)
- or strong family pressure for stable job
- or strong desire to go abroad

So here's the Year-1 skill strategy that works in real life:

Pick **one income skill** that:

- is sellable online/offline
- takes 3–6 months to reach basic competence
- has real demand

Examples:

- sales + closing (real estate, insurance, SaaS, education)
- performance marketing (Meta/Google ads)
- video editing + content packaging
- basic web development/no-code
- logistics + supply chain operations
- real estate documentation/broker systems
- accounting basics (Tally + GST basics)

Speaker Singh rule:

Year 1 is not about "passion." It's about **income power**.

YEAR 2 – "ACCELERATION" (INCOME GROWTH + DISCIPLINE INVESTING)

Year 2 is where you stop being a saver and become an allocator.

Goal of Year 2

1. Increase income by 20–50% (through skill, job switch, business)
2. Increase SIP by 25–100% (step-up)

3. Build credit discipline (for future leverage)
4. Create first micro-cashflow stream

The Step-Up System

If your SIP is ₹2,000/month in Year 1, your Year-2 job is to push it to ₹3,000–₹5,000/month depending on income.

Why step-up works:

- it matches your rising capacity
- it avoids "one big decision" fear
- it becomes automatic wealth

Build Your "Anti-Gambling Firewall"

This is mandatory because youth risk is high.

SEBI's data shows the majority of individual F&O traders lose money; losses exceeded ₹1.8 lakh crore over FY22–FY24.

So in Year 2, you build a firewall:

- no options trading as "income"
- no borrowing to invest
- no "Telegram tips"
- no "guaranteed returns"

Aggressive line:

If you need excitement, go to the gym. Not the market.

First Cashflow Stream (micro level)

Options:

- freelancing income (skill-based)
- commission-based sales

- micro business: resale, services, agency model
- real estate referral (with ethics)

The purpose is not big money.

The purpose is **second income identity**.

Most people stay stuck because they have one identity:

"I earn only if I work."

Year 2 begins the shift:

"I earn from systems."

YEAR 3 – "ASSET POSITIONING" (PROPERTY THINKING WITHOUT PROPERTY MISTAKES)

Year 3 is where Punjab youth must become smart about property because Punjab culture is property-heavy. If you don't learn property math, you'll become emotional and trapped.

Goal of Year 3

1. Build down payment reserve/business reserve
2. Add a cashflow asset layer (REIT or rental system planning)
3. Strengthen legal and documentation discipline

If Your Family Has Land or Property (Punjab reality)

From my experience, many young Punjabis have "assets" on paper—land, plot, house—but cashflow is weak and disputes are common.

Your Year-3 mission:

- treat family property like a business asset
- measure cashflow and risk
- fix documentation gaps (titles, mutation, will planning where appropriate)

Cashflow Strategy: Don't Buy Property for Ego

You learned earlier in this book:

- rent is evidence, appreciation is opinion
- cashflow gives holding power

So Year 3 is where you decide:

- Do I want landlord-style cashflow?
- Do I want REIT cashflow?
- Do I want business cashflow?

You don't need to buy property in Year 3.

But you must become **property-intelligent** in Year 3.

REIT's (Practical Bridge)

If you want property exposure with liquidity:

REIT's can be a practical tool to access real estate cashflows without buying a flat.

(We covered REIT logic in Part 3. Here, it becomes a portfolio tool.)

YEAR 4 – "EXPANSION" (DIVERSIFICATION + REAL LEVERAGE DISCIPLINE)

Year 4 is when your empire becomes visible in numbers:

- your SIP is meaningful
- your emergency fund is real
- your income is higher
- your credit profile is strong
- your second income stream exists

Goal of Year 4

1. Diversify: equity + debt + gold + property exposure
2. Prepare for conservative leverage (only if cashflow supports it)
3. Begin global awareness (optional)

Why leverage is delayed until Year 4

Because leverage is a magnifier.

If your system is weak, leverage magnifies stress.

And remember: household debt is rising in India, and a large portion is consumption-driven.

You will not build an empire with consumption debt.

Global Diversification (Optional but strategic)

If you becomc financially stable and want global exposure:

RBI LRS allows up to **USD 250,000 per financial year** for permissible transactions.

For Punjab youth, global diversification becomes relevant because:

- many families have overseas connections
- many youth plan relocation
- currency risk becomes personal

But again: you earn this level through stability.

The Overseas Dream — Do It Cleanly or Don't Do It

Because Punjab has high complaints about illegal recruiting agents.

Year 4 rule if you are moving abroad:

- verify agents
- avoid under-the-table deals
- don't destroy family finances for a fake promise

YEAR 5 – "THE EMPIRE STAGE" (MULTIPLE INCOME STREAMS + ASSET PAYROLL)

Year 5 is not "Ferrari."

Year 5 is **freedom.**

Goal of Year 5

1. Your assets start paying meaningful income ("asset payroll")
2. You have 2–3 income streams
3. You can handle shocks without panic
4. You can invest globally if needed
5. You have a clear 10-year vision

What an "Empire" looks like (realistic)

Not one big jackpot.

Instead:

- an emergency fund that protects you
- a compounding core growing every month
- one cashflow system (business or property income)
- a disciplined reputation (people trust your money behavior)

This is how millionaire families operate:

They don't chase money.

They build **structure.**

4. THE PRACTICAL PUNJAB YOUTH PLAYBOOKS

Now I'll give you "choose your lane" versions—because Punjab youth isn't one type.

Playbook A — The Job Track (Private job/Govt prep/corporate)

Core focus: stable income + aggressive investing discipline

Rules:

- SIP starts immediately (₹500–₹2,000 minimum)
- step-up annually
- avoid F&O "income" trap
- build skill to switch jobs and raise income

Playbook B — The Business Track (Punjab's natural strength)

Core focus: cashflow + reinvestment + discipline

Rules:

- keep business and personal accounts separate
- build 6 months business buffer
- reinvest profits into scalable assets (inventory, distribution, marketing)
- still invest personally (SIP as "personal retirement engine")

Playbook C — The Abroad Track (Study/work abroad)

Core focus: capital protection + clean compliance + skill income

Rules:

- do not borrow blindly through shady channels (Punjab complaints data is a warning)
- build a written budget: fees, living costs, emergency buffer

- understand LRS framework for remittance limits
- avoid "agent debt" that forces your family to sell assets

Playbook D — The Farm/Property Family Track

Core focus: turn inherited assets into systems, not conflicts

Rules:

- legal clarity first
- measure real cashflow
- do not sell core assets for lifestyle
- monetize assets responsibly (lease, storage, small commercial, etc. — depending on legality and feasibility)

(This book teaches strategy; local execution requires local professional guidance.)

5. THE "MONDAY MORNING" CHECKLIST (SO THIS IS ACTUALLY PRACTICAL)

If you do nothing else, do this.

Week 1

- Make your net worth sheet
- List all debts and interest rates
- Start emergency fund auto-transfer
- Start SIP auto-debit (even small)

Week 2

- Cut one waste expense permanently
- Build a "no debt for lifestyle" rule
- Choose one income skill to learn (3–6 months)

Week 3

- Start one side income action (freelancing, sales, service)
- Track every rupee for 7 days (discipline training)

Week 4

- Review: net worth, spending, investments
- Increase SIP if possible
- Plan Year-1 targets (emergency fund months, debt reduction)

This is what separates dreamers from builders: **builders review numbers.**

6. COMMON PUNJAB YOUTH MONEY LOSS STORIES (COMPOSITE, BUT REAL PATTERNS)

Loss Story 1: The "Option Trading Hero"

A young man (composite) turned ₹10,000 into ₹30,000 once.

Then borrowed money, increased risk, and lost ₹2–₹5 lakh within months.

This isn't rare. It's statistically normal.

SEBI's study shows most retail derivatives traders lose.

Loss Story 2: The "Agent Promise"

A family mortgaged gold and borrowed to pay an agent for overseas placement.

The offer was fake. The debt stayed real.

Punjab's high complaint share against illegal recruiting agents is exactly why I warn you: verify everything.

Success Story 1: The "Boring SIP + Skill Switch"

A youth (composite) started a ₹2,000 SIP, upskilled, switched job, stepped SIP to ₹8,000 over 3 years.

No drama. No trading.

By Year 5, the portfolio became a real asset base and confidence engine—because the habit stayed.

This is why SIP culture in India has grown so large—SIP inflows ~₹31,000 crore in Jan 2026 show massive adoption.

Success Story 2: The "Small Business Reinvestment"

A small service business owner reinvested profits into systems: staff + marketing + process.

They still maintained personal investing discipline.

After 5 years, they had both:

- a cashflow business
- and a compounding portfolio

That's an empire.

7. THE EMPIRE SCOREBOARD (TRACK THIS MONTHLY)

If you want to build a wealth empire, track these 7 numbers every month:

1. Net worth (assets – liabilities)
2. Emergency fund months (how many months you can survive)
3. Total SIP amount per month
4. Income growth (monthly income trend)

5. Debt-to-income ratio
6. Cashflow assets income (rent/business/REIT distributions)
7. Skill pipeline (what are you learning to increase income)

You don't rise to your goals.

You fall to your systems.

CLOSING: SPEAKER SINGH'S FINAL LINE FOR PUNJAB'S YOUTH

Let me end this chapter with something I truly believe from my experience:

Punjab doesn't have a talent shortage. Punjab has a system shortage.

You don't need luck.

You don't need a miracle.

You need:

- discipline
- compounding
- cashflow thinking
- and protection from scams and shortcuts

And if you follow the 5-year roadmap in this chapter, you will build something the old world can't take from you:

A wealth empire that is earned, structured, and survivable.

READER NOTE

This chapter is educational and designed as a general roadmap, not personalized financial advice. Investing involves risk, and results vary based on income, discipline, market conditions, and life events. For major decisions (insurance, property purchase, international investing, taxes), consult qualified professionals.

Chapter 19

THE 10-YEAR FREEDOM FORMULA

A Practical, Punjabi-Youth Proof Blueprint to Build Assets, Cashflow, and Choices

*(Narrated in the voice of Speaker Singh — **The New Wealth Order**)*

Let me speak like a consultant, not like a poet.

When I sit with young people—especially Punjab's youth—the pattern is painfully consistent:

- You're ambitious.
- You're hungry.
- You're ready to work.
- But the money system around you is either **too slow** (jobs scarcity, delayed growth) or **too toxic** (fast money traps, debt, scams, fake overseas promises).

And then people say, "10 years is too long."

No.

From my journey—managing wealth for millionaires and billionaires across markets—the truth is the opposite:

10 years is not long. 10 years is a superpower.

Because most people waste 10 years *reacting.*

The wealthy use 10 years *building systems.*

This chapter is your system.

Not a motivational speech.

A **freedom formula**.

1. WHAT "FREEDOM" ACTUALLY MEANS

Before we talk strategy, we must define the destination.

Financial freedom is not "never work again."

Financial freedom is:

When your life decisions stop depending on your next salary.

Freedom is when you can say:

- "I won't tolerate this job."
- "I can start a business without begging."
- "I can handle an emergency without panic."
- "I can support my parents without destroying my future."
- "I can choose to go abroad—or choose to stay—without being forced."

For Punjab's youth, this matters more than ever because the numbers are not soft.

A Periodic Labour Force Survey (Oct–Dec 2025) based report showed Punjab's youth unemployment (15–29) at **19.3%,** with rural youth unemployment **22.5%**, and a sharp gender gap (female unemployment higher).

So my first aggressive statement in this chapter is this:

If the job market is uncertain, your asset plan must be certain.

2. THE PUNJAB REALITY YOU MUST ACCEPT (WITHOUT DRAMA)

In Punjab, wealth psychology has three powerful forces:

Force A: "Status spending" pressure

Car, iPhone, wedding show, lifestyle on EMI—so you look settled.

Force B: "Property is the only real investment" belief

Property is important—yes—but many people buy property as emotion and then bleed cashflow for years.

And the data shows how dominant property is in India's household wealth:

A Government of India press release on the All India Debt & Investment Survey stated that **land and buildings together formed ~91% of total household asset value in rural India** (as of 30.06.2018), and in urban India land (~49%) and buildings (~38%) were major components.

Force C: "Go abroad fast" urgency

Punjab's overseas dream is real, and there are genuine pathways—but the scam ecosystem is also real.

A report citing Ministry of External Affairs data said Punjab accounted for **53% of complaints** (in the region) against illegal recruiting agents between 2023–2025, and the eMigrate portal listed **3,505 unregistered agents** by January 2026.

So the New Wealth Order reality is:

Punjab's youth doesn't just need an investment plan. You need an anti-trap plan.

3. THE 10-YEAR FREEDOM FORMULA (SIMPLE, BRUTAL, PRACTICAL)

I will give you the formula first, then we build the roadmap.

Freedom = (Income Power × Allocation Rate × Time) + (Cashflow Systems - Debt Stress)

That's it.

Most people focus on one piece (like "which stock?").

We build the whole machine.

This chapter is built on 5 engines:

1. **Income Engine** — skills + career + business
2. **Allocation Engine** — how much you invest automatically
3. **Compounding Engine** — equity/asset growth over time
4. **Cashflow Engine** — rental income, business cashflow, REIT income
5. **Protection Engine** — emergency fund, insurance, fraud avoidance, risk control

If one engine fails, your freedom slows.

If two fail, your freedom dies.

4. YOUR FREEDOM NUMBER (SO YOU STOP GUESSING)

People talk about freedom like it's a vibe. It's not. It's a number.

A common retirement planning framework (based on historical U.S. data) is the "safe withdrawal rate" approach—popularized by William Bengen's 1994 paper and later the Trinity/Cooley-Hubbard-Walz study—testing how long portfolios survived at different withdrawal rates.

In very simple terms, the "4% rule" idea says:

If your portfolio can support roughly ~4% withdrawal (inflation-adjusted) over long periods, then:

Freedom Fund ≈ Annual Expenses ÷ 0.04 = Annual Expenses × 25

But I want Punjab's youth to be more conservative and more intelligent than copy-paste America.

Because:

- India has different inflation patterns
- careers are more volatile for many families
- sequence risk (bad early years) can hit hard
- family responsibilities are heavier

So I often teach a range:

- **Aggressive benchmark:** 4% (×25)
- **Strong benchmark:** 3.5% (×28–29)
- **Ultra-safe benchmark:** 3% (×33)

Example (simple and real):

If your family lifestyle requires **₹6 lakh/year** (₹50,000/month), then:

- at 4% → **₹1.5 crore**
- at 3.5% → **~₹1.7 crore**
- at 3% → **₹2 crore**

Now here's the truth:

Your goal is not to hit this in one jump. Your goal is to climb the Freedom Ladder.

5. THE FREEDOM LADDER (PUNJAB-PRACTICAL)

In my experience, you build freedom in levels—not one jackpot.

Level 1: Safety (Year 1–2)

You can survive 6 months without borrowing.

Level 2: Stability (Year 2–4)

You invest monthly, debt is controlled, you can handle emergencies.

Level 3: Strength (Year 4–7)

You have one additional income stream + real portfolio size.

Level 4: Choice (Year 7–10)

Your assets begin paying meaningful cashflow. Your life decisions change.

Level 5: Empire (beyond 10)

Your cashflow systems + compounding become bigger than your effort.

6. A HARD TRUTH: "FAST MONEY" IS MOSTLY A WEALTH TRANSFER

This is where I get aggressive, because soft talk destroys young people.

SEBI reported that **93% of individual traders** incurred losses in equity F&O between FY22–FY24, with aggregate losses exceeding **₹1.8 lakh crore**.

If you are Punjab's youth trying to become free in 10 years, here is the rule:

**You do not build freedom with instruments where the majority of beginners statistically lose. **

If you want thrill, play sports.

If you want wealth, build systems.

7. THE 10-YEAR ROADMAP (YEAR-BY-YEAR, PUNJABI-YOUTH PROOF)

YEAR 1: "BASE CAMP" — You Become Unbreakable

Goal: stop financial bleeding + build your first investing habit.

Non-negotiables:

1. **Debt cleanup plan** (especially high interest)
2. **Emergency fund** (start with 1 month → 3 months → 6 months)
3. **Health risk control** (basic health cover; don't gamble with hospital bills)
4. **SIP starts immediately**

AMFI explains SIPs can start as low as **₹500/month** (and **₹250/month** under "Chhoti SIP").

I don't care if you start small.

I care that you start **automatic**.

Punjab-specific Year 1 discipline:

Do not build a lifestyle you must maintain through loans.

Because once you start "status EMIs," your investing rate dies.

YEAR 2: "INCOME UPGRADE" — You Increase Earning Power First

Freedom is easier when income rises.

Punjab's per-capita income (2023–24) was estimated at **₹1,95,621** (current prices) in PRS budget analysis—useful as context, but it does not represent what most youth personally earn.

Year 2 is where you pick **one income skill** that can raise you 20–50%:

Examples (practical, not fancy):

- sales + closing
- performance marketing
- video editing + content packaging
- basic analytics/Excel/finance ops
- real estate documentation + broking systems (ethical)
- logistics/supply chain ops
- coding/no-code for small businesses
- online tutoring/coaching

The rule:

Increase income without increasing lifestyle at the same speed.

That gap is your investing fuel.

YEAR 3: "ALLOCATION MACHINE" — You Become an Allocator

Year 3 is where you stop being "a saver" and become "a capital allocator."

You do 3 things:

1. **Step-up SIP annually**
2. **Build a second income stream**
3. **Create a rules-based asset plan (not random picks)**

And you stop believing "I'll invest when I earn more."

You invest so you *become* more powerful.

Reality check (how big India's investing culture is becoming):

AMFI noted that the mutual fund industry's AUM grew from **₹12.74 trillion (Jan 31, 2016)** to **₹81.01 trillion (Jan 31, 2026)**—more than 6× over 10 years.

This matters because it shows a structural shift: India is moving toward market-linked investing as a mainstream habit.

YEAR 4: "CASHFLOW THINKING" — You Learn Property Like a Professional

Property is a Punjab reality. But we treat it like a business, not emotion.

Also understand the pressure many farm families carry:

A report noted Punjab's outstanding Kisan Credit Card debt at **₹57,536 crore (March 2025)**, rising while the number of KCC accounts fell—meaning burden per borrower increased.

So for many households, land exists—but debt exists too.

Year 4 is where you learn:

- rental yield vs appreciation
- net yield after costs

- vacancy reality
- legal clarity
- conservative leverage

And you decide the path:

- direct rental property system
- REIT exposure (property cashflow with liquidity)
- business cashflow first, property later

New Wealth Order rule:

If your property doesn't pay you (net), it is not an asset—it is a stress machine.

YEAR 5: "SCALE" — The Two-Stream Rule Begins

By Year 5, you must have:

1. **One core income** (job/business)
2. **One secondary stream** (freelancing, sales, rental, REIT, commission, side business)

If you still have only one stream, you're not building an empire.

You're just surviving.

Investment habit proof (India-wide):

Reports citing AMFI data said SIP inflows stayed above **₹31,000 crore** in January 2026 (second consecutive month), indicating a strong retail habit.

YEAR 6–7: "ASSET ACQUISITION YEARS" — You Buy/Build What Pays You

This is where freedom becomes visible.

You now have:

- emergency fund
- compounding portfolio
- stronger income
- better discipline

So you start acquiring **cashflow-producing assets**, depending on your lane:

- scalable business profits
- rental income systems
- REIT allocations
- conservative leverage only if cashflow supports it

Also, you get serious about debt risk because India is seeing rising household leverage in consumption categories.

RBI's Financial Stability Report (as covered by Reuters) noted household debt around **41.9% of GDP** (and highlighted non-housing retail loans forming over half of household debt and about **25.7% of disposable income** as of March 2024 in that reporting).

This is why the New Wealth Order rule exists:

Borrow to build assets, not to buy lifestyle.

Lifestyle debt is the enemy of freedom.

YEAR 8–9: "CONSOLIDATION" — You Upgrade from Hustle to Structure

At this stage, millionaires stop acting like "hard workers" and start acting like "operators."

You build:

- automated investing
- automated savings

- clear asset allocation
- tax and legal discipline
- emergency + opportunity cash reserves
- portfolio rebalancing habit

This is also the stage where you plan for family stability:

- avoid property disputes
- documentation clarity
- nomination, will basics
- insurance alignment

Because in Punjab, many families lose wealth not in markets— but inside family conflict.

YEAR 10: "FREEDOM YEAR" — Your Assets Start Paying Your Life

Year 10 doesn't mean you stop working.

Year 10 means:

If you choose to work, it's power. If you must work, it's slavery.

Your income becomes optional.

Your assets become your base.

And your identity changes from:

"I need money."

to:

"I allocate capital."

That is the New Wealth Order.

8. THE PRACTICAL "HOW" (SO THIS IS NOT JUST THEORY)

A. The Allocation Rule (Your Real Wealth Accelerator)

The fastest way to freedom is not picking the perfect investment.

It is increasing your **allocation rate**.

Allocation rate = (Invested money per month) ÷ (Monthly income)

Targets (practical, not perfect):

- **Year 1:** 10–15%
- **Year 2–3:** 20–30%
- **Year 4–6:** 30–40% (if income supports)
- **Year 7–10:** 40%+ for aggressive wealth builders

Punjab youth often has one advantage: family support or shared household costs can sometimes allow higher allocation rates early—if you don't destroy it with lifestyle EMIs.

B. The Automation Rule (Because Discipline Is Not a Mood)

I've seen this across millionaires and billionaires:

They don't "decide" every month.

They automate.

Your freedom plan must run even when:

- you feel lazy
- you feel emotional
- you feel unlucky
- you feel distracted

Automation is how you beat your own psychology.

C. Compounding in Real Numbers (10-Year Proof)

Let's make this practical.

If you invest **₹10,000/month** for 10 years, and you get an average 12% annual return (not guaranteed), your portfolio might reach roughly **₹23 lakh**.

If you start at **₹30,000/month** and increase it by **10% each year** (step-up), at 12% annual return, you might reach roughly **₹1 crore** in 10 years (illustrative math, not a promise).

This is why compounding is not magic—it is *math + time + consistency.*

And to show how real compounding can look in the market-linked world: one illustration reported that a ₹10,000 SIP over 20 years in a particular ELSS fund grew to ~₹1.03 crore (CAGR ~12.9%)—again, this is an example of compounding behavior, not a guarantee or recommendation.

Speaker Singh rule:

Don't chase 1 crore in one year. Build a system that can produce crores over decades.

9. PUNJAB YOUTH LANES (CHOOSE YOUR LANE, SAME FORMULA)

Lane 1: Job Track (Private/Govt/Corporate)

Winning move: job switch + skill + SIP step-up

If Punjab youth unemployment is high, you must become rare.

Rare skill → better job → higher allocation → faster freedom.

Lane 2: Business Track (Punjab's natural strength)

Winning move: business cashflow + reinvestment + personal investing discipline

Most business owners fail because:

- they mix business money and personal money
- they don't build buffers
- they don't invest outside the business

You do both:

- build the business engine
- build the personal portfolio engine

Lane 3: Abroad Track (Study/work abroad)

Punjab has huge overseas ambition—respect it, but do it with clean intelligence.

Reality check: Canada reduced international student permits again in 2025 (continuing caps introduced in 2024), citing strain on housing and services; applicants required attestation letters and rules tightened further.

So the New Wealth Order abroad rule is:

- plan for policy change
- build buffers
- don't take blind debt for "dreams"
- verify agents (Punjab complaint data is a warning)

Also remember: remittances are powerful—India received a record **$135.46 billion** in remittances in FY25, showing diaspora money is a real economic force.

But diaspora wealth is not built by scams. It is built by clean skills and clean pathways.

Lane 4: Farm/Land Family Track

Many youth have "assets" on paper. But paper doesn't pay EMIs.

You focus on:

- legal clarity
- measuring cashflow
- risk control (debt discipline)
- monetization strategies that are lawful and sustainable

Because farmer debt stress is real in Punjab's KCC numbers.

10. THE FREEDOM SAFETY KIT (PUNJAB EDITION)

If you want freedom, you need protection.

1. Anti-Scam Protocol

If someone promises:

- "Guaranteed return"
- "Double in 3 months"
- "Visa pakka" without documentation
- "No risk, sir"

You walk away.

Punjab's complaints against illegal recruiting agents are not theory.

2. Anti-Gambling Protocol

If you're under 30 and your "plan" depends on F&O profits, stop.

SEBI's data is the warning label.

3. Inflation Awareness Protocol

RBI operates a flexible inflation targeting framework—targeting 4% CPI inflation with a tolerance band of 2%–6%.

Meaning: prices will keep rising over your life.

So your money must grow faster than inflation.

4. Global Optionality Protocol

RBI's Liberalised Remittance Scheme allows resident individuals up to **USD 250,000 per financial year** for permissible transactions.

You don't need to use it early.

But in the New Wealth Order, you must *understand* global options.

11. STORIES FROM MY JOURNEY (COMPOSITE, BUT REAL PATTERNS)

Loss Story 1: "Trading made me feel powerful... until it made me broke."

A young man (composite) turned small money into quick profit once.

Then he started thinking: "I'm talented."

He increased position size.

He lost.

He chased.

He lost again.

His biggest loss wasn't money.

It was confidence.

And the harsh truth is: this is statistically common among retail derivatives traders.

Loss Story 2: "Agent said Dubai/Canada/Europe job pakka."

Family borrowed. Gold went. Money paid.

Then the job disappeared.

The phone switched off.

The debt remained.

Punjab's high share of complaints against illegal recruiting agents is why I'm strict about verification.

Success Story: "Boring investing made me unstoppable."

A young woman (composite) began with a tiny SIP.

She increased it every year.

She upskilled.

She switched jobs.

She built a second income stream.

Her friends were chasing fast money.

She was building a machine.

Today she has the most powerful asset in the world: **options**—real options in life.

And across India, the scale of SIP behavior (₹31,000+ crore monthly inflows in Jan 2026) shows this habit is becoming mainstream wealth building.

12. THE "10-YEAR WEEKLY ROUTINE" (SO YOU ACTUALLY EXECUTE)

Every week (30 minutes)

- Track spending
- Track investing
- Track debt reduction
- Track one skill improvement action

Every month (60 minutes)

- Update net worth
- Raise SIP if possible
- Rebalance (basic)
- Review goals: safety fund, cashflow targets

Every quarter

- income strategy review (job switch/business expansion)
- portfolio review (risk concentration, emergency fund adequacy)
- paperwork review (banking, nominations, insurance)

Wealth is not built by intensity.

Wealth is built by repetition.

13. CLOSING: THE SPEAKER SINGH MESSAGE TO PUNJAB'S YOUTH

Let me end this chapter with the truth I've learned watching wealthy families behave:

They don't "hope" for freedom. They engineer freedom.

Punjab's youth has talent.

Punjab's youth has hunger.

Punjab's youth has global ambition.

But ambition without a system becomes anxiety.

So here is your New Wealth Order promise (if you follow the formula):

In 10 years, you won't just have money.

You will have **position**.

And position is the real wealth.

Because money can come and go.

But a system that produces money—stays.

READER NOTE

This chapter is educational and provides a general roadmap, not personalized financial advice. Investing involves risk, including loss of capital. Returns are not guaranteed. Laws, taxes, and regulations vary by jurisdiction and can change. For major decisions (insurance, property, overseas migration, taxes, portfolio construction), consult qualified professionals.

Chapter 20

DESIGNING A FREEDOM PORTFOLIO

The Punjab-Practical Blueprint to Build Wealth That Buys You Options

*(Narrated in the voice of Speaker Singh — **The New Wealth Order**)*

Let me start with a line that may offend people who love comfort more than truth:

Most Indians don't have an investing problem. They have a portfolio design problem.

They buy what's trending.

They copy what a friend bought.

They follow a tip from a cousin.

They chase a "sure shot" plot.

They jump into F&O because it looks like fast money.

And then they call it "investing."

No.

That is financial gambling wrapped in motivational language.

A **freedom portfolio** is different. It's not built to impress people at weddings. It's built to protect your family, grow your net worth, and eventually produce cashflow that gives you choices.

And for Punjab's youth—where unemployment for ages 15–29 was reported at **19.3%** in Oct–Dec 2025 (with rural youth unemployment higher) —your money strategy cannot be casual. It has to be engineered.

From my journey and experience working with wealthy families across markets, I can tell you something very clearly:

Wealthy people don't "pick investments."

They design portfolios—like engineers design bridges.

A bridge doesn't collapse because the steel was bad.

It collapses because the design didn't respect real-world forces: load, stress, wind, time.

Money works the same way.

Your portfolio must survive:

- inflation
- job shocks
- health emergencies
- market crashes
- bad decisions made in emotion
- and the one enemy nobody talks about: **lifestyle debt**

This chapter is how you build a portfolio that survives all that—and still grows.

1. WHAT IS A FREEDOM PORTFOLIO? (SIMPLE DEFINITION)

A freedom portfolio is a collection of assets designed to do **three jobs**:

1. **Keep you unbreakable** (liquidity + protection)
2. **Grow your net worth** (compounding assets)
3. **Build cashflow systems** (rental income, business cashflow, REIT income, dividends)

Most people only focus on job #2 (growth).

That's why they get destroyed by job #1 (shocks).

Your freedom portfolio is not a single product.

It is not "mutual funds."

It is not "real estate."

It is a **structure**.

2. THE PUNJAB REALITY: WHY PORTFOLIO DESIGN MATTERS MORE HERE

Punjab youth faces three realities—no drama, only facts:

Reality A: Job volatility is real

If youth unemployment is elevated, your income may not be stable early on.

So your portfolio must assume volatility, not hope against it.

Reality B: Property is culturally dominant

In India, land and buildings dominate household assets. A Government of India press release on AIDIS data noted that **land + buildings were ~91% of total asset value in rural India** (as of 30.06.2018).

This creates a dangerous national habit: people become **asset-rich on paper and cash-poor in life**.

Reality C: "Go abroad" is both opportunity and risk

Punjab has strong migration ambition. India's diaspora also sends massive money home—FY25 remittances were reported at **$135.46 billion**, a record.

But the scam ecosystem is real too: a report citing MEA data said Punjab accounted for **53% of complaints** against illegal recruiting agents in the region (2023–2025), and the eMigrate portal listed **3,505 unregistered agents** by Jan 2026.

So a Punjab-practical freedom portfolio must include:

- a **shock absorber**
- an **anti-trap policy**
- and an **optionality plan** (India + global)

3. THE FOUR ENEMIES THAT KILL MIDDLE-CLASS WEALTH

Before I teach you what to buy, I want you to understand what you're fighting.

Enemy 1: Inflation (silent thief)

India runs under a flexible inflation targeting framework—**4% target with a 2%–6% band** (government retained it for April 2021–March 2026).

Meaning: prices will rise over your lifetime.

If your money grows slower than inflation, you are working—but moving backwards.

Enemy 2: Consumer debt (loud thief)

RBI's Financial Stability Report (June 2025) reporting noted household debt at **41.9% of GDP**, and highlighted non-housing retail loans (personal/credit card/auto, etc.) forming over half of household debt and **25.7% of disposable income** (as referenced in reporting).

Translation: more people are borrowing for consumption.

Consumption debt kills allocation rate. Allocation rate kills freedom.

Enemy 3: Concentration (property-only mindset)

When a family has 90% net worth in one property, they don't have wealth.

They have a **single-point failure**.

Enemy 4: "Fast money" instruments (especially F&O)

I'm going to be blunt because soft talk ruins young people.

SEBI reported that **93% of individual traders** incurred losses in equity F&O between FY22–FY24, and aggregate losses exceeded **₹1.8 lakh crore**.

Reuters also reported retail derivatives traders' net losses of about **₹1.81 trillion** over three years, and that **43%** of retail traders were under 30.

If you want freedom, you don't build it in an arena where the majority of beginners statistically lose.

4. THE FREEDOM PORTFOLIO ARCHITECTURE: "THE FIVE-LAYER TOWER"

From my experience, the best portfolios are built like buildings—layer by layer.

Layer 1: Protection Layer (You don't invest without it)

This includes:

- health risk planning (because one hospital bill can liquidate years of investing)
- basic life cover planning (if others depend on your income)

This is not "investment."

This is **anti-destruction.**

Speaker Singh rule:

If your family's survival depends on luck, you don't have a portfolio. You have a prayer.

Layer 2: Liquidity Layer (Your freedom oxygen)

This is your emergency fund: money that prevents forced selling.

For Punjab youth, this is non-negotiable because job volatility + family obligations + sudden expenses are common.

Target:

- Start with **1 month** expenses
- Then **3 months**
- Then **6 months**

Instruments (examples, not recommendations):

- high-quality bank deposits
- liquid mutual funds (if appropriate for you)
- short-term safe instruments

Purpose: survival and flexibility.

Not returns.

Layer 3: Stability Layer (To reduce portfolio violence)

This includes conservative debt allocation for:

- near-term goals
- tuition
- travel
- upcoming wedding expenses (yes, I said it)
- business buffer capital

If you invest short-term money in long-term volatile assets, you will hate the market and quit at the worst time.

Layer 4: Growth Layer (Compounding engine)

This is where equity investing lives.

And if you think "equity is risky," understand the truth:

Equity is volatile in the short term.

Equity is historically one of the strongest compounding engines in the long term.

But only for people who:

- stay diversified
- invest consistently (SIP mindset)
- avoid emotional exits

India's SIP culture is becoming massive—SIP inflows stayed above **₹31,000 crore** in January 2026 for the second straight month (as reported), showing disciplined retail participation.

AMFI also notes SIPs can be as small as **`500/month**, and **₹250/ month** under "Chhoti SIP."

That's important for Punjab youth: you don't need big money to start. You need a system.

Layer 5: Cashflow & Real Assets Layer (Wealth that pays you)

This is where:

- rental income systems
- REIT's
- business cashflow
- selective property investing
- gold hedging
- and global diversification

come into play.

This layer is where people get excited.

But I want you to earn the right to this layer by building Layer 1–4 first.

Because real assets with weak cashflow discipline become chains.

5. THE FREEDOM PORTFOLIO DESIGN PROCESS (7 STEPS)

Step 1: Define your Freedom Goal (Number, not emotion)

Freedom means: your life decisions stop depending on your next salary.

A widely cited framework in retirement planning uses a "safe withdrawal rate" concept (popularized through research and later discussions around the "4% rule").

In very simple terms, a common rule-of-thumb is:

Freedom Fund ≈ Annual Expenses × 25 (for a 4% withdrawal concept)

But I teach Punjab youth a range (more conservative, more realistic):

- ×25 (aggressive)
- ×28–29 (strong)
- ×33 (ultra-safe)

Example:

If you want a lifestyle of ₹8 lakh/year:

- ×25 → ₹2 crore
- ×30 → ₹2.4 crore

This is not a promise. It's a planning compass.

Step 2: Put your money into "time buckets"

Instead of thinking "where to invest," ask:

When do I need this money?

Buckets:

- **0–2 years:** safety > returns
- **2–5 years:** balanced

- **5–10 years:** growth focused
- **10+ years:** compounding focused

Punjab youth often fails here because they invest wedding/visa/ urgent money into volatile markets—and then blame markets.

Markets didn't fail you.

Your time bucket design failed you.

Step 3: Measure your risk capacity (not your ego)

Risk tolerance is psychological.

Risk capacity is mathematical.

If your income is unstable, your risk capacity is lower—even if you're brave.

Youth unemployment data is a reminder that many young families have fragile income stability.

Speaker Singh rule:

If a 20% fall will force you to sell, you are overexposed.

Step 4: Decide your "Core Allocation" (the heart of your portfolio)

A beginner-friendly freedom portfolio often has three core engines:

1. **Growth engine** (equity)
2. **Stability engine** (debt/cash equivalents)
3. **Real asset hedge** (gold/property/REIT)

But the percentage depends on your age, income stability, responsibilities, and goals.

Step 5: Choose instruments that reduce your worst enemy: behavior

This is the truth I've learned managing wealth:

The best portfolio is not the one with the highest theoretical return.

It's the one you can hold through real life.

That's why SIP discipline matters.

AMFI's data shows the mutual fund industry has structurally expanded: from **₹12.74 trillion (Jan 2016)** to **₹81.01 trillion (Jan 31, 2026)**.

This indicates growing adoption—but also means more people need portfolio design, not product addiction.

Step 6: Automate the plan (discipline must be a machine)

SIP inflows around ₹31,000 crore show many investors are building discipline through automation.

You should too—because motivation is unreliable.

Automation beats mood.

Step 7: Rebalance once a year (so greed and fear don't drive)

Rebalancing is the adult version of investing:

- when equity rises too much → book some gains into stability
- when equity crashes → add gradually (if your emergency fund is solid)

This keeps your risk stable.

6. THREE MODEL FREEDOM PORTFOLIOS (PUNJAB-PRACTICAL TEMPLATES)

These are **templates**—not personal advice. Your correct allocation depends on your goals and risk capacity.

Template A: The Starter Portfolio (Net worth under ₹5 lakh)

Goal: survival + habit + compounding starts

- **Liquidity + emergency fund:** 40–60% until you reach 3–6 months expenses
- **Growth (equity via diversified funds/index approach):** 30–50%
- **Hedge (gold/simple diversifier):** 0–10%
- **Skill/career investment:** always (this is your highest ROI asset early)

If you're starting with ₹250–₹500 SIP, you are not "small."

You are building identity.

Template B: The Builder Portfolio (Net worth ₹5–₹25 lakh)

Goal: expand compounding + build stability + prepare for opportunity

- **Liquidity:** 10–20% (6 months expenses maintained)
- **Stability:** 20–35% (goal-based)
- **Growth:** 40–60%
- **Hedge (gold):** 5–10%
- **Cashflow exploration:** 0–10% (REIT's/small business reinvestment, depending on knowledge)

This is the stage where many Punjab youth get distracted by:

- car upgrades
- "look successful" spending
- EMIs that kill allocation rate

Remember: RBI reporting shows consumption-led non-housing retail loans are a growing part of household debt.

That's the national warning label.

Template C: The Accelerator Portfolio (Net worth ₹25 lakh+)

Goal: diversify, add cashflow systems, global optionality

- **Liquidity:** 6–12 months expenses (because your lifestyle is higher)
- **Stability:** 15–30%
- **Growth (India equity):** 35–55%
- **Global equity diversification:** 5–20% (based on your plan and compliance)
- **Real assets/Cashflow:** 10–30% (property, REIT's, rental systems, business cashflow)
- **Gold hedge:** 5–10%

This is where wealth starts behaving like an empire.

7. THE ANTI-TRAP RULES (READ THIS LIKE A CONTRACT)

Rule 1: No F&O as a "wealth plan"

If 93% lose, it is not a "strategy" for the masses.

If you still want to trade, treat it like entertainment money—small, capped, and not your freedom fund.

Rule 2: No "guaranteed returns" from unknown people

If someone says "guaranteed monthly return," they are either:

- lying
- hiding risk
- or running a wealth transfer scheme

Rule 3: No lifestyle debt that steals your allocation rate

If your EMI eats your investing capacity, you are building someone else's wealth.

Rule 4: Property is not an emotion

Property must be evaluated as a business:

- legal clarity
- location logic
- conservative leverage
- vacancy reality
- net yield after costs

If you buy property to feel secure, you may become financially insecure.

8. THE REAL ASSET DEBATE: GOLD, PROPERTY, REIT's (HOW A FREEDOM PORTFOLIO THINKS)

Gold: Not a growth engine—an insurance asset

Reuters reported that in January 2026, gold ETFs in India saw strong inflows and even surpassed equity mutual funds in net inflows in that period, reflecting demand for diversification during volatility.

AMFI-linked reporting also noted record inflows into passive funds driven by gold ETFs.

Your freedom portfolio uses gold for:

- hedge
- crisis stability
- diversification

Not for "get rich."

Property: Best when treated as a system

Property can create generational wealth because:

- land is limited
- replacement costs rise over time
- rent can rise with economic growth
- leverage can amplify outcomes

But leverage is a weapon. If used emotionally, it becomes self-harm.

REIT's: Property cashflow with liquidity (when appropriate)

REIT's can be a bridge for young investors who want property exposure without full property ownership complexity.

And when you look at global examples, you see how REIT structures can operate at scale.

For instance, Dubai Residential REIT reported FY2025 revenue of **AED 1.95 billion** and average occupancy of **98.3%** (as reported in its communications).

Reuters also reported Dubai Residential REIT's IPO and expected dividend distribution levels in 2025, highlighting how institutional property vehicles are positioned in Dubai's market cycle.

Important: This is not a guarantee of returns.

It's a reminder that professional property markets often create structured, income-focused vehicles—while retail investors often buy property like emotion.

9. GLOBAL DIVERSIFICATION (PUNJAB YOUTH MUST UNDERSTAND THIS)

If Punjab youth is globally mobile—study abroad, work abroad, business abroad—then your portfolio should understand global rules.

LRS: the legal doorway for residents

RBI states that under the Liberalised Remittance Scheme (LRS), resident individuals can remit up to **USD 250,000 per financial year** for permissible current/capital transactions.

RBI also clearly lists prohibited items under LRS, including remittances for **margins/margin calls to overseas exchanges** and **trading in foreign exchange abroad**, among others.

And RBI's FAQ explicitly mentions consolidation rules for **acquiring immovable property outside India** (under certain conditions), showing that global asset ownership can be part of a legal portfolio plan when done correctly.

Speaker Singh rule:

Global investing is powerful—but compliance is non-negotiable. A freedom portfolio is built on clean structure.

Policy risk is real abroad

Countries change rules. For example, Canada extended its ban on foreign ownership of Canadian housing to **January 1, 2027** (government announcement).

The lesson isn't "don't invest abroad."

The lesson is: **don't assume rules stay constant.**

10. THE PUNJAB YOUTH "FREEDOM PORTFOLIO ROADMAP" (HOW IT EVOLVES OVER 10 YEARS)

Years 1–2: Build the base

- emergency fund to 3–6 months
- start SIP (even ₹250–₹500)
- skill upgrades to increase income
- remove toxic debt

Years 3–5: Build the engine

- step-up SIP annually
- diversify (equity + stability + hedge)
- add a second income stream
- avoid "fast money" traps
- SIP discipline is proven by the scale: inflows stayed above ₹31,000 crore in Jan 2026.

Years 6–8: Build cashflow systems

- property decisions become mathematical
- REIT exposure can be considered (if it fits the plan)

- business cashflow reinvestment becomes structured
- global diversification begins (if relevant)

Years 9–10: Consolidate and protect

- rebalancing habit becomes mature
- documentation, nominations, risk controls
- freedom fund milestones become real
- money becomes optionality, not stress

11. STORIES FROM MY JOURNEY (COMPOSITE PATTERNS, REAL LESSONS)

Story 1: The F&O Trap (how young wealth gets stolen)

A young man from a Tier-2 city (composite) starts trading because he wants "freedom fast."

He wins once.

He increases size.

He loses.

Then he chases.

What he didn't understand: the game is structurally tilted.

SEBI and Reuters reporting show the scale of retail losses and the dominance of young traders in derivatives.

His biggest loss wasn't money.

It was time—years of compounding destroyed.

Story 2: The Boring SIP Winner (how freedom is actually built)

A young woman (composite) starts small—₹500/month.

Every year she steps up.

She upgrades skills.

She stays consistent.

Ten years later, she doesn't just have an investment account.

She has a new identity: allocator.

And she is not alone—India's investing habit is becoming a national phenomenon, with mutual fund AUM growing dramatically over a decade.

Story 3: The "Go Abroad" Scam (how dreams become debt)

A family borrows to pay an agent.

The job vanishes.

The agent vanishes.

The debt remains.

Punjab's share of complaints against illegal recruiting agents and the listing of thousands of unregistered agents are a warning label for every ambitious youth.

A freedom portfolio includes a rule:

Dreams must be verified like investments.

12. THE SPEAKER SINGH FREEDOM PORTFOLIO CHECKLIST (PRACTICAL & SIMPLE)

If you do only one thing after this chapter, do this:

✅** **The 10-Point Freedom Portfolio System**

1. Emergency fund exists (3–6 months)
2. Health risk plan exists
3. No toxic debt (or it's in a clear payoff plan)
4. SIP is active and automated
5. Portfolio has at least 2–3 asset categories
6. You are not dependent on one property for net worth
7. You are not using F&O as your "plan"
8. You step-up investment annually
9. You rebalance yearly
10. You have an optionality plan (India + global) within rules

This is not complicated.

But it is rare—because most people want entertainment, not engineering.

CLOSING: THE NEW WEALTH ORDER PROMISE

Let me end with a line I want Punjab's youth to remember:

You don't become free by earning more.

You become free by keeping more, allocating better, and compounding longer.

Income is important.

But design is everything.

From my journey, the world's wealthy aren't magical.

They are structured.

They treat money like a system.

And that is exactly what you are building now:

A freedom portfolio—built to survive reality, not fantasies.

READER NOTE (IMPORTANT)

This chapter is educational and intended for general financial literacy. It does not constitute personalized financial advice, investment recommendations, or solicitation. Investing involves risk, including loss of principal. Laws, taxes, and regulations change and vary by jurisdiction. Consult qualified professionals for decisions related to insurance, taxation, cross-border investing, and property transactions.

Chapter 21

CASE STUDIES

Real People. Real Mistakes. Real Comebacks. Real Wealth Systems.

*(Narrated in the voice of Speaker Singh — **The New Wealth Order**)*

Let me be brutally honest with you.

Most finance books fail because they teach **concepts** without teaching **consequences**.

Concepts sound intelligent.

Consequences change lives.

So in this chapter, I'm not giving you philosophy. I'm giving you **case studies**—the kind I've seen again and again through my journey and experience advising serious wealth builders across different income levels and geographies.

And a note before we begin:

These are "truthful composites."

Names, locations, and some numbers are adjusted to protect privacy—but the patterns are 100% real. Because the goal isn't gossip.

The goal is: **you see yourself in these stories before life forces you to learn the hard way.**

HOW TO READ THESE CASE STUDIES

Each case study is structured like this:

1. **Starting Point** (age, income, family pressure, debt, mindset)
2. **The Trap** (what went wrong—usually behavior, not returns)
3. **The Pivot** (the one decision that changed the direction)
4. **The Roadmap** (what they did—month by month, year by year)
5. **Outcome** (what improved and why)
6. **Speaker Singh's Rule** (the New Wealth Order lesson)

Also, because this book is for real life, we are grounding these stories in today's India—especially Punjab's youth reality:

- Punjab's youth unemployment (15–29) was reported at **19.3%** in Oct–Dec 2025, with rural youth unemployment **22.5%** and female youth unemployment even higher in that period.

That means your wealth plan must survive job uncertainty, not assume stable salary growth.

And we'll also anchor the "fast money" danger with hard regulator data:

- SEBI's study (press release) said **93% of individual traders** lost money in equity F&O (FY22–FY24) and aggregate losses exceeded **₹1.8 lakh crore**.
- The SEBI study PDF noted average losses of around **₹2 lakh per losing trader** (inclusive of transaction costs).
- Reuters reported retail traders' net losses at **₹1.81 trillion** in derivatives over three years to March 2024, with only **7.2%**

making profits; it also noted about **43%** of retail traders were under 30 and most earned under ₹5 lakh annually.

Now—let's get to the real stories.

CASE STUDY 1

"The Options Trap": How a 24-Year-Old Burned 3 Years of Savings in 4 Months

Profile: Gurpreet, 24, Mohali. Entry-level job + side hustle.

Monthly income: ₹32,000–₹40,000 (variable)

Goal: "Freedom fast" + prove himself

The Trap

He wasn't lazy. He was aggressive. And that's what made him vulnerable.

He started watching reels:

- "Options is income"
- "Daily 5k profit"
- "Bro, this strategy is guaranteed"

First month: small wins.

Second month: bigger bets.

Third month: borrowed money + leverage.

Fourth month: collapse.

He didn't just lose money. He lost **identity**.

He came to me (in this story, as a composite of many young clients) with one sentence:

"Sir, I think I'm not made for money."

That sentence is a lie that the market sells to beginners.

The truth is simpler:

He wasn't doing investing. He was playing a professional game without professional tools.

And the data supports how common this is:

- SEBI reported 93% of individual F&O traders lost money (FY22–FY24).
- SEBI's study also referenced average losses around ₹2 lakh per losing trader.
- Reuters described the structural imbalance: institutions/proprietary traders (often algorithmic) making profits while retail loses, and highlighted how young and lower-income participants dominate retail trading.

The Pivot

I told him something harsh:

"Your problem is not bad luck. Your problem is bad structure."

So we created a **24-month recovery plan**.

The Roadmap (24 months, very practical)

Month 1–2: Stop the bleeding

- Close the "trading as income" identity
- Freeze the apps (not delete in emotion—freeze with rules)
- Write a debt map: who, how much, interest, due dates
- Start emergency cash buffer—even ₹500/day

Month 3–6: Rebuild trust with money

- No "big decisions"
- Only automation: small SIP + debt payoff
- One new income skill: sales/marketing/analytics/real estate documentation (choose one)

Month 6–12: Upgrade income

- Switch job or increase earnings through skill
- Raise allocation rate
- Build 3 months emergency fund

Month 12–24: Become an allocator

- Portfolio becomes boring: diversified, consistent, rule-based
- If he wants trading later: only with "fun money" capped at 1–2% of net worth

Outcome

His biggest win wasn't returns. It was self-respect.

He stopped chasing "daily profit" and started building "monthly allocation."

That is how wealth begins.

Speaker Singh's Rule

If your wealth plan requires adrenaline, it's not a plan. It's a trap.

CASE STUDY 2

"Chhoti SIP, Badi Soch": How a ₹500 SIP Became a Wealth Identity

Profile: Simran, 22, Patiala.

Monthly income (Year 1): ₹18,000 (internship + part-time)

Goal: "I want to be financially independent before marriage pressure starts."

The Trap She Avoided

The trap wasn't markets. The trap was society telling her:

"You earn too little to invest."

But SIP is designed exactly for this.

AMFI states SIP instalments can be as small as **₹500/month**, and even **₹250/month** under "Chhoti SIP."

The Pivot

She didn't wait for confidence.

She built confidence through action.

She started tiny. But she started automatic.

The Roadmap (10 years, clean and practical)

Year 1

- ₹500/month SIP
- Emergency fund target: ₹10,000 first
- Skill upgrade focus

Year 2

- SIP to ₹1,500/month (income improved)
- Emergency fund to 2 months expenses

Year 3–5

- Step-up SIP by 10–15% yearly
- Add stability bucket (goal-based)

Year 6–10

- Portfolio becomes meaningful
- Adds diversified exposure (growth + stability + hedge)

Now, to ground the "why" behind long-term investing:

An NSE publication on the "25-year journey of Nifty 50" noted that from June 30, 1999, the **Nifty 50 Total Return index** delivered about **14.2% CAGR** up to Dec 15, 2021 (with dividends reinvested), while also showing real volatility.

This isn't a guarantee—this is evidence that **time + discipline** can be powerful.

Also, the culture of SIP is now massive in India:

- January 2026 SIP inflows stayed above **₹31,000 crore** for the second consecutive month, per AMFI data reported in business coverage.

That means Simran wasn't doing something weird.

She was doing something **rare—but increasingly mainstream among long-term builders.**

Outcome

Her biggest victory:

"I stopped asking 'Can I invest?' I started asking 'How much can I allocate this month?'"

That is the New Wealth Order.

Speaker Singh's Rule

Small investing is not small thinking. It is big thinking with humility.

CASE STUDY 3

"The EMI Prison": How Lifestyle Debt Quietly Kills Wealth

Profile: Manpreet, 27, Ludhiana.

Monthly income: ₹55,000

Lifestyle: Bike EMI + phone EMI + credit card revolve

Goal: Buy property, "settle life"

The Trap

He looked successful. But he was financially fragile.

One salary delay and everything shook.

This isn't a "him" problem. It's a national pattern:

RBI's Financial Stability Report (as covered by Reuters) noted household debt around **41.9% of GDP**, and highlighted that **non-housing retail loans** dominate household debt—over half—and were about **25.7% of disposable income** (as of March 2024 in that reporting).

Translation for a normal reader:

A lot of people are borrowing—not for assets—but for lifestyle and consumption.

And consumption debt steals the one thing that creates freedom:

Allocation rate (how much you invest every month).

The Pivot

I told him:

"If you don't control your EMIs, your EMIs will control your future."

We built a **90-day reset**.

The Roadmap (90 days)

Day 1–7: Reality audit

- List all EMIs and interest rates
- Identify "toxic debt" (highest interest)

Day 8–30: Restructure

- Stop credit card revolving
- Negotiate repayment terms where possible
- Pause lifestyle upgrades
- Build ₹25,000 emergency buffer

Day 31–90: Rebuild investing

- Start SIP even if small
- Every bonus goes 70% to debt, 30% to investing
- Track net worth monthly

Outcome

Within months, he felt lighter—not because money increased, but because stress reduced.

And when stress reduces, discipline becomes possible.

Speaker Singh's Rule

You can't invest your way out of a debt lifestyle. You must restructure your behavior first.

CASE STUDY 4

"Land-Rich, Cash-Poor": How a Punjab Family Turned Property Into a System

Profile: Family in rural Punjab.

Assets: Land + house, but low cashflow

Debt: Kisan Credit Card burden

Goal: "We have land, but why are we always stressed?"

The Trap

In India, property dominates household assets.

Government press release data from AIDIS noted:

- In rural India, **land + building were ~91%** of total household asset value (land ~69%, buildings ~22%) as of 30.06.2018.

Punjab adds another reality: rising farm credit stress.

A report noted Punjab's Kisan Credit Card outstanding loans rising to **₹57,536 crore** by March 2025, even as KCC accounts declined—meaning heavier burden per borrower.

So you get this dangerous situation:

Asset-rich on paper. Cash-poor in life. Debt-heavy in reality.

The Pivot

I told them something they didn't like at first:

"Your land is not your pride. Your land is your balance sheet. Treat it like a business asset."

The Roadmap (18 months)

Step 1: Cashflow audit

- What does land generate annually?
- What does it cost?
- What is net?

Step 2: Debt clarity

- KCC repayment plan
- Remove unnecessary leakages
- No new borrowing without ROI logic

Step 3: Convert assets into systems

Depending on the family situation:

- better leasing structures
- storage/warehouse possibilities
- legal documentation cleanup
- or partial monetization only if it improves long-term stability

Step 4: Diversify

A small portion of surplus moves into:

- emergency buffer
- systematic investing for future education and stability

Outcome

The family didn't become "rich overnight."

They became **stable**.

And stability is the foundation of generational wealth.

Speaker Singh's Rule

Generational wealth is not land ownership. It's land ownership plus cashflow, legal clarity, and diversification.

CASE STUDY 5

"The Punjabi Micro-Entrepreneur": How Small Business Becomes a Wealth Engine

Profile: Harleen, 25, Jalandhar

Start: small service business (skills-based)

Goal: "I don't want to depend on one employer."

The Trap She Avoided

Most small business owners do this:

- earn money
- spend money
- repeat
- no investing
- no buffer
- one shock kills the business

Harleen did the opposite.

The Pivot

She treated her business like a machine with three accounts:

1. **Business operations**
2. **Business buffer** (survival fund)
3. **Owner investing** (personal wealth engine)

The Roadmap (5 years)

Year 1

- build client flow
- keep costs lean
- start small SIP (identity building)

Year 2

- build 3-month business buffer
- reinvest in growth (tools/marketing/process)

Year 3–5

- increase owner allocation rate
- diversify beyond business (because one business is still one point of failure)

Outcome

Her power wasn't just income.

Her power was: **she built two engines**—business cashflow and compounding portfolio.

Speaker Singh's Rule

A business becomes wealth only when profits become assets.

CASE STUDY 6

"The Abroad Dream": One Path Built Wealth. One Path Built Debt.

This is not one case. This is Punjab's reality.

Punjab's youth has global ambition. Respect it.

But respect it with intelligence.

Story A — The Scam Path (Debt + shame)

A report citing MEA data said Punjab accounted for **53% of complaints** against illegal recruiting agents in the region (2023–2025), and noted 3,505 unregistered agents listed on the eMigrate portal by Jan 2026.

That statistic is not decoration. It is a warning label.

The pattern:

- social media promise
- "job pakka"
- money paid
- delays
- blame games
- phone switched off
- family left with debt

Story B — The Clean Path (Budget + compliance + skills)

Now the wealth-building version.

India's diaspora remittances were reported at a record **$135.46 billion** in FY25, up 14% year-on-year in that coverage.

Meaning: done right, overseas earning can be a powerful asset engine for families.

But policies abroad can change quickly.

Canada, for example:

- Reuters reported Canada would issue **437,000** study permits in 2025 (a 10% decline from 2024), continuing caps introduced due to pressure on housing/services.
- Canada's government also announced a two-year extension of the foreign homebuyer ban to **January 1, 2027**.

So the clean path requires: **planning, buffers, and realistic expectations.**

The Roadmap (Abroad done right)

Before leaving

- verify institution/agent/legal pathway
- written budget: fees + rent + emergency buffer
- no blind high-interest debt

After landing

- first goal: stabilize cashflow
- second goal: skill + income growth
- third goal: systematic investing

Cross-border clarity

RBI's LRS FAQ states residents can remit up to **USD 250,000 per financial year** for permissible transactions.

Speaker Singh's Rule

Going abroad is not a lottery ticket. It's a project. Treat it like one.

CASE STUDY 7

"Dubai Done Right": Yield, Structure, and a Real System (Not Blind Hype)

Profile: Karan, 33, Punjabi entrepreneur with India income + Gulf exposure

Goal: Build a cashflow asset outside India + diversify currency/geography

Let me speak carefully here.

Dubai real estate can be a powerful part of a freedom portfolio **when done right**.

And it can destroy investors **when done emotionally**.

The Opportunity (why people consider Dubai)

Dubai's government communications reported:

- 2025 saw **270,000+ transactions** worth **AED 917 billion**, up 20% YoY—record performance.

Rental yield data points (market research—not guarantees):

- REIDIN's UAE Residential Property Price Report (Nov 2025) showed Dubai residential **gross rental yields ~6.55%**, and Dubai apartment gross rental yields around **7.03%** (in that snapshot).
- Savills (World Cities Prime Residential Index 2025) highlighted Dubai as a standout for prime residential, and Savills commentary notes yields in Dubai around **5.3%** in that context.

Tools that support "system investing":

- Dubai Land Department provides a **Rental Index** service to check rental benchmarks and legal rent increase guidance.
- DLD also provides a **Service Charge Index** to check approved service fees for jointly owned properties.

Transaction fee reality (because investors must budget properly):

- DLD's page on registering the sale of a mortgaged property shows **4% of sales value** for registration and notes a **mortgage fee of 0.25%** of mortgage value (if any).

Currency framework:

- UAE dirham is effectively pegged within a narrow band; the Central Bank of the UAE lists intervention rates around **3.672–3.673 USD/AED**.

The Risk (why "Dubai hype" can punish people)

- Reuters reported Fitch warning Dubai residential prices could face a **double-digit fall (up to 15%)** in late 2025 into 2026 due to a large supply pipeline (210,000 units projected).
- UBS Global Real Estate Bubble Index 2025 placed Dubai in an **elevated risk** category and noted it had one of the strongest risk increases versus the prior edition.

So the message is not "Dubai always goes up."

The message is:

Dubai rewards structure and punishes emotion.

The Pivot

Karan didn't buy because of Instagram.

He bought only after building a **Dubai underwriting checklist**.

The Roadmap (Dubai property, system approach)

Step 1: Decide the role in the freedom portfolio

- growth?
- cashflow?
- diversification?

If you can't answer this, you're not investing—you're shopping.

Step 2: Underwrite net yield (not gross)

Gross yield looks sexy. Net yield pays your life.

He calculated:

- rent
- vacancy assumption
- service charges (checked via DLD tool)
- maintenance
- agent fees
- registration costs

Step 3: Stress test

- What if rent drops 10%?
- What if vacancy lasts 3 months?
- What if price falls 15% temporarily? (Fitch scenario warning)

Step 4: Conservative leverage

Only if cashflow supports EMI even during vacancy.

Step 5: Compliance

If investor is India-resident, cross-border capital movement must be within legal frameworks—LRS exists, but needs proper process via authorized dealers.

Outcome

He didn't become "rich overnight."

He built a second cashflow pillar and reduced single-country dependence.

Speaker Singh's Rule

Dubai is not magic. Dubai is mathematics + regulation + cycle awareness.

CASE STUDY 8

"Dubai Done Wrong": The Flipper Who Confused a Cycle for a Skill

Profile: Raj, 29

Goal: "Buy off-plan, flip in 12 months, repeat"

The Trap

He thought:

- one successful flip = talent
- rising prices = proof
- leverage = accelerator

He ignored cycle risk.

When supply and sentiment shift, flippers become forced sellers.

And again, there are public warnings that cycles exist:

- Reuters reported Fitch's view about potential correction due to supply.
- UBS flagged elevated bubble risk for Dubai in its 2025 index framework.

The Pivot

I told him:

"You don't control the market. You control your leverage."

So we rebuilt his plan:

- stop flipping as identity
- convert strategy to holdable cashflow assets
- increase liquidity
- diversify

Outcome

He survived. But he learned the expensive lesson:

Speaker Singh's Rule

If your plan collapses when appreciation pauses, you didn't buy an asset—you bought a hope.

CASE STUDY 9

"The Freedom Portfolio Couple": How Two Salaries Became One Empire

Profile: Aman (31) + Neha (29)

Combined income: ₹1.2 lakh/month

Goal: "In 10 years, we want choices."

The Trap They Avoided

They avoided two common Indian traps:

- property-only wealth
- equity-only arrogance

They built layers.

The Roadmap (Freedom Portfolio — simplified)

Layer 1: Protection + liquidity

- emergency fund 6 months
- insurance planning mindset (anti-destruction)

Layer 2: Stability bucket

- goal-based stability (wedding, family obligations)

Layer 3: Growth bucket

They understood that equity is volatile but can compound over time.

NSE material on Nifty 50's long history noted strong long-run return potential (TR index example ~14.2% CAGR from 1999 to Dec 2021), but also meaningful volatility.

Layer 4: Diversification

- gold as hedge (small allocation)
- REIT/property exposure as cashflow layer later
- global optionality if relevant (within legal frameworks)

Behavior rule

- annual rebalancing
- automatic SIP step-ups
- lifestyle growth slower than income growth

Outcome

By year 6–7, their portfolio started influencing decisions:

- ability to switch jobs without panic
- ability to support parents
- ability to invest during downturns instead of fearing them

Speaker Singh's Rule

A freedom portfolio is not a product. It is a behavior system with asset layers.

CASE STUDY 10

"The Punjab Youth Roadmap": From Uncertainty to Control in 5 Years

This one is for the reader who says:

"Sir, I'm young. Jobs are uncertain. How do I even begin?"

Remember: Punjab youth unemployment data shows the environment is challenging.

But difficult environments create strong builders—if you build structure.

Profile: "You" (18–26), Punjab

Goal: 5 years to stability, 10 years to freedom

The Roadmap (5 years, ultra practical)

Year 1

- emergency fund seed
- avoid toxic debt
- start SIP even tiny (₹250/₹500)
- skill selection (one high-income skill)

Year 2

- income upgrade through job switch or higher-paying role
- step-up SIP
- second income stream begins

Year 3

- diversification
- build credit discipline
- avoid "fast money" traps (SEBI data is the warning label)

Year 4

- cashflow asset planning begins (business expansion/REIT/ rental strategy)

Year 5

- portfolio becomes meaningful
- decisions become calmer
- life becomes less dependent on one paycheck

Speaker Singh's Rule

The youth advantage is time. Waste it on gambling, and you lose your biggest weapon.

The Patterns That Separate Winners from the Financially Stuck

After all these case studies, here are the truths that repeat:

Winners do these things:

- automate investing early
- build emergency buffers before chasing returns
- treat property as a business (cashflow + legal clarity + cycle awareness)
- diversify and rebalance
- upgrade income skills consistently

Losers repeat these errors:

- confuse speculation with investing
- borrow for lifestyle and then call it "success"
- buy property emotionally and ignore net yield
- fall for overseas scams because of urgency
- wait for "perfect timing" instead of building a system

Reader Worksheet: Write Your Own New Wealth Order Case Study

Take a notebook and answer:

1. My current income: ______
2. My fixed expenses: ______
3. My debts + interest rates: ______
4. My emergency fund months: ______

5. My monthly allocation rate today: ______
6. My biggest money weakness (behavior): ______
7. My next 90-day goal: ______
8. My next 12-month goal: ______
9. My 5-year freedom milestone: ______
10. My "one skill" to increase income: ______

Because wealth is not built by reading.

Wealth is built by execution.

CLOSING: THE NEW WEALTH ORDER PROMISE (FROM MY JOURNEY)

If you remember one sentence from this chapter, remember this:

Case studies are not entertainment. They are warnings and blueprints.

Learn from other people's consequences.

That is the cheapest education in the world.

And if Punjab's youth builds systems—not fantasies—then 5 years from now, you won't just have money.

You will have **position**.

That is the New Wealth Order.

www.ingramcontent.com/pod-product-compliance
Lightning Source LLC
LaVergne TN
LVHW100248210926
848480LV00003B/862